New ENTERPRISE

Student's Book

Jenny Dooley

CONTENTS

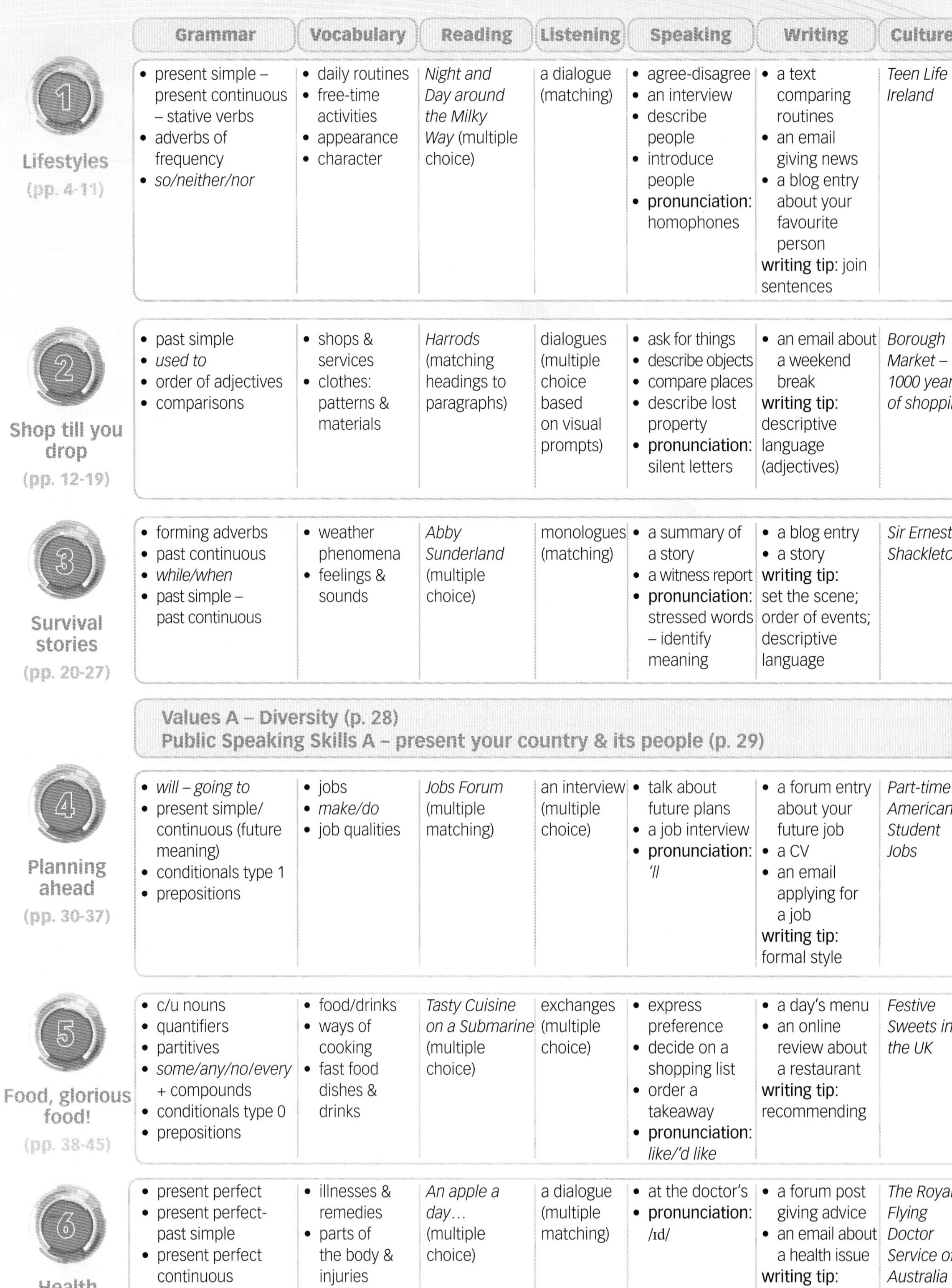

Values C – Good citizenship (p. 80)
Public Speaking Skills C – present how to save electricity (p. 81)

Values D – Cooperation (p. 106)
Public Speaking Skills D – present a new piece of technology (p. 107)

Vocabulary:	daily routines, free-time activities, appearance & character
Grammar:	present simple, present continuous, stative verbs; adverbs of frequency, *so/neither/nor*
Everyday English:	introducing people; expressing agreement/disagreement
Writing:	a blog entry describing your favourite person

Lifestyles

Listening & Reading

1 THINK **What is the Milky Way? What can life be like on a space station?**

2 **Listen and circle the correct answer.**

1 The crew wakes up with **messages/music**.
2 Each day the crew work on science **projects/systems**.
3 The crew **work/don't work** after lunch.

3 **Read the article. For questions 1-4, choose the correct answer, A, B or C. Then, explain the words in bold.**

1 How long does it take a mission to go around the Earth once?
A one and a half hours
B sixteen hours
C twenty-four hours

2 How do astronauts stay clean in space?
A They have long baths.
B They have quick showers.
C They use a towel.

3 What is true about spacewalks?
A They don't happen all the time.
B They usually don't take long.
C They always take place in the 'morning'.

4 Astronauts like sitting by the window because
A it's a good place to read.
B it's near their beds.
C there's a great view.

4 **Fill in:** *daily*, *crew*, *science*, *space*, *running*, *short*, *typical*, *ordinary*. **Then make sentences using the completed phrases.**

1 .... station
2 .... routine
3 .... member
4 .... day
5 .... water
6 .... clothes
7 .... project
8 .... break

VIDEO

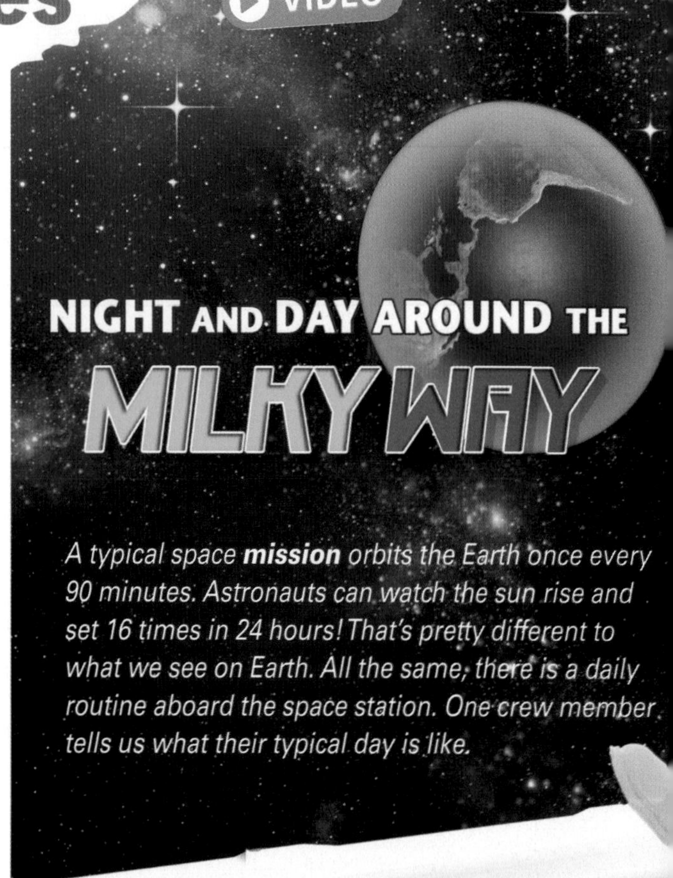

*A typical space **mission** orbits the Earth once every 90 minutes. Astronauts can watch the sun rise and set 16 times in 24 hours! That's pretty different to what we see on Earth. All the same, there is a daily routine aboard the space station. One crew member tells us what their typical day is like.*

"Every 'morning', Mission Control wakes us up with music. We have a couple of hours to wash, have breakfast and get the 'morning' messages from Mission Control. It's impossible to have a shower in space so we use a wet **towel** to wash ourselves. Shaving and brushing our teeth are also difficult, as there is no running water. Next, we get dressed. Inside the space station we wear ordinary clothes like T-shirts and jeans. Then we're ready for work.

Most of the 'morning' we work on science projects **involving** life on the station. We also check all our **equipment** and systems are working properly. Sometimes, we put on our **spacesuits** and go on a spacewalk, but not every day. There's a short **break** for lunch and then we go back to work for the 'afternoon'.

Fortunately, it's not all work and no play aboard the space station. In the 'evening', everyone has a couple of hours to have dinner and relax. Most of us video call our families in this free time. We also read books, watch films or listen to music. Sometimes we sit by the window and **admire** the Earth spinning around under us! After that, it's time to go to bed and get our eight hours' sleep. Mission Control and the computers can take over for the 'night'!"

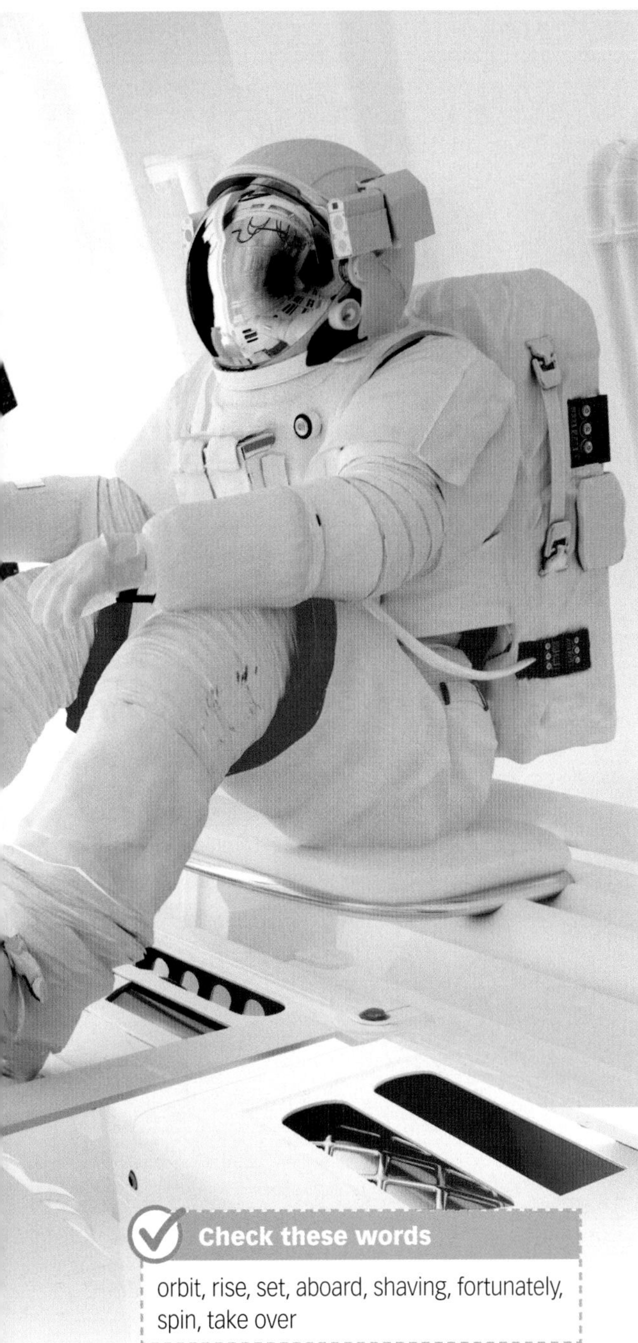

Check these words

orbit, rise, set, aboard, shaving, fortunately, spin, take over

5 **PREPOSITIONS** **Fill in:** *around, in, for, on (x2), by, to (x2).* **Then, make sentences based on the text using the completed phrases.**

1 *around* the Earth
2 .... space
3 work .... projects
4 go .... a spacewalk
5 break .... lunch
6 go back .... work
7 listen .... music
8 sit .... the window

Vocabulary

Daily routine & Free-time activities

6 **Fill in the gaps with the verbs:** *meet, play, watch, listen to, have, do, ride, wash, go, read.*

1 .... video games, tennis, cards
2 .... a bicycle, a motorbike
3 .... shopping, ice skating, fishing, to bed
4 .... a book, a magazine, a newspaper
5 .... friends
6 .... a film, the news on TV
7 .... dinner, a shower, coffee, a lesson, breakfast
8 .... music, the radio
9 .... the dishes, the car, my clothes
10 .... my homework, the washing-up, the ironing, the housework

7 **Use phrases from Ex. 6 and your own ideas to say two things you ...** *do every day, do every weekend, don't like doing, hate doing, don't mind doing, like doing.*

8 **Fill in:** *crew, club, staff, team.* **Check in your dictionary.**

1 The .... welcomed the passengers onto the ship.
2 All the .... started shouting when their best player scored a goal.
3 All members of the .... must be at next month's meeting.
4 The new restaurant is looking for .... to work in the kitchen.

Speaking & Writing

9 a) **Read the article again and make notes about the astronauts' daily routine under the headings:** *the morning – the afternoon – the evening.*

b) **You are a reporter and your partner is an astronaut. Interview him/her about a typical day in his/her life aboard a space station.**

10 THINK **Write a short text comparing a typical day in your life to that of an astronaut's in a space station.**

Grammar in Use

Hi Ann,

*Greetings from Bergen. **1) I'm having** a fantastic time here in Norway. Lee and I **2) are staying** at the historic Royal Hotel. At the moment, we **3) are having** a cup of hot chocolate by the harbour.*

*The weather's cold, but it's lovely and sunny, too. Most mornings, we **4) go** hiking in the mountains. Lee sometimes **5) goes** skiing. The food is delicious. All the restaurants **6) serve** seafood, especially salmon and shrimp. I just **7) love** eating fresh bread and smoked salmon for lunch.*

*Next week **8) we're going** to Oslo for three days. Lee **9) doesn't like** the idea, but I can't wait. Our flight **10) leaves** for Oslo next Friday at 9:20 pm. How **11) are you enjoying** your holiday?*

See you soon.

Susan

1 **Read the theory. Identify the tenses in bold in the email, then match them to the uses in the theory box. Find two examples of stative verbs.**

Present simple – Present continuous

We use the **present simple** for:
- habits/routines/repeated actions
  *He always **gets up** early.*
- permanent states
  *She **works** in a seafood restaurant.*
- timetables
  *The train **arrives** at 9 o'clock.*

We use the **present continuous** for:
- actions happening at the moment of speaking
  *I**'m having** my lunch now.*
- fixed arrangements in the near future
  *Pat **is meeting** Tom at 6 pm this evening.*
- actions happening around the time of speaking
  *They**'re sightseeing** in Rome all this week.*

Stative verbs are verbs that do not usually have continuous forms because they describe a state rather than an action (***want***, ***like***, ***love***, ***hate***, ***know***, ***believe***, ***need***, etc.). *She **knows** Laura.* (NOT: *She's knowing Laura.*)

2 **Choose the correct tense. Give reasons.**

1 What **do you do/are you doing** on Sunday afternoons?
2 She **likes/is liking** watching TV in the evenings.
3 **Do you want/Are you wanting** to go to the shopping centre?
4 She usually **plays/is playing** video games on Saturdays.
5 Oh no! It **rains/is raining** now.
6 They **get/are getting** married in June.
7 The bus **leaves/is leaving** at 6:15 am.
8 We **stay/are staying** with Molly these days.
9 Tony **lives/is living** in Los Angeles.
10 We **don't want/aren't wanting** to go abroad this summer.

3 **Fill in:** *am*, *is*, *are*, *do*, *does* **or** *isn't*. **Identify the tenses of the verbs (1-13), then explain their uses.**

A: So, Sergio, where **1)** .... you from?
B: I **2)** .... from Lisbon.
A: Ah, Lisbon! That **3)** .... a beautiful city. So, what **4)** .... you do, Sergio?
B: I **5)** .... an actor.
A: And what **6)** .... you doing here in the UK?
B: I **7)** .... working. I work with the Royal Theatre Company, and this year we **8)** .... touring Britain.
A: What **9)** .... you think of London?
B: Well, it **10)** .... like Lisbon at all! I **11)** .... not like the food very much and the sun **12)** .... not shine very often. The people **13)** .... great, though, and I love shopping here!

Adverbs of frequency

Adverbs of frequency tell us how often something happens. They go *before* the main verb, but *after* the verb ***to be***. They are:

always	100%
usually	90%
often	70%
sometimes	50%
occasionally	30%
seldom	10%
hardly ever/rarely	5%
never	0%

4 Use adverbs of frequency to say how often you do the following activities:

- make your bed • do the washing-up • cook
- do online shopping • go to the gym
- do the ironing

5 SPEAKING Use the prompts to ask and answer questions about each person, as in the example.

Ann, England, married, secretary – send emails

Glen, Australia, single, mechanic – fixes cars

Marie, France, divorced, doctor – treats sick people

Hans, Germany, married, lawyer – advises people about the law

A: Where does Ann live?
B: She lives in England.
A: Is she married?
B: Yes, she is.
A: What does she do?
B: She's a secretary.
A: What does she do at work?
B: She sends emails.
A: What is she doing now?
B: She's reading a newspaper.

6 Read the theory.

Agreeing – Disagreeing (*so/neither/nor*)

- We use ***so*** + **auxiliary verb** + **subject** to agree with an affirmative statement.
  A: I always walk to work.
  *B: **So do** I.*
- We use ***neither/nor*** + **auxiliary verb** + **subject** to agree with a negative statement.
  A: I don't have cereal for breakfast.
  *B: **Neither/Nor do I**.*
- We use **subject** + **auxiliary verb** to disagree with what someone says.
  A: I never drink coffee.
  *B: Oh, really? **I do**.*
  A: I often go to the cinema.
  *B: **I don't**.*

7 a) Fill in the missing words. Listen and check.

1 A: I always drive to work.
B: .... do I.

2 A: I never play video games in my free time.
B: .... do I.

3 A: I never make my bed in the morning.
B: Oh, really? I ....

4 A: I often go fishing at weekends.
B: I .... I hate going fishing.

b) Act out similar dialogues using the prompts below.

- walk to college/work
- go to the gym in my free time
- hang out with friends after college/work
- do the housework at weekends

8 Put the verbs in brackets into the present simple or the present continuous. Give reasons.

Hi Nancy,
How **1)** .... **(you/be)**? I **2)** .... **(be)** on holiday in Ho Chi Minh City with Rob and Sheila! We **3)** .... **(stay)** at a beautiful hotel in the city centre. Every morning we **4)** .... **(visit)** famous sights and then we **5)** .... **(go)** shopping. The malls here are amazing. Right now we **6)** .... **(visit)** a street food market. It **7)** .... **(not/rain)** now, so there are a lot of people. Sheila **8)** .... **(buy)** souvenirs while I **9)** .... **(have)** coconut water. Rob **10)** .... **(want)** to try some Vietnamese noodles. Tonight we **11)** .... **(go)** on a cruise on the Saigon River. We **12)** .... **(come)** back in a week.
Hope you are OK. See you soon!
Pam

9 WRITING Imagine you are on holiday. Write a short email to your English-speaking friend (80-100 words). In your email write: *where you are – who with – where you are staying – what you do everyday – what you are doing now/tonight – when you are coming back.*

Skills in Action

Vocabulary

Describing people

1 Choose the correct item.

C

Ann is **1) tall/short** and **2) plump/thin** with a **3) dark/pale** complexion. She's in her **4) late/early** thirties and she's got blue eyes, **5) thin/full** lips and **6) long/short**, **7) straight/wavy** fair hair. She's really attractive.

Mark is a very handsome **1) young/old** man. He's of medium **2) height/complexion**, **3) slim/well-built** with **4) straight/wavy**, **5) brown/fair** hair, thin lips, a beard and **6) a moustache/freckles**.

James is **1) middle-aged/in his late seventies**. He's **2) tall/short** and **3) overweight/thin** with green eyes, **4) thin/full** lips and **5) wrinkles/freckles**. He's **6) bald/chubby** with some white hair and has a friendly **7) height/smile**.

2 Match the character adjectives to the definitions. Check in your dictionary. Then, use them to describe people you know well, as in the example.

calm	not like hard work
kind	like talking to people
jealous	want things others have
lazy	do what you say you will do
reliable	learn new things quickly
careful	not be afraid of anything
clever	always help others
brave	rarely make mistakes
friendly	not get angry easily

Tom is very calm. He doesn't get angry easily.

Listening

3 Listen and match the colours (1-5) to the characters (A-E).

1 ☐ **Red**	A jealous & friendly
2 ☐ **Blue**	B lazy & clever
3 ☐ **Green**	C kind & careful
4 ☐ **Purple**	D calm & reliable
5 ☐ **Pink**	E brave & happy

Everyday English

Introducing people

4 a) Listen and read the dialogues. Then, match them to the situations (a-c).

a introducing a family member
b introducing two people at work
c welcoming a friend to your house

1 ☐

A: Hi, John! Come on in! Great you could make it!
J: Hi, Anna. Thanks for inviting me.
A: My pleasure. Have you met my flatmate Carol?
J: No, I haven't. Hello, Carol. Nice to meet you.
C: Nice to meet you, too, John.

2 ☐

B: Tony! Welcome to London! Great to see you again. How are things in the Leeds branch?
T: Great to see you, too, Bob. Everything's fine, thanks.
B: This is my boss, Mark Mills. Mr Mills, this is Tony Jones.
T: Pleased to meet you, Mr Mills.
M: Pleased to meet you, Tony.

3 ☐

R: Uncle Brad, this is Samuel, my roommate. Samuel, this is my uncle Brad.
B: Nice to meet you, Samuel.
S: Pleased to meet you. Are you here on business?
B: No – my son studies here, too.

b) Act out similar dialogues to introduce:

- your flatmate to your best friend.
- your business partner to a trainee.
- your friend to your grandmother.

Pronunciation: homophones

5 Listen and circle the odd word out. Listen again and repeat.

1 where – wear – we're	3 hair – hear – here
2 she – sea – see	4 know – no – now

Reading & Writing

6 **Read the blog. What is Sally like?**

Describing a person's character
When we describe a person's character, we support our description with examples. When we describe negative qualities, we need to use mild language (*tends to be*, *can be*, *is a bit*, etc). *She's kind. She always helps others. She can be rude at times. She doesn't always mind her manners.*

Log out

Thelma's blog

'm sure everyone's got someone that's very special to them. My favourite person is my flatmate Sally. She's a vet and oves looking after animals. I really admire her.

Sally is in her late twenties and she's very pretty. She's slim with long straight brown hair and big brown eyes. I love her freckles and her friendly smile!

Sally is sociable and likes meeting her friends. Actually, she can be a bit too talkative at times! The other person can't get a word in! But she's still a lovely person.

n her free time, Sally likes doing exercise so she's very fit. She usually rides her bicycle at weekends. She also goes running every evening in the park.

Sally makes a big difference in my life because she always makes me feel happy. She's not just a flatmate – she's a real friend! Who's your favourite person?

7 **Copy and complete the spidergram in your notebook about Sally.**

my favourite person → comments/feelings, name, relationship, age, appearance, character, interests

8 **Join the sentences. Use the words in brackets.**

1 Paul is a young man. He's got a beard. **(with)**
Paul is a young man with a beard.
2 He's short and plump. He's got brown eyes. **(with)**
3 She's got short, curly, dark brown hair. She's got full lips. **(and)**
4 Pam's got short, straight, fair hair. She's got blue eyes. **(and)**
5 He's tall and well-built. He's got short, fair hair. **(with)**

9 **Complete with:** *loves*, *knows*, *listens*, *needs*, *supports*.

1 Ben is always ready to help. He .... to me when I have a problem.
2 Nora isn't perfect, but she's a good person and .... me in her own way.
3 Sue is a great friend. She .... me no matter what I do or I say.
4 Ann usually .... what to say to make me feel better.
5 Keith is always there when someone .... him.

Writing (a blog entry about your favourite person)

10 **Read the task. Think of your favourite person. Copy the spidergram from Ex. 7 in your notebook and make notes under the headings. Use your notes to write your entry. Follow the plan.**

Write a blog entry for an international online teens magazine about your favourite person (80 -100 words). In your entry:
- mention his/her relationship to you & age.
- describe his/her appearance and character.
- state what activities he/she likes doing.
- say why he/she is special to you.

Plan

Para 1: name of person & relationship to you
Para 2: his/her age & appearance
Para 3: his/her character
Para 4: his/her interests
Para 5: your comments/feelings

VALUES
Growth
Good habits formed at youth make all the difference.
Aristotle

TEEN LIFE IN IRELAND

Interests & Preferences

Irish teens like doing what most teens do: playing video games, shopping, watching films and hanging out with friends. They also enjoy listening to music and can tell you all about famous Irish singers and **bands**. Chatting online is also extremely popular and is an important way for Irish teenagers to contact each other.

Families

The **traditional** Irish family is big with five or six children, maybe more. These days, though, it is more common to have just two children. Most families have two parents while some others are single-parent families.

Favourite activities

It rains a lot in Ireland but this doesn't stop people from doing activities outdoors. Teens love playing sports such as football and hockey. There are traditional sports, too, like Gaelic football and hurling. Another favourite is going to festivals – Ireland has lots of **different** kinds all year round, so there's always something fun for young people to do.

Check these words

hang out, contact, single-parent, outdoors

Listening & Reading

1 **Read the text quickly. Find two things that teens in your country like doing.**

2 **Listen to the text. What can you remember about teen life in Ireland? Tell the class.**

3 **Read the text and decide if the sentences are *T* (True), *F* (False) or *DS* (Doesn't say). Then, explain the words in bold.**

1 Irish teenagers only listen to Irish music. ....
2 Irish teens use the Internet to keep in touch. ....
3 Irish families today tend to be large. ....
4 The weather in Ireland is usually warm and sunny. ....
5 Teens play both Irish and international sports. ....

Speaking & Writing

4 THINK **How does teen life in Ireland compare to teen life in your country? Write a few sentences. Read them to the class.**

Review 1

Vocabulary

1 Match the words in the two columns.

1	☐ listen to	A	a motorbike
2	☐ read	B	my face
3	☐ play	C	the radio
4	☐ ride	D	cards
5	☐ meet	E	a lesson
6	☐ do	F	fishing
7	☐ watch	G	a newspaper
8	☐ have	H	the housework
9	☐ wash	I	a film
10	☐ go	J	friends

(10 x 2 = 20)

2 Circle the odd word out.

1 middle-aged – chubby – old – young
2 well-built – slim – reliable – thin
3 calm – pale – friendly – kind
4 light – dark – full – fair
5 thin – plump – overweight – dark
6 patient – brave – lazy – bald
7 wrinkles – freckles – moustache – build
8 straight – late – wavy – long

(8 x 2 = 16)

Grammar

3 Choose the correct item.

1 "I ride my bike to college." "**So/Nor** do I."
2 "I don't have lessons on Mondays." "**So/Neither** do I."
3 "I don't like studying in the library." "Oh really? I **do/don't**."
4 "I have lunch at college." "I **do/don't**. I prefer having lunch at home."

(4 x 5 = 20)

4 Put the verbs in brackets into the present simple or the present continuous.

1 A: .... **(she/go)** to Brussels next week?
B: Yes, she .... **(visit)** her brother.
2 A: .... **(you/know)** where Simon is?
B: He .... **(watch)** TV in his room.
3 A: .... **(they/live)** in London?
B: Yes, but this week they .... **(stay)** with my aunt in Bournemouth.
4 A: Paul .... **(study)** a lot these days.
B: Yes, his exams .... **(start)** at 9 o'clock on Monday.
5 A: Mr Clark .... **(wash)** his car every Saturday!
B: He .... **(hate)** having a dirty car!
6 A: He always .... **(have)** a yoga class on Monday evenings.
B: Yes, but he .... **(be)** never on time for it!

(6 x 4 = 24)

Everyday English

5 Match the exchanges.

1	☐ Thanks for inviting me.	A	Great to see you, too.
2	☐ Are you here on business?	B	Pleased to meet you, too.
3	☐ Great to see you again.	C	No, I'm visiting family.
4	☐ Have you met my sister?	D	You're welcome.
5	☐ Nice to meet you.	E	No, I haven't. Nice to meet you.

(5 x 4 = 20)

Total 100

Competences

Lexical Competence

Understand words/ phrases related to:

- daily routines & free-time activities
- people's appearance & character

Reading Competence

- understand texts related to daily routines & free-time activities (read for specific information – multiple choice)

Listening Competence

- listen & understand dialogues related to character (listen for specific information – multiple matching)

Speaking Competence

- introduce people

Writing Competence

- write an email while on holiday
- write a blog entry about my favourite person

Vocabulary: shops and services, clothes, patterns and materials
Grammar: past simple – *used to*, order of adjectives, comparisons
Everyday English: asking for things in a shop, describing lost property
Writing: an email

Shop till you drop

Vocabulary
Shops & Services

1 **Choose words from the list to label the pictures.**

• antique shop • baker's • bank • bookshop • butcher's • chemist's • department store • florist's • greengrocer's • hair & beauty salon • jeweller's • newsagent's • post office • supermarket • travel agent's

A

....

B

....

C

....

D

....

E

....

F

....

2 **a) In which of the shops in Ex. 1 can you buy these things:** *apples? a plane ticket? old clocks? a book? a comb? a pair of trousers? a diamond ring? flowers? an armchair? grapes? a bottle of perfume? lamb chops? a leather suitcase? stamps? a woollen skirt? a leather jacket? a bouquet of roses? a magazine? sugar? a gold necklace? a loaf of bread? medicine?* **What else can you buy in each place?**

You can buy apples at a greengrocer's.

b) In which of the shops can you: *book tickets? post a letter? have a haircut? send flowers?*

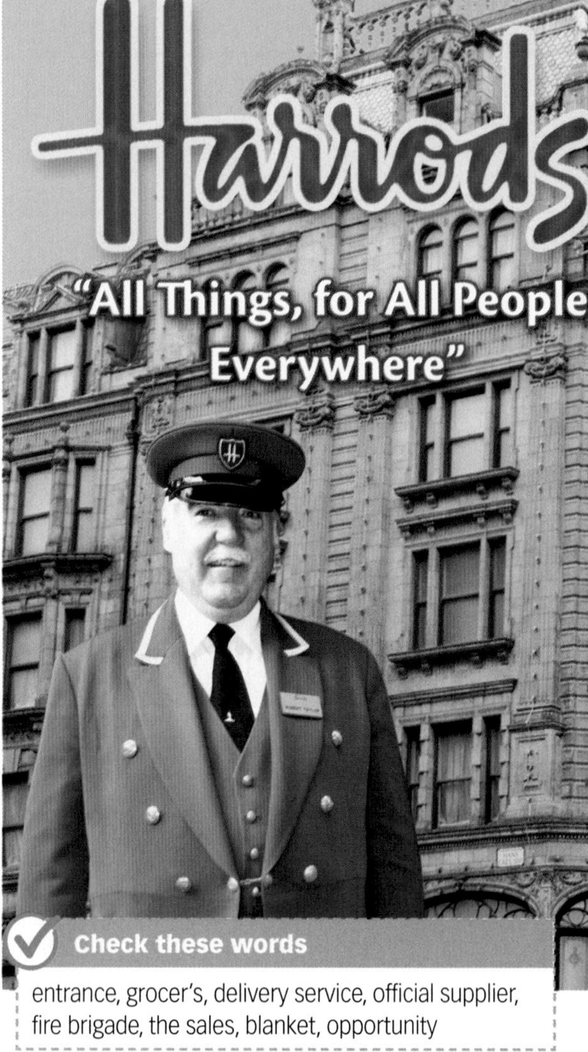

Check these words

entrance, grocer's, delivery service, official supplier, fire brigade, the sales, blanket, opportunity

3 **Use the items and the phrases in the language box to act out dialogues, as in the example.**

• caviar • green apples • sausages • milk • sugar • flour • a loaf of bread

Asking for things	
• Can/Could I have ..., please? • Do you happen to have any ...?	• Do you have ...? • I'd like ..., please.
Responding	
• Yes, of course./Yes, we do. It's in Aisle 2. • Certainly. How much/many would you like? • I'm afraid we haven't got any left, but how about ...? • Sorry, no, but we've got these ...	

A: *Do you have any caviar?*
B: *Yes we do. It's in Aisle 2.*
A: *Thank you.*

A ....

"Enter a Different World," it says in the entrance of Harrods in Knightsbridge, London, and visitors do just that. Harrods is not the oldest, but it's probably the most famous department store in the world.

B ....

In the beginning, Harrods was just a small grocer's. Charles Henry Harrod opened it in 1849. His son **took over** and added fruit, flowers, sweets and a delivery service. It became an official supplier to the Royal Family. It is now more than just a shop. It is a London landmark, a must-see UK tourist attraction.

C ....

35,000 people visit Harrods every day. **In addition to** its 300 departments, selling everything from clothes to caviar, there are twenty-six restaurants and cafés, a bank, a travel agent's and the biggest hair and beauty salon in Europe. It **employs** over 4,000 staff, including the famous doormen (known as 'Green Men'), security guards dressed as **ordinary** shoppers, doctors and nurses – even its own fire brigade!

D ....

The busiest month for Harrods is December, with 100,000 Christmas shoppers per day. But the busiest day of all is Boxing Day, the first day of the January sales, with over 300,000 **customers**! A lot of people sleep outside all night to be first in when the doors open. Harrods makes things easier for them by **handing out** food, hot drinks and blankets!

E ....

"All things, for all people, everywhere" is the store's motto, because there's nothing you can't find there. There even used to be a pet department where you could buy lions and alligators! But today most people come to look around and buy something small so they can get one of the famous green bags. So if you're in London, don't **miss** the opportunity to visit this historic department store!

Listening & Reading

4 **Guess which statements are true about Harrods, the famous London department store. Listen and check.**

1. Harrods is the oldest department store in the world. ....
2. Harrods started as a grocer's in 1849. ....
3. 300,000 people visit Harrods every day. ....
4. The largest hair and beauty salon in the world is in Harrods. ....
5. There is no pet department in Harrods now. ....

5 **Read the article and fill in the headings. Then, explain the words in bold.**

History of the Store | The Sales | Location & Reputation | Recommendation | Departments & Services

6 THINK **Why is Harrods a popular tourist attraction? Give three reasons.**

7 **Fill in the words from the list, then make sentences using the completed phrases.**

• delivery • fire • hot • January • security • tourist

1. .... guard
2. .... service
3. .... drink
4. .... attraction
5. .... brigade
6. .... sales

Speaking & Writing

8 **Look at the headings in Ex. 5. Use them to present Harrods to the class.**

9 **In groups, design your own department store. Think about:** *name – location – motto – products – opening hours*. **Present your store to the class.**

Grammar in Use

Shopping in Ancient Athens

Ancient Athenians didn't use to have supermarkets or department stores. They had the agora – a large open market where people bought and sold things. The agora was usually the most crowded and noisiest place in the city. Traders shouted out their prices while buyers tried to get things for a lower price. There was a great variety of things to choose from. Traders selling similar goods had their shops together in a specific area in the agora. But people didn't go to the agora just to shop. It was full of life! In Athens, the agora was famous for its philosophers. Socrates, for example, used to go there and talk to people. Imagine going shopping and hearing someone say: 'I know one thing, and that is that I know nothing!'

1 **Read the theory. Find examples in the article.**

Past simple – *used to*

- We use the **past simple** or ***used to*** to describe past habits and states which don't happen/exist anymore.
  *I **worked/used to** work as a cleaner.* (past habit)
  *I **didn't have/didn't use to have** long hair.* (state)
- We use the **past simple** for an action which happened at a specific time in the past. *We **went** to the beach last Sunday. What **did you do** last Sunday?*
  (NOT: *We ~~**used to go**~~ to the beach last Sunday.*)

What are the spelling rules for regular verbs in the past simple?

2 **Match the present simple forms to the past simple forms. Which verb forms are irregular?**

1	☐ be	a	was/were
2	☐ live	b	sang
3	☐ sing	c	lived
4	☐ go	d	bought
5	☐ learn	e	went
6	☐ travel	f	wrote
7	☐ start	g	started
8	☐ eat	h	had
9	☐ have	i	learnt
10	☐ enjoy	j	enjoyed
11	☐ buy	k	ate
12	☐ write	l	travelled

3 **Complete the dialogues with the correct past simple form of the verbs in brackets.**

1
A: .... **(you/get)** the bus to the mall?
B: No, I .... **(travel)** by train. Ann .... **(come)** with me. We .... **(have)** a great time and .... **(buy)** lots of things.

2
A: .... **(you/go)** to the baker's?
B: No, I didn't. I .... **(get)** the tickets from the travel agent's and then I .... **(meet)** Sue for coffee, but I .... **(forget)** about the baker's!

3
A: .... **(the high street/be)** different when you .... **(be)** a kid?
B: Oh, yes! In fact, my grandfather .... **(own)** a butcher's there.

4 **Ask and answer questions. Use the ideas below. You can use your own ideas as well.**

watch TV	last Monday?
upload videos	last night?
go shopping	last weekend?
text a friend	yesterday?
eat pizza	yesterday morning?

A: Did you watch TV last Monday?
B: No, I didn't. I went shopping.

5 **a) Complete the gaps with the correct form of *used to* and the verbs from the list.**

• be • not/buy • grow • go • not/drive • cost • not/be

When I was a girl, bread **1)** .... 8½p. There **2)** .... any big super markets. There **3)** .... a butcher's, a baker's, a grocer's and a greengrocer's on the high street. We **4)** .... to the shops – we **5)** .... on foot. And we **6)** .... many vegetables – my dad **7)** .... most of them in the garden.

b) What did/didn't your grandparents use to do when they were young?

6 **Read the theory. Find examples of opinion and fact adjectives in the article on p. 14, then number the adjectives in the correct order.**

Order of adjectives

- **Opinion adjectives** *(beautiful, expensive, etc)* describe what we think of someone or something. **Fact adjectives** *(short, red, etc)* describe what someone or something really is. Opinion adjectives go before fact adjectives. *She's wearing a **beautiful red** dress.*
- When there are **two or more fact adjectives** in a sentence, they usually go in this order:
  size: small, big, etc
  age: old, new, etc
  weight: heavy, light, etc
  shape: triangular △, round ○, rectangular ▭, square □, etc
  colour: dark/light blue, yellow, pink, red, etc
  origin: Australian, Spanish, etc
  material: cotton, silk, plastic, etc
  *She bought a **beautiful, blue, cotton** shirt.*

1 a **brown** (*2*) **wooden** (*3*) **beautiful** (*1*) box
2 a **cotton** (.....) **large** (.....) **grey** (.....) shirt
3 a **heavy** (.....) **metal** (.....) **black** (.....) saucepan
4 a **silk** (.....) **blue** (.....) **Japanese** (.....) scarf

7 **SPEAKING Describe the objects, as in the example.**

It's a rectangular grey suitcase with stickers on it.

8 a) **Read the theory.**

Comparisons

We use the **comparative** to compare two people, things, objects, places etc. We use the **superlative** to compare more than two people, things, objects, places etc. We use ***than*** in the comparative. We use ***the ... of/in*** in the superlative.
as ... as: for two people, animals, things that are the same *His car is **as fast as** yours.*
not so/as ... as: for two people, animals, things that aren't the same *Her car isn't **so/as fast as** yours.*

b) **Complete the table, then say how we form the comparative and superlative forms of adjectives. Find examples in the text on p. 14.**

Adjective	Comparative	Superlative
big		the biggest
short	shorter than	
dry		the driest
large		the largest
expensive	more expensive than	

Irregular forms:
bad – worse – the worst, good – better – the best,
little – less – the least, much/many – more – the most

9 **Put the adjectives in brackets into the correct form.**

1 The .... **(large)** mall in the world is in Dubai.
2 Supermarkets these days sell .... **(many)** products than they used to.
3 Colchester is the .... **(old)** market town in England.
4 High street shopping is not as .... **(convenient)** as shopping in a mall.
5 Corner shops have .... **(little)** product variety than supermarkets.
6 The .... **(cheap)** way to travel long distances is usually by coach.
7 The service in a small shop is often .... **(good)** than in a big one.
8 The .... **(bad)** shopping experience for most people is when shops are crowded.
9 This leather coat is not as .... **(warm)** as the woollen one, but it's .... **(light)**.
10 People say that Harrods is one of the .... **(beautiful)** buildings in London.

10 **SPEAKING Compare the three markets, as in the example.**

	Green Market	Holland Market	Hillside Market
expensive	✓✓✓	✓✓	✓
convenient	✓	✓✓✓	✓✓
crowded	✓✓	✓	✓✓✓
large	✓	✓✓	✓✓✓

Holland Market is more expensive than Hillside Market, but Green Market is the most expensive of all.

Skills in Action

Vocabulary

Clothes – Patterns & Materials

1 **Listen and learn. List the words in bold under the headings:** *materials – patterns*.

2 **Choose one of your classmates. Describe what he/she is wearing. Make three mistakes. Your partner corrects your mistakes.**

Listening

3 **Look at the pictures. What can you see?**
Now listen and tick (✓) the correct answer (A, B or C).

1 What did Anna buy yesterday?

A ☐ B ☐ C ☐

2 What did Mary give Sue as a present?

A ☐ B ☐ C ☐

3 What did Kate buy from the market?

A ☐ B ☐ C ☐

Everyday English

Describing lost property

4 a) **Read the first exchange. What seems to be the problem?**

b) **Which of these objects were in the bag?**
Listen and read to find out.

A: Welcome to Hadley's Department Store. How can I help you?
B: I was shopping here yesterday, and I think I left my bag in your fitting rooms.
A: What does it look like?
B: It's a blue denim handbag with brown leather handles.
A: What's it got in it?
B: My purse, a pair of plain red woollen gloves and my yellow sunglasses.
A: Where and when did you lose it exactly?
B: It was in the first fitting room near the entrance. It was just before closing time.
A: I think you're in luck. Is this it?
B: Oh, yes! Thank you very much!

5 **Use the prompts to act out similar dialogues. Record yourselves.**

wallet: money, photos, driving licence
rucksack: notebooks, wallet, scarf, four books

Pronunciation: *silent letters*

6 **Listen and underline the silent letters. Listen again and repeat.**

• know • talk • listen • autumn • write • design • comb • honest

Reading & Writing

7 Read the email. Which paragraph (a-c) contains ...

1 a recommendation & invitation? ....
2 descriptions of shops? ....
3 opening remarks & where writer was? ....

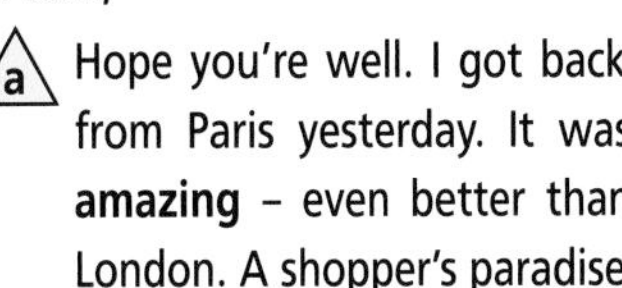

From: Kristin
To: Sam
Subject: Back from Paris trip!

Hi Sam,

a Hope you're well. I got back from Paris yesterday. It was **amazing** – even better than London. A shopper's paradise!

b The sales were on, so I went to the department stores and found some great bargains. Department stores in Paris are **huge**, so I was on my feet for hours at a time. **Exhausting**! There were also some **fantastic** antique shops on Bonaparte and Jacob Streets, and interesting bookstalls along the River Seine. I discovered the Marais, an area with **tiny** boutiques selling the trendiest clothes. I picked up a cool coat (see attachment)!

c I really recommend Paris as a shopping destination. Actually, I'm planning to go again. Why don't you come with me? Write back.

Love

Kristin

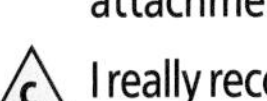

Writing Tip

Descriptive language

Use adjectives to bring your descriptions to life. Avoid adjectives like *good*, *bad*, *nice*, etc because the reader soon gets bored with them.

8 Replace the adjectives in the paragraph below with the ones in bold from the email.

New York has got some **good** shops. I went to Macy's, the **big** department store, and found some **good** bargains. It was very busy, though, so that was **bad**. I preferred the **small** shops on Bleecker Street, Greenwich Village.

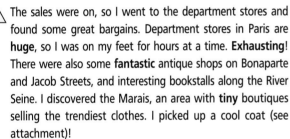

Recommending

9 Complete the sentences. Use: *like*, *miss*, *recommend*, *worth*.

1 I really .... Madrid as a shopping destination.
2 Don't .... the chance to go shopping if you're in Marrakesh.
3 If you .... shopping, you should definitely visit New York.
4 It's well .... visiting Dubai just for the shops.

Writing (an email about a weekend break)

10 Read the task. Copy the spidergram and complete it in your notebooks.

Imagine you went to the capital city in your country or in another country on a weekend break. Write an email to your English-speaking friend describing what shops you visited and what you bought (80-120 words).

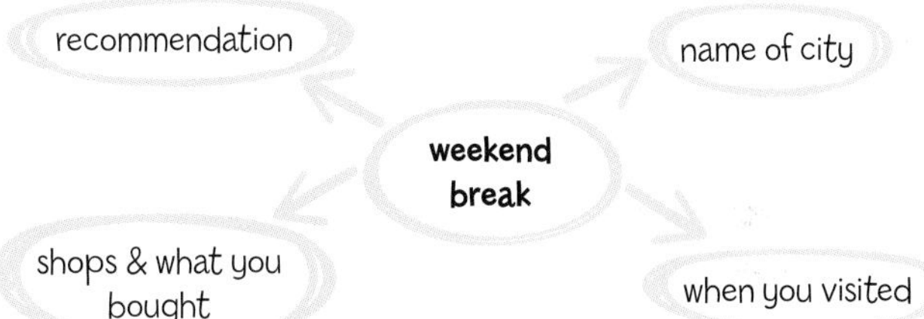

11 Use your notes in the spidergram in Ex. 10 to write your email. Follow the plan.

Plan

Hi/Hey, (+ first name)

Para 1: name of city, when you went there, what the shopping was like

Para 2: names of shops, what you bought

Para 3: recommendation

Bye for now/See you,

(your first name)

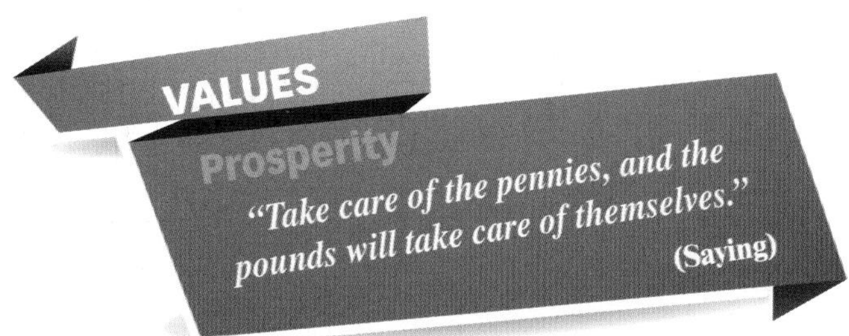

VALUES
Prosperity
"Take care of the pennies, and the pounds will take care of themselves."
(Saying)

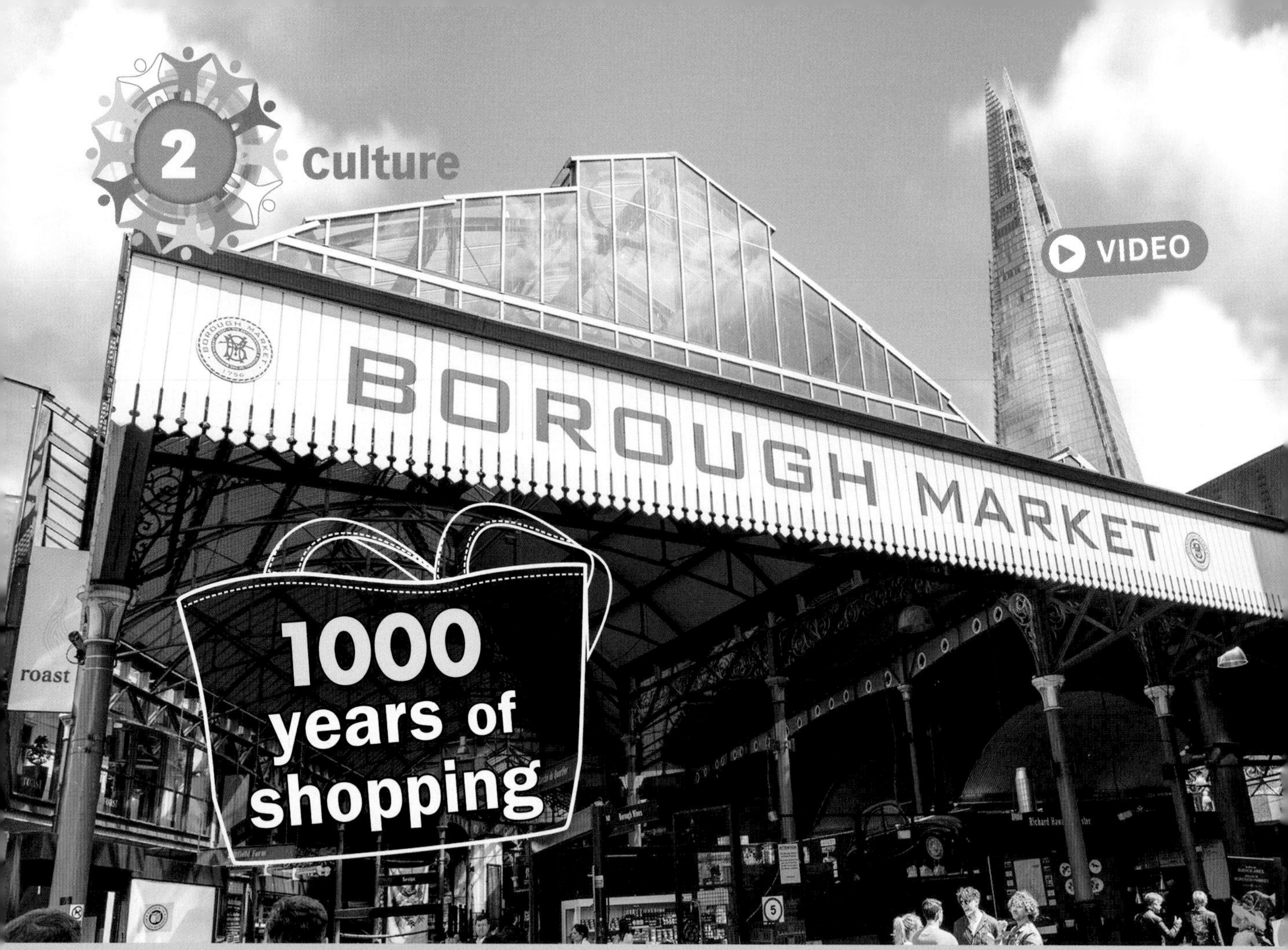

VIDEO

1000 years of shopping

"First they made their way to London, and so up into the Thames, but the Danes held the city. On the other side of the river is a great market town called Southwark ..."

Snorri Sturluson, the great Icelandic storyteller, wrote those words in 1014. That same Southwark is now the London borough of Southwark, and the market is still there! In 2014, Borough Market celebrated its 1000th anniversary – though it's probably much older.

Its success is all about **location**. It is on the south bank of the River Thames, just by London Bridge. The Romans built the first bridge there in around 55 CE, and until 1729, it was the only place you could cross the river into London. So farmers and fishermen came to Southwark to sell their **produce**.

Today's Borough Market is different from the old one in lots of ways. It is smaller and more **organised**. It is a green market, with a 'zero food waste' philosophy. It is also famous for its restaurants and street food. There's even a demo kitchen, so you can learn the secrets of cooking from top chefs.

But just like then, it is a food market, and sells food of all kinds from all around the British Isles and **beyond**. Many of the people you buy from are also the producers, so you get bread from the baker, cheese from the farmer and fish straight from the fisherman. Borough Market is a brilliant part of London, full of life and history.

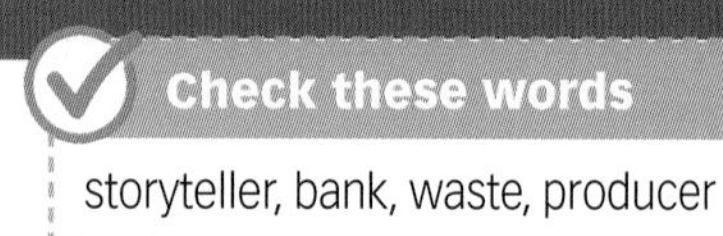

Listening & Reading

1 **Read the title and the quotation, then look at the picture. What do you think you'll find out about Borough Market?**

Listen and read to find out.

2 **Read again and complete the sentences. Then, explain the words in bold.**

1. Borough Market is more than .... years old.
2. It is next to .... , opposite the City of London.
3. A lot of people go to Borough Market to eat at the ....
4. The market sells food from within Britain and ....

Speaking & Writing

3 THINK **What makes a market popular with customers? Has Borough Market got these features?**

4 THINK ICT **What old or historic market is there in your country? Collect information, then write a short text for an online travel magazine. Write about:** *name – location – history – what it sells.*

Review 2

Vocabulary

1 **Fill in:** *handed, took, looked, employed, designed.*

1 Jo .... clothes for a big fashion company.
2 I .... around the shop while my friend tried on jeans.
3 Joan .... over the business from her father.
4 They .... out food and blankets.
5 The supermarket .... 200 staff in 2012.

(5 x 3 = 15)

2 **Choose the odd word out.**

1 woollen – cotton – scarf – silk – denim
2 plain – striped – spotted – floral – linen
3 shirt – jacket – cardigan – comb – trousers
4 leather – round – triangular – square – rectangular
5 butcher's – florist's – magazine – chemist's – bank
6 tights – bread – sugar – grapes – chops

(6 x 2 = 12)

Grammar

3 **Put the verbs in brackets into the past simple.**

1 Henry .... **(buy)** a coat yesterday.
2 I .... **(get)** this spotted scarf in Milan.
3 .... **(he/travel)** to Asia last summer?
4 Sam .... **(study)** fashion design.
5 Liam .... **(not/take)** your hat.

(5 x 4 = 20)

4 **Correct the mistake in each sentence.**

1 Did you used to go to college on Wednesday?
2 Gemma use to have longer hair.
3 Ken's uncle didn't used to work as a doorman.
4 We used to meet for coffee yesterday.

(4 x 3 = 12)

5 **Put the adjectives in brackets in the correct order.**

1 a(n) .... bag **(Italian, lovely, leather)**
2 a .... hat **(round, red, small)**
3 a .... scarf **(woollen, striped, long)**
4 a(n) .... ring **(expensive, gold, old)**
5 a .... bat **(wooden, short, heavy)**

(5 x 2 = 10)

6 **Fill in the correct form of the adjectives in brackets. Add *than* or *the* where necessary.**

1 London is .... Rome, but New York is .... of all. **(big)**
2 Cotton is not as .... as wool, but silk is .... of all. **(expensive)**
3 This wooden clock is .... the metal one, but it's not as .... as the gold one. **(old)**
4 "That was .... food ever!" "Come on – it wasn't as .... as Mum's!" **(tasty)**

(4 x 4 = 16)

Everyday English

7 **Match the exchanges.**

1 ☐ Could I have four red apples?
2 ☐ What's it got in it?
3 ☐ What does it look like?
4 ☐ Where and when did you lose it exactly?
5 ☐ How can I help you?

A In the fitting rooms.
B Sorry, we haven't got any left.
C I think I lost my purse here yesterday.
D Just my keys and a pair of glasses.
E It's a long black-and-white woollen scarf.

(5 x 3 = 15)
Total 100

Competences

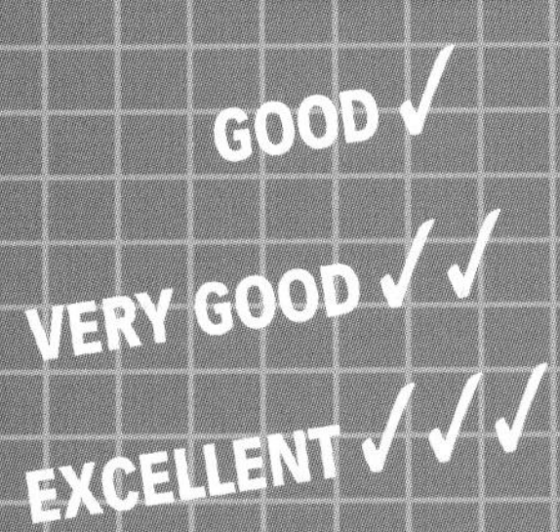

Lexical Competence
Understand words/ phrases related to:
- shops and shopping
- clothes
- patterns and materials

Reading Competence
- understand texts related to shops & shopping (read for gist – matching headings to paragraphs)

Listening Competence
- listen and understand dialogues related to products (listen for specific information – multiple choice questions)

Speaking Competence
- ask for things in a shop
- describe objects

Writing Competence
- write an email about a weekend break

Vocabulary: Weather phenomena; Feelings & Sounds
Grammar: past continuous – *while/when*, past continuous vs past simple
Everyday English: Giving a witness statement
Writing: A story

3 Survival stories

Vocabulary

Weather phenomena

1 **Listen and learn. Which of these weather phenomena happened in your country last year?**

1 blizzard

2 tornado

3 tsunami

4 hurricane

5 lightning

6 flood

2 **Fill in:** *blowing, shining, coming, pouring, raining.*

1 A flash of lightning lit up the dark sky; a violent storm was ....
2 It was .... heavily as we were driving.
3 The day after the flood, the sun was .... brightly, but the streets were still under water.
4 The wind was .... hard and it was .... with rain.

Reading

3 **Read the background information about Abby Sunderland. What do you think happened to Abby in the Indian Ocean?**
Listen and read to find out.

Surviving Solo

Abby Sunderland was 16 years old when she set sail from the USA in January 2010, on her boat *Wild Eyes*. Her goal? To sail around the world – alone. After five months, she headed into the Indian Ocean – one of the most remote and dangerous places on Earth.

4 **Read the blog entries and for questions 1-4, choose the best answer (A-C).**

1 At first Abby found the bad weather
A exhausting. **B** scary. **C** exciting.
2 The boat was damaged by
A the wind. **B** a wave.
C the broken mast.
3 Abby communicated with the rescue plane using
A her satellite phone.
B signals.
C her radio.
4 How does Abby feel about her experience?
A relieved that it's finished
B unhappy that the weather was so bad
C proud that she kept herself alive

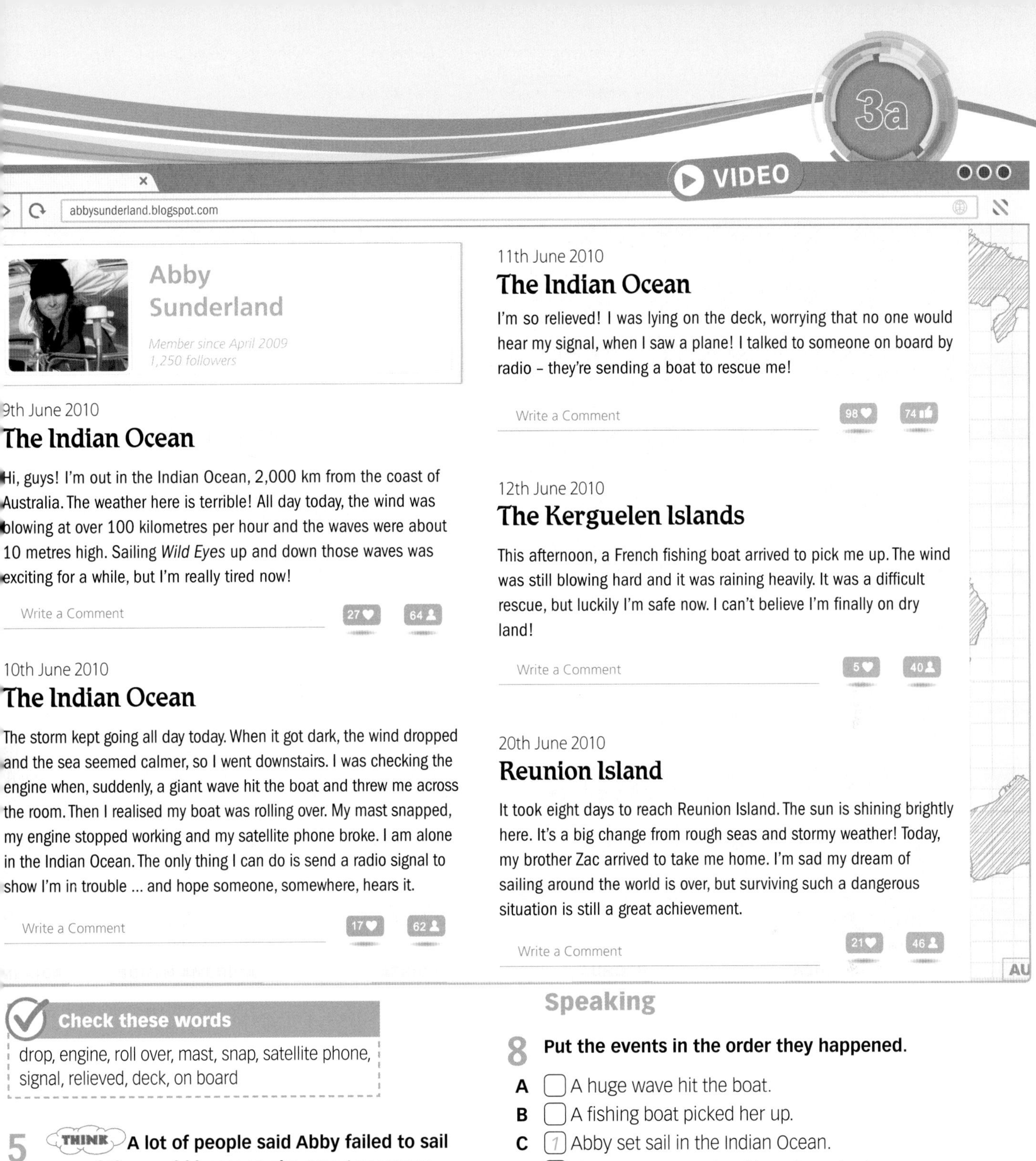

VIDEO

abbysunderland.blogspot.com

Abby Sunderland

Member since April 2009
1,250 followers

9th June 2010

The Indian Ocean

Hi, guys! I'm out in the Indian Ocean, 2,000 km from the coast of Australia. The weather here is terrible! All day today, the wind was blowing at over 100 kilometres per hour and the waves were about 10 metres high. Sailing *Wild Eyes* up and down those waves was exciting for a while, but I'm really tired now!

Write a Comment 27 64

10th June 2010

The Indian Ocean

The storm kept going all day today. When it got dark, the wind dropped and the sea seemed calmer, so I went downstairs. I was checking the engine when, suddenly, a giant wave hit the boat and threw me across the room. Then I realised my boat was rolling over. My mast snapped, my engine stopped working and my satellite phone broke. I am alone in the Indian Ocean. The only thing I can do is send a radio signal to show I'm in trouble ... and hope someone, somewhere, hears it.

Write a Comment 17 62

11th June 2010

The Indian Ocean

I'm so relieved! I was lying on the deck, worrying that no one would hear my signal, when I saw a plane! I talked to someone on board by radio – they're sending a boat to rescue me!

Write a Comment 98 74

12th June 2010

The Kerguelen Islands

This afternoon, a French fishing boat arrived to pick me up. The wind was still blowing hard and it was raining heavily. It was a difficult rescue, but luckily I'm safe now. I can't believe I'm finally on dry land!

Write a Comment 5 40

20th June 2010

Reunion Island

It took eight days to reach Reunion Island. The sun is shining brightly here. It's a big change from rough seas and stormy weather! Today, my brother Zac arrived to take me home. I'm sad my dream of sailing around the world is over, but surviving such a dangerous situation is still a great achievement.

Write a Comment 21 46

Check these words

drop, engine, roll over, mast, snap, satellite phone, signal, relieved, deck, on board

5 THINK **A lot of people said Abby failed to sail around the world because she was too young. Do you think this is true? Why or why not?**

6 **Fill in:** *satellite, stormy, giant, dry, fishing.*

1 .... land
2 .... weather
3 .... phone
4 .... boat
5 .... wave

We form adverbs by adding ***(-i)ly*** to the adjective.
nice – nicely, angry – angrily
BUT: ***good – well, hard – hard, fast – fast, late – late***

7 **Find the adverbs in the text formed from these words:** *bright, hard, lucky, sudden, heavy.*

Speaking

8 **Put the events in the order they happened.**

A ☐ A huge wave hit the boat.
B ☐ A fishing boat picked her up.
C [1] Abby set sail in the Indian Ocean.
D ☐ The mast snapped and her phone broke.
E ☐ She sent a radio signal.
F ☐ She went to check the engine.
G ☐ Her brother took her home.
H ☐ She saw a plane.
I ☐ They reached Reunion Island.

9 **Use your answers from Ex. 8 to give a summary of Abby's story to the class.**

Writing

10 **Imagine you were a rescue worker on the plane that spotted Abby's boat. Write a blog entry about it. Include:** *where you were – what happened – how you felt*. **Tell the class.**

Grammar in Use

Fast Facts **News**

Avalanche in the Alps

At 8:46 am yesterday morning, an avalanche struck at Tignes in the French Alps. It crashed down onto the resort's main ski slope, close to the Grande Hotel where a lot of the guests were having breakfast.

Luckily, because of the bad weather, only a few people were skiing at that time. Four tourists though – Mr and Mrs Jones and their two teenage children – were missing.

Theo Bisset, the manager of the hotel, called the emergency services. Snow was falling heavily and strong winds were blowing. The rescue helicopters couldn't fly, so Bisset grabbed his boots and set out to look for them himself. He was searching the area furthest from the hotel when he heard a shout. It took him another hour to dig the family out.

"We were afraid." said Mr Jones later. "But we knew the people at the resort would find a way to rescue us." Fortunately for Mr Jones and his family, he was right.

1 **Read the table. How do we form the past continuous?**

Past continuous

Affirmative	Negative
I/he/she/it **was eating** we/you/they **were eating**	I/he/she/it **wasn't eating** we/you/they **weren't eating**
Interrogative	**Short Answers**
Was I/he/she/it **eating**? **Were** we/you/they **eating**?	Yes I/he/she/it **was**./ No, he/she/it **wasn't**. Yes, we/you/they **were**./ No, we/you/they **weren't**.

Time expressions with the past continuous:
at 9 o'clock yesterday morning/evening; at 10 o'clock last night, etc.

2 **Match the underlined verb forms in the news report with the uses:**

a) *two or more actions happening at the same time in the past*
b) *background information in a story*
c) *action in progress interrupted by another action in the past*
d) *action in progress at a stated time in the past*

3 **Look at the notes. Write sentences as in the example.**

3 – 4 pm Pam/play basketball
5 – 6 pm George and Pam/shop
6 – 7 pm Sue/cook dinner
6 – 7 pm Kate/drive home
7 – 8 pm George/chat online

1 Pam *was playing basketball* at 3:30 pm.
2 George and Pam .... at 5:30 pm.
3 Sue .... at 6:40 pm.
4 Kate .... at 6:55 pm.
5 George .... at 7:45 pm.

4 SPEAKING **What were you doing at these times:** *last Monday*? *last Sunday*?

• 6 am • 8:30 am • 11 am • 3:30 pm • 7 pm

At 6 am last Monday, I was getting dressed.
At the same time last Sunday, I was sleeping.

5 **Read the theory, then choose the correct word.**

while/when

while + **past continuous**:
- two past actions happening at the same time. *Tony **was reading** a book **while** Sam **was surfing** the Net.*
- a past action in progress interrupted by another action. ***While** Paul **was cooking**, the lights went off.*

when + **past simple**: past action that interrupted a past action in progress.
***When** the lights **went off**, Paul was cooking.*

1 Jane was driving **while/when** Kate was sleeping.
2 He was driving on the motorway **when/while** the police stopped him.
3 Sue was walking back home **when/while** it was raining.
4 Paul was waiting in the car **while/when** Tim was trying to find a petrol station.
5 Bob was sleeping **when/while** the phone rang.

6 **These people were in the garden last Sunday at midday. Look at the pictures and correct the sentences.**

Paul

Ann

Sue

Jane & Mary

Bob

1 Paul was playing with the dog.
Paul wasn't playing with the dog. He was painting the door.

2 Ann was eating an apple.
....
....

3 Sue was watering the flowers.
....
....

4 Jane and Mary were cutting the grass.
....
....

5 Bob was painting the door.
....
....

7 **Ask and answer questions, as in the example.**

1 at 6 o'clock yesterday afternoon?
A: What were you doing at 6 o'clock yesterday afternoon?
B: I was having a lesson.

2 last Saturday morning at 10:30?

3 yesterday afternoon at 3:30?

4 at this time last Wednesday?

5 at 10 o'clock last Sunday night?

8 **Form questions, then answer them, as in the example.**

1 Bob/send emails/at 10 o'clock/last night? – No/vlog
Was Bob sending emails at 10 o'clock last night?
No, he wasn't. He was vlogging.

2 Paula/fly/to New York/yesterday morning? – No/have/a meeting

3 Mark and Terry/watch/TV/on Sunday afternoon? – No/chat online

4 you/work/yesterday afternoon? – No/study/at the library

9 **Choose the correct tense. Give reasons.**

1 Kate got her bag and **walked/was walking** out of the room.

2 He **slept/was sleeping** at 8 o'clock, and so he didn't answer the phone.

3 They were **climbing/climbed** the mountain when an avalanche struck.

4 I **didn't go/wasn't going** out yesterday afternoon.

5 They were hiking through the forest when it **started/was starting** raining.

6 While Daniel was talking on the phone, Max **watched/was watching** the news.

10 a) **Put the verbs in brackets into the past simple or the past continuous.**

It was a bitterly cold morning. Grey clouds **1)** .... ***(hang)*** *low in the sky and snow* **2)** .... ***(fall)****. It* **3)** .... ***(be)*** *the beginning of the winter holidays and Laura* **4)** .... ***(travel)*** *home from university to spend the holidays with her family.*

Suddenly, an elderly gentleman **5)** .... ***(enter)*** *her carriage. He* **6)** .... ***(wear)*** *a black coat and he* **7)** .... ***(carry)*** *a briefcase. He* **8)** .... ***(sit)*** *opposite Laura,* **9)** .... ***(open)*** *his briefcase,* **10)** .... ***(take)*** *out an envelope and* **11)** .... ***(give)*** *it to Laura.*

b) THINK **Continue the story in Ex. 10a.**

Skills in Action

Vocabulary

Feelings & Sounds

1 **Use the words** *thrilled*, *anxious*, *sad*, *puzzled*, *relieved*, *angry*, *proud*, *frightened* **to say how each person felt.**

1 Alex had no idea who the mysterious parcel was from.
2 She finally had her very own horse! This was the best day of her life.
3 Mandy thought she heard footsteps behind her. She started walking more quickly.
4 Mike's parents were so pleased when he won the award.
5 Becky screamed when she saw the snake.
6 "You lied to me!" she shouted. "I can never forgive you!"
7 Evan couldn't believe it. His brother was alive, after all these years – and he was coming home!
8 Emma couldn't stop crying while her sister was driving away.

2 **Listen and tick (✓) the sounds in the order you hear them.**

A a siren wailing ☐
B the wind blowing ☐
C car brakes screeching ☐
D someone knocking on the door ☐
E rain falling ☐
F a dog barking ☐

3 THINK **Use the phrases from Ex. 2 to continue the story.**

The wind was blowing as John was walking back home. He heard a dog. It was barking. ...

Listening

4 **Listen and match the speakers to how they feel.**

Speaker 1 ☐ a thrilled
Speaker 2 ☐ b puzzled
Speaker 3 ☐ c sad
Speaker 4 ☐ d frightened

Everyday English

A witness report

5 **Put the verbs in the past simple or past continuous, then listen and check.**

A: So, Mr Jeffries, where **1)** .... **(you/be)** at the time of the burglary?
B: I **2)** .... **(be)** in my garden.
A: What **3)** .... **(you/do)**?
B: I **4)** .... **(cut)** the grass.
A: What **5)** .... **(happen)** exactly?
B: Well, I **6)** .... **(hear)** someone shout from number 15, and then I **7)** .... **(see)** a man in jeans and a black top running down the street. I **8)** .... **(try)** to chase after him, but he was too fast.
A: **9)** .... **(you/see)** his face?
B: No, I'm afraid not. But I **10)** .... **(see)** him get into a car at the end of the street. I **11)** .... **(write)** down the number of the car as it **12)** .... **(drive)** away.
A: That's really helpful. Thank you.
B: You're welcome.

6 **Use the prompts to act out a similar dialogue. Use phrases from the Useful Language box.**

• robbery • come out of post office
• 2 men in black • blue van

Asking questions	Giving information
• What were you doing ...? • Where were you/did you ...? • What did you *(hear/see, etc.)*?	• I was ... . • I (was) ... . • I *(heard/saw, etc.)* ... .
Thanking	**Responding**
• Thank you for your time. • That's really helpful.	• I'm glad I could help. • You're welcome.

Pronunciation: stressed words

7 **Listen and underline the stressed word, then tick (✓) the correct meaning. Listen again and repeat.**

1 I was here at <u>six</u> o'clock.
☐ not somewhere else ☐ not at seven o'clock
2 A young woman was standing at the door.
☐ not an old woman ☐ not a young man
3 They were both very sad.
☐ not just one of them ☐ they weren't happy

Writing Tip

Setting the scene

We start a story by setting the scene, that is we write **where** and **when** the story takes place, **who** the people are, **what** the weather is like and **what** happened first.

Reading

8 **Read the story and put the events in the correct order. How did the writer set the scene?**

As soon as Fay woke up, she knew this day was going to be very special. The sun was shining brightly through her bedroom window and a gentle breeze was blowing. An hour later, her cousin Alex picked her up for a ride in a hot-air balloon!

Fay was thrilled when the huge, yellow balloon began to rise slowly into the air. "This is fantastic!" she shouted cheerfully.

Suddenly, the happy smile disappeared from her face. Dark clouds were gathering in the sky and the wind started blowing hard. The balloon shook violently from side to side. Fay screamed loudly and covered her eyes, then she felt the balloon crash into something.

"Are you alright?" Alex asked anxiously. "The wind blew us into a tree, but we're OK. I'm calling for help." A fire engine arrived and soon Fay and Alex were safely on the ground. It was a day to remember.

A [8] A fire engine arrived.
B [ ] Alex picked Fay up.
C [ ] The balloon crashed into a tree.
D [1] Fay woke up.
E [ ] The balloon rose into the air.
F [ ] Alex called for help.
G [ ] The balloon shook violently from side to side.
H [ ] Dark clouds gathered in the sky.

Writing Tip

Descriptive language

We can use a variety of adverbs and adjectives in our stories to make them more interesting to the reader.

*She was holding a bouquet of **pretty flowers**.*
*"Excuse me," the young woman **said sweetly**.*

9 **Find the adjectives the writer used to describe:** *the breeze, the balloon, the smile, the clouds.*

10 **Fill in the correct adverb from the story, then say how we form adverbs.**

1	bright →	5	hard → ....
2	slow →	6	loud → ....
3	cheerful →	7	anxious → ....
4	sudden →	8	safe → ....

Writing (a story)

11 **a) Listen and put the events in the correct order. Then, use the events to retell the story.**

A [ ] Two fishermen pulled the canoe to safety.
B [1] Mark & Dan pushed their canoe onto the river.
C [ ] They stopped to have some coffee.
D [ ] They thanked the fishermen.
E [ ] They got back into the canoe.
F [5] They saw a waterfall.
G [ ] They saw a kingfisher.

b) Use the list of events in Ex. 11a and the plan below to write a story entitled *The Waterfall*, for a teen magazine short story competition. (100-120 words).

Plan

Introduction

Para 1: set the scene *(who, when, where, what)*

Main body

Paras 2-3: develop the story (events before the main event, the main event itself)

Conclusion

Para 4: end the story (what happened in the end, how people felt)

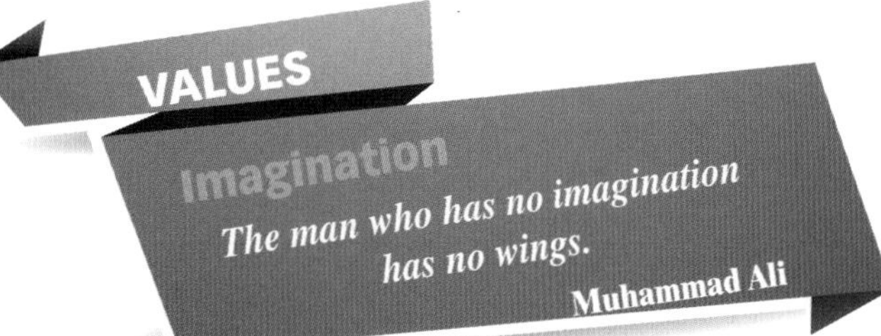

VALUES
Imagination
The man who has no imagination has no wings.
Muhammad Ali

3 Culture

Sir Ernest Shackleton

VIDEO

5th December 1914
Today we left South Georgia, an island off the coast of South America, and started our journey to Antarctica. I am on the ship *Endurance* with 27 men. I feel very excited. We are trying to be the first people to cross Antarctica!

19th January 1915
We are one day away from Antarctica, but the *Endurance* is trapped. The ice froze around it and we can't get out. We have to stay here until the ice melts.

21st November 1915
The ice was **destroying** our ship so, two days ago, I ordered my men to leave the *Endurance*. Now we are camping in tents on the ice. Today, the Endurance **sank**. We saved the dogs, the food and three lifeboats, but we've got no radio.

16th April 1916
After six months, the ice finally broke up on 9th April. We jumped into the lifeboats and headed for Elephant Island, 160 km away. It was crazy – we didn't have a map – but Captain Worsley found the island! It took seven days, and we are all so **relieved** to stand on dry land again.

24th April 1916
I'm going to South Georgia – in a tiny lifeboat. It's 1,300 km away, but I have to do it. I have to **save** my men.

20th May 1916
I sailed in the lifeboat with five other men. It was a terrible journey but, on 10th May, we landed in South Georgia. I **left** three men with the boat, and Crean, Worsley and I went to find help. We walked for 36 hours, up and down snowy mountains. We didn't stop and we got so tired, but we found a boat!

30th August 1916
I tried to **reach** Elephant Island three times. Every time the ice stopped me, but today I **rescued** my men! It's the best day of my life! We wanted to cross Antarctica – we didn't even land on it. But we **survived**! All my men are alive.

Listening & Reading

1 **In December 1914, British explorer Sir Ernest Shackleton and his team, set out to cross Antarctica. They didn't return until 1916, but they never set foot on the continent of Antarctica. What happened to them? Can you guess?**
Listen and read to find out.

Check these words

trap, melt, sink, break up, survive, alive

2 **Read the diary entries and complete the sentences. Then explain the words in bold.**

1 The *Endurance* was a ....
2 Shackleton and his men wanted to be the first people to ....
3 The ship sank because the ....
4 Shackleton went to South Georgia to ....

Speaking & Writing

3 THINK **Imagine you were one of the men on Elephant Island. How did you feel when Shackleton finally rescued you? Tell the class.**

4 ICT **Collect information about an explorer from your country or another country. Write a short paragraph about him/her.**

Review

Vocabulary

1 Read the definitions and write the correct word.

1 This is a storm with very strong winds. h _ _ _ _ _ _ _ _
2 This is a huge wave. t _ _ _ _ _ _
3 This is a flash of light in a storm l _ _ _ _ _ _ _ _
4 You can see them in the sky. c _ _ _ _ _
5 This is a storm with strong winds and snow. b _ _ _ _ _ _ _.

(5 x 2 = 10)

2 Fill in: *snapped, poured, raining, blowing, dropped*.

1 The wind was .... hard when we left the harbour.
2 The rain .... down for three days and nights.
3 After the storm, the wind .... and the sea became calm.
4 When the boat rolled over, the mast .... into two pieces.
5 It was .... heavily all day yesterday.

(5 x 3 = 15)

3 Fill in: *thrilled, anxious, heavy, thick, stormy*.

1 We couldn't see through the .... fog.
2 The rain is very .... – you can't go outside to play.
3 They sailed for 17 days on .... seas.
4 Paul was .... when he got sailing lessons for his birthday present.
5 Maria felt .... while she was waiting for her brother to return from the Antarctic.

(5 x 3 = 15)

Grammar

4 Choose the correct tense.

1 What **did you do/were you doing** at 9 pm last night?
2 Her parents **bought/were buying** her a boat last year.
3 I **didn't see/wasn't seeing** her at school yesterday.
4 Tony **didn't ride/wasn't riding** his bike when I saw him outside the cinema – he was in his sister's car.
5 Why **did you call/were you calling** him last night?

(5 x 4 = 20)

5 Put the verbs in brackets into the past simple or the past continuous.

1 He .... **(find)** his seat on the train, ... **(sit)** down and .... **(take)** out a book.
2 .... **(you/see)** the accident while you .... **(drive)** to work?
3 The wind .... **(blow)** and the rain .... **(pour)** down yesterday morning.
4 At 8:30 last night, I .... **(read)** a book. I .... **(not/hear)** the phone ringing.
5 She .... **(visit)** the museum last Sunday.

(5 x 4 = 20)

Everyday English

6 Choose the correct response.

1 A: What were you doing yesterday evening?
B: **a** At about 7:30. **b** I was watching TV.

2 A: Thank you for your time.
B: **a** You're welcome. **b** I'm afraid not.

3 A: What did you see?
B: **a** A black car outside the house.
b I tried calling the police.

4 A: I took a photo of the car with my phone.
B: **a** Thank you for your time.
b That's really helpful.

(4 x 5 = 20)

Total 100

Competences

Lexical Competence
Understand words/ phrases related to
- weather phenomena
- feelings & sounds

Reading Competence
- understand texts related to weather (read for specific information – multiple choice)

Listening Competence
- listen and understand monologues about feelings (listen for attitude – multiple matching)

Speaking Competence
- give a witness report

Writing Competence
- write a story
- write a blog entry about an experience of yours

Values: Diversity

VIDEO

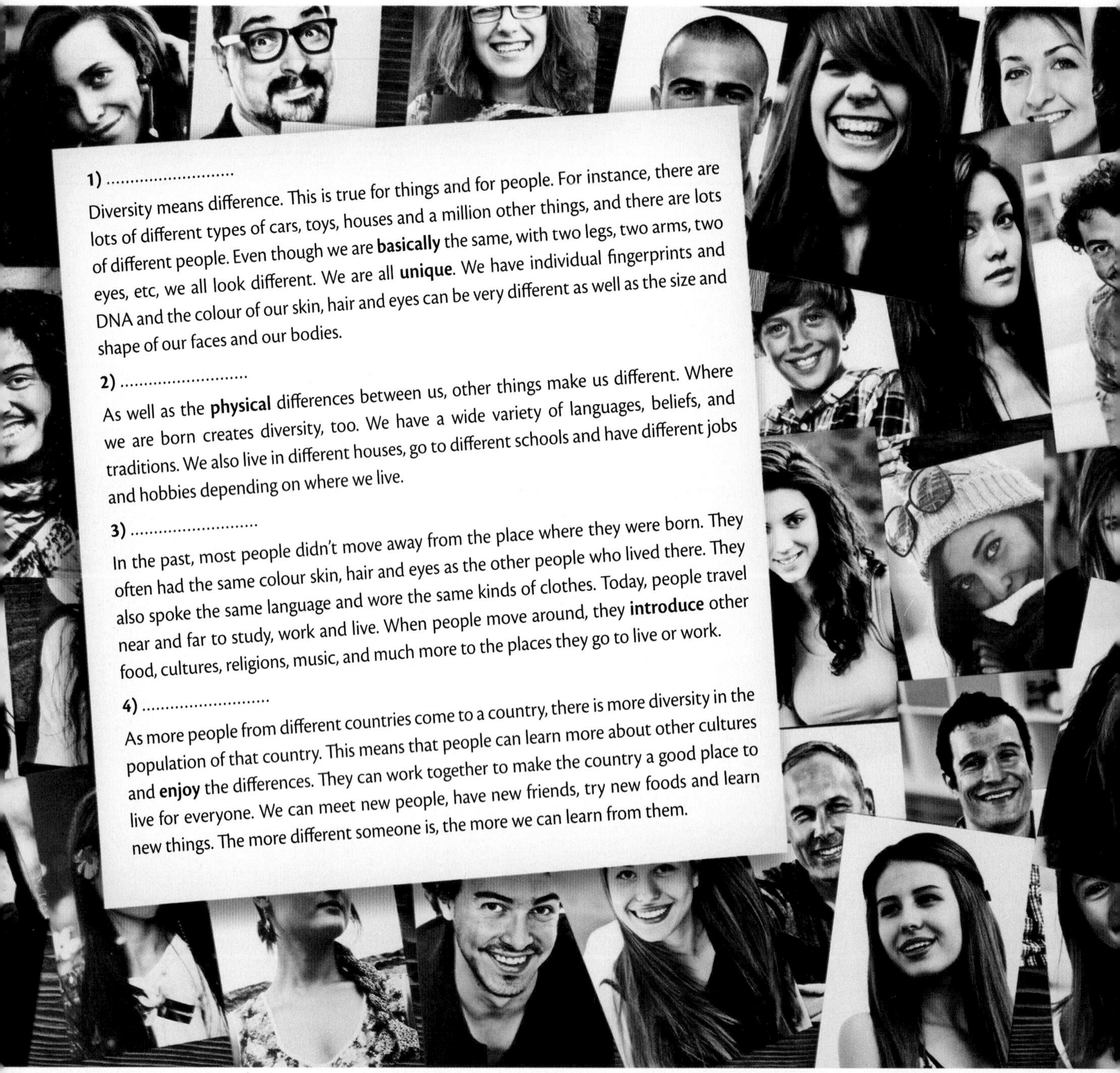

1) ....

Diversity means difference. This is true for things and for people. For instance, there are lots of different types of cars, toys, houses and a million other things, and there are lots of different people. Even though we are **basically** the same, with two legs, two arms, two eyes, etc, we all look different. We are all **unique**. We have individual fingerprints and DNA and the colour of our skin, hair and eyes can be very different as well as the size and shape of our faces and our bodies.

2) ....

As well as the **physical** differences between us, other things make us different. Where we are born creates diversity, too. We have a wide variety of languages, beliefs, and traditions. We also live in different houses, go to different schools and have different jobs and hobbies depending on where we live.

3) ....

In the past, most people didn't move away from the place where they were born. They often had the same colour skin, hair and eyes as the other people who lived there. They also spoke the same language and wore the same kinds of clothes. Today, people travel near and far to study, work and live. When people move around, they **introduce** other food, cultures, religions, music, and much more to the places they go to live or work.

4) ....

As more people from different countries come to a country, there is more diversity in the population of that country. This means that people can learn more about other cultures and **enjoy** the differences. They can work together to make the country a good place to live for everyone. We can meet new people, have new friends, try new foods and learn new things. The more different someone is, the more we can learn from them.

1 **What is diversity? Can you give two examples?**

2 **Read the article and fill in the headings. Then explain the words/phrases in bold.**

A How does diversity happen?
B What's so great about diversity?
C What does diversity look like?
D What is diversity?

3 THINK **Listen to and read the text. Is it OK to be different? Discuss.**

4 **Think of people in a different country than yours. In what ways are they different from you? Make notes. Tell the class.**

Public Speaking Skills

Purposes of presentations

We give presentations to:

- **entertain** the audience
- **narrate** events
- **inform** the audience about something they may not know
- **persuade** the audience to do something

1 Read the task. What is the purpose of the presentation?

You are in the UK on a student exchange programme. It is Culture Day and everyone is presenting their country and its people. Present yours.

2 Listen to and read the model. What opening/closing techniques did the speaker use: *a riddle/humour*? *addressing the listeners directly*? *a statement*? *a quote/saying*? *a rhetorical question*? *a rhyme/short poem*?

Hello, everybody! My name's Kannika.

Do you know where I'm from? My country is in Southeast Asia, it's got a tropical climate, white sandy beaches and many beautiful ancient temples. Let me give you a clue – its nickname is 'The Land of Smiles'... That's right – it's Thailand! Thailand is a beautiful country, but what makes it really special is its people.

Thai people usually have delicate features. We've often got black hair, dark eyes and a golden, light tanned complexion. The Thais are friendly people who are well known for being welcoming, generous and kind. We are a happy people and we're very proud of our history.

A lot of people in Thailand still live in villages. A typical Thai village consists of wooden houses, a school and a Buddhist temple. Most of the people in the villages are farmers and fishermen. The men usually work in the fields or catch fish in the rivers and the women plant the crops.

Family life is very important in Thailand, and families often eat together. Thai food is spicy and includes curries, fish, seafood, soups and noodles. We eat lots of rice, too! In our free time we like watching sports, going to the cinema and eating out.

Thailand is one of the most wonderful countries to visit. Its fascinating sights, rich cultural history and warm-hearted people make it unique. 30 million visitors a year can't be wrong, can they?

3 Copy the spidergram in your notebook. Complete it with information about your country and people.

Country
- location, climate & nickname
- people's appearance & character
- lifestyle, food & free time
- reasons to visit

4 Use your notes in Ex. 3 to present your country and people to the audience.

Vocabulary: jobs; job qualities
Grammar: *will – going to –* present simple/continuous (future meaning)
Everyday English: having a job interview
Writing: A CV; an email applying for a job

Planning ahead

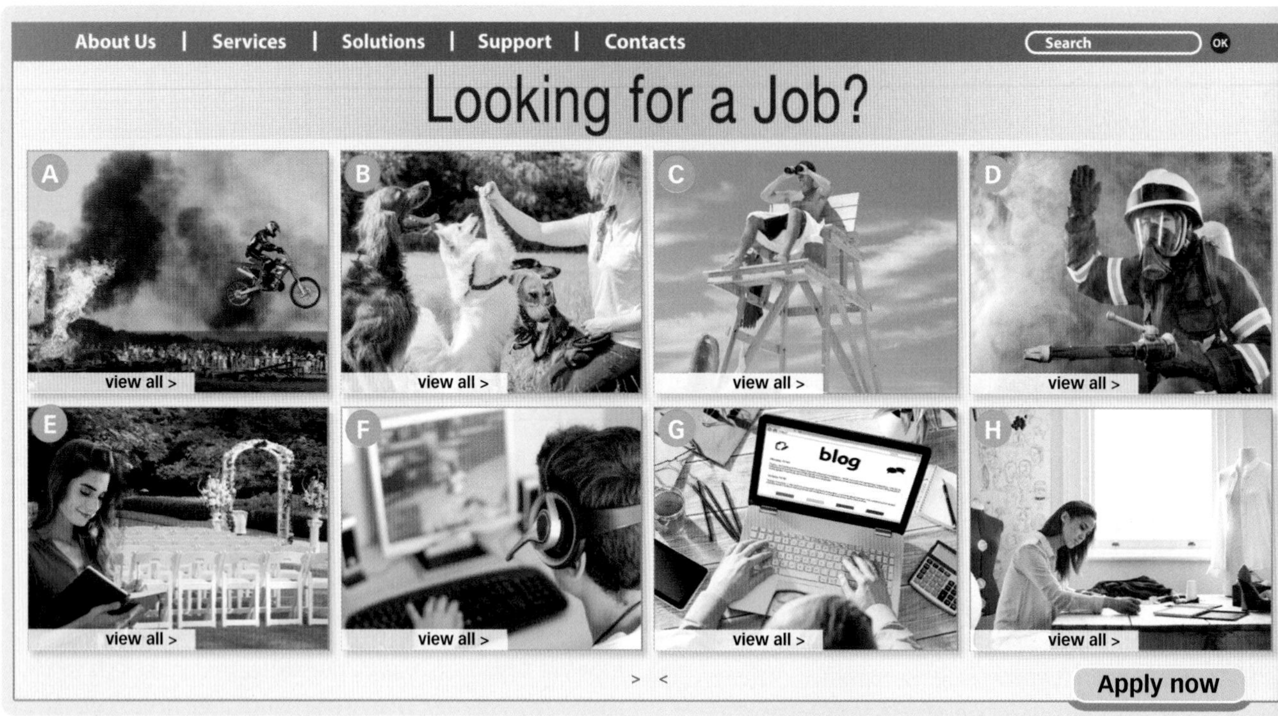

Vocabulary

Jobs

1 **a) Which of the jobs in the list can you see in the pictures?**

• animal trainer • app/software developer
• builder • doctor • event planner
• fashion designer • firefighter • gardener
• lifeguard • nurse • public relations specialist
• social media editor • stuntman • tour guide
• video game tester • web designer

b) Which of the jobs in Ex. 1a asks for: *physical skills – computer skills – creative skills – social skills – communication skills – organisational skills*?

2 **a) Which of the jobs in Ex. 1a would be appropriate for the following speakers?**

1 "I like giving companies feedback on their blogs and profile pages." ....
2 "I enjoy being outside taking care of plants." ....
3 "I love meeting new people and showing them new places." ....
4 "I like organising parties." ....
5 "I'm good at looking after sick people." ....
6 "I like being outdoors repairing houses." ....

b) Ask and answer questions about the jobs in Ex. 2a, as in the example.

A: *Which job would you most like to do?*
B: *I'd like to work as a nurse because I like looking after sick people. What about you?*
A: *I'd like to ...*

Listening & Reading

3 **Listen and match the people to the job they want to do and the reason why.**

Ito	event planner	wants to treat sick people
Chiara	firefighter	has great organisational skills
Neil	doctor	wants to save lives

4 **Read the text. For questions 1-6, choose from the people (A-C). Who ...**

1 ☐ believes in hard work?
2 ☐ exercises regularly?
3 ☐ is going to start their own business?
4 ☐ is at university?
5 ☐ has only just realised what job they want to do?
6 ☐ needs to take a training course?

One question has more than one answer. Then, explain the words in bold.

I'm Ellie from the USA and I'm 22 years old. I just finished college, and I still have no idea what job I want to do. Help!

A

Hi, Ellie! Ito from Japan here. When I was a kid, I wanted to be a firefighter – and I still do! Firefighters **save** lives and they have to be **fit** and strong, so I **work out** twice a week at the local gym to be ready for the entrance test. I'm sure I'll pass it. Then, I'm going to begin a training course and I'm going to work really hard. Good luck with finding your dream job!

B

Hey, guys! My name's Chiara and I'm from Italy. When I finished school, I didn't know what I wanted to do, either. Then, my brother got his **degree**. I **arranged** his graduation party – the guest list, the venue, the decorations, the food and the music. Everyone said they had a great time! That's when I realised I've got great organisational skills. So I made a decision – I'm going to be an event planner! I'm going to **set up** my own company and do what I'm good at. Think of what you are good at and I'm sure you will find the job that suits you.

C

This is Neil from Scotland. I agree with Ito and Chiara. You should follow your dreams and do something you're good at – **otherwise** you aren't going to be happy. But you need to work hard, too. My dream was always to treat sick people, so I'm studying to be a doctor. I know doctors work very **long hours** and they need to be careful not to make mistakes. When I finish, I'm going to start a full-time job in a hospital.

Check these words

entrance test, pass, venue, suit, agree

5 **Use the words from the list to complete the gaps, then make sentences using the completed phrases.**

• make • training • have • organisational • full-time • entrance • long • set up

1 to .... a company
2 to .... a decision
3 to work .... hours
4 to .... no idea
5 to have .... skills
6 a(n) .... course
7 a(n) .... job
8 a(n) .... test

6 **Choose the correct word. Check in your dictionary.**

1 He **took/passed** the test because he worked hard.
2 Gill is **learning/studying** Architecture at university.
3 Freddie decided to **follow/take** his dream.
4 Being a nurse isn't an easy **job/work**.

7 **WORDS EASILY CONFUSED** **Fill in *make* or *do*. Check in your dictionary. Choose four phrases and make sentences using the completed phrases.**

1 to .... mistakes
2 to .... a phone call
3 to .... my homework
4 to .... the beds
5 to .... the washing-up
6 to .... money
7 to .... a noise
8 to .... the shopping
9 to .... the ironing
10 to .... my best

8 **PREPOSITIONS** **Fill in:** ***at*, *from*, *of*, *for*, *with*, then make sentences using the completed phrases.**

1 to be .... (a country)
2 to be ready .... a test
3 to be good .... something
4 to think .... something
5 to agree .... somebody

Speaking

9 **Read the text again and take notes under these headings:** *Dream job – Reason – Job Qualities – Plans/ Fixed Arrangements*, **then talk about each person.**

Writing

10 THINK **What job would you like to do? Why? Write an entry for the forum.**

Grammar in Use

CALLING ALL FUTURE NURSES!

What are you doing next week?

Come along to **Careers Week**
19th - 23rd October at **Alexandra Hospital**.

There are going to be:

- tours of the new Children's Ward every two hours.
- nurses and doctors to answer your questions.

If you come on Monday, you will get the chance to meet the Chairman of the Board of the hospital.

The event starts at **10 am** and finishes at **4 pm** each day.

Be there!

1 **Read the theory. Find examples in the advert.**

***will* – *be going to* – Present continuous – Present simple**

- We use ***will*** to:
  - make **on-the-spot decisions**. *These boots are nice. I'**ll take** them, please.*
  - make **predictions** based on **what we think or imagine**. *I think the weather **will get** warmer soon.*
- We use ***be going to*** to:
  - talk about **future plans** and **intentions**. *I'**m going to** move to Seattle as soon as I get my degree.*
  - make **predictions** based on **what we can see or know**. *Look at him! He'**s going to fall**!*
- We use ***present continuous*** to: talk about **fixed arrangements**. *I'**m leaving** tonight. Here's my ticket.*
- We use ***present simple*** to: talk about **timetables/ programmes**. *The train **leaves** at 8.45.*

2 **Choose the correct item.**
Listen and check.

Ann: Your new flat is great, Pam! By the way, have you decided what you **1) are going to/will** do after graduation?
Pam: **2) I'm going to/I will** travel around Australia for a year. Actually, **3) I'm picking up/I will pick up** my ticket tomorrow. I can't wait! What about you?
Ann: I'm not sure. Maybe **4) I'm going to/I'll** work for my father for a while, but after that, I don't know. Hang on, let me get something to drink ...
Pam: What would you like?
Ann: **5) I'm going to/I'll** have a cup of tea, please.
Pam: OK. Oh, was that the doorbell? Saaam! The door, please!
Ann: Don't worry! **6) I'll/I'm going to** get it.
Pam: Thanks. **7) I'm going to/I'll** bring you your tea.

3 **Complete the short dialogues below with *will*, *won't*, *is going to* or *am going to*.**

1 A: Your appointment is at 9:00 tomorrow morning.
B: Don't worry. I .... be late.
2 A: I'm tired.
B: Have some rest. I .... cook dinner for you.
3 A: Your shirt is dirty.
B: I know. I .... wash it later.
4 A: Why is Steve wearing his suit?
B: He .... meet some new customers.
5 A: Did you send those emails this morning?
B: Oh, I forgot! I .... send them right now.

4 **Look at the notes, then listen and tick (✓) what Robin is going to do in the summer.**

1 travel abroad ....
2 work as a waiter ....
3 volunteer at a summer camp ....
4 buy a car ....
5 take driving lessons ....
6 move house ....
7 study Maths ....
8 join a gym ....

Ask and answer questions, as in the example.

A: Is Robin going to travel abroad this summer?
B: No, he isn't. He isn't going to travel abroad.

5 **SPEAKING** **Use the ideas below to make sentences about what you *are* and *aren't going to do* after work/college today.**

- drive home • go shopping • have a snack
- visit friends • listen to music
- do my homework • watch a film
- clean my house • get some exercise
- have a dance class • have a board game night
- watch an episode of my favourite TV show

6 **Read the short texts, then put the verbs in brackets into the present continuous or the present simple.**

Dr Jean Harris
LECTURE: **THE FUTURE OF MEDICINE**
The Old Theatre, 8:00 - 9:00

Fast Bus
Departure: Saturday 17th, 19:30, Newark Station
Arrival: Sunday 18th, 1:30, Boston Central

Dentist Thursday 11 am
Luke pick up 10:45

Meet me outside the cinema at 8:15. Film is at 8:30. Kate

1 Dr Harris .... **(give)** a lecture tomorrow morning. The lecture .... **(begin)** at 8:00 and .... **(finish)** at 9:00.
2 We .... **(travel)** to Boston on Saturday. The bus .... **(leave)** at 19:30 and .... **(arrive)** at 1:30.
3 I .... **(go)** to the dentist on Thursday. Luke .... **(pick)** me up at 10:45.
4 The film .... **(start)** at 8:30, so we .... **(meet)** outside the cinema at 8:15.

7 **Put the verbs in brackets into the correct future form. Then, in pairs, use the prompts to act out similar dialogues.**

1 A: What are your plans for the summer?
B: We .... **(visit)** Jamaica.
A: Wow! When .... **(you/leave)**?
B: On 28th July.
• winter break – Switzerland – 20th December

2 A: It's very cloudy today.
B: Yes. I think it .... **(rain)** soon.
• cold – snow

3 A: Which extra subjects .... **(you/study)** next year?
B: I'm not sure yet, but I think I .... **(choose)** Music and Drama.
• languages – Spanish and French

8 **Study the examples and complete the rule. Find an example in the advert on p. 32.**

Conditionals Type 1

*If you **don't hurry up**, you **will miss** the bus.*
*If I **have** enough money, I'**ll move** to a bigger house.*

Form
.... + present simple → .... + infinitive without ***to***

Use
We use conditionals type 1 to talk about **real** or **very probable situations** in the **present** or **future**.
When the ***if***-clause precedes the main clause, we separate them with a comma. When the main clause precedes the ***if***-clause, we do not separate them with a comma.
- We use ***when*** to show that something **will certainly happen.** *When I go into town, I'll buy you a newspaper.*
- We use ***if*** when we **are not certain that something will happen.** *If I go into town, I'll buy you a newspaper (but I'm not sure I'll go).*
- ***Unless*** = ***If not***. *Unless it rains, we'll go out. (= if it doesn't rain, ...)*

9 **Choose the correct verb form. Put commas where necessary.**

1 If you **study/will study** hard you **pass/will pass** the test.
2 When she **starts/will start** work as a taxi driver she **isn't/won't be** at home very often.
3 He **becomes/will become** a doctor if he **gets/will get** a degree in Medicine.
4 You **are/will be** fitter if you **work out/will work out** at the gym three times a week.
5 Unless you **work/will work** full-time you **don't/won't** earn much money.
6 If they **open/will open** their own café they **work/will work** long hours.

10 THINK **Use the ideas to act out dialogues, as in the example.**

1 haven't got enough money
A: What will you do if you haven't got enough money?
B: If I haven't got enough money, I'll get a part-time job.
2 car breaks down
3 a sunny day tomorrow
4 get hungry
5 go to London

Skills in Action

Vocabulary

Job qualities

1 Complete the sentences with the adjectives in the list.

• brave • patient • imaginative • sociable • hard-working • caring • careful

1 Accountants need to be .... It's important that they don't make mistakes in their figures.
2 Farmers need to be .... They have to work more hours than most people.
3 Vets need to be .... Sick and injured animals need a lot of love.
4 Public relations specialists need to be .... Their job often involves meeting and entertaining clients.
5 Fashion designers need to be .... They aim to create original and interesting styles.
6 Teachers need to be .... They often have to repeat things before children understand them.
7 Firefighters need to be .... They put their lives at risk to do their job.

Listening

2 You will hear part of an interview. For questions 1-5, choose the correct answer (A, B or C).

1 Julia's job is
A in an office. **B** part-time.
C writing her blog.

2 Julia says vlogs are
A hard work. **B** popular.
C only on YouTube.

3 Julia advises new vloggers to
A watch other vlogs.
B make their vlogs look nice.
C do some online research.

4 She tells us that her first vlog
A wasn't popular.
B only had 11 subscribers.
C got 100,000 views in the end.

5 Julia thinks people should vlog about
A what they love.
B their own ideas.
C whatever their viewers are interested in.

Everyday English

Having a job interview

3 a) Read the job adverts (A, B). Then, read the dialogue and fill in the missing words.

A
WANTED!
Friendly, hard-working, enthusiastic shop assistant
Sports Warehouse, Town Centre
Part-time
(9 am – 1 pm weekdays)
Ask inside the shop

B
Are you polite, careful and hard-working?
The **Rose Garden Restaurant** on Penny Lane is looking for **weekend serving staff**
Hours: Saturday 18:00 – 00:00 and Sunday 18:00 – 22:00
Call Eileen Wright on 078569873

A: Hello. Please have a seat.
B: Thank you.
A: **1)** ....'s your full name?
B: Anna Smith.
A: **2)** .... you give me a contact phone, Ms Smith?
B: Yes, sure. It's 0732675643.
A: OK. What can you **3)** .... us about yourself?
B: Well, I'm still a student, studying Biology, but I'm very hard-working and polite and I need a job.
A: **4)** .... old are you?
B: I'm 22.
A: **5)** .... you live near the restaurant?
B: Yes, I live at 35 Kings Road.
A: Can you work at weekends?
B: Yes, no problem. Can I ask how much the wage is?
A: It's £7 per hour. **6)** .... you start this Saturday?
B: Yes, I'd be happy to.
A: OK. I'll see you at six in the evening, then.

b) Listen and check. Which advert does it match?

4 Now look at the other job advert. Act out a dialogue for this job, similar to the one in Ex. 3.

Pronunciation *('ll)*

5 Listen and repeat the sentences.

1 I'll see you then.
2 She'll be back soon.
3 He'll meet us outside the shop.
4 We'll tell them tomorrow.
5 They'll work on this.
6 You'll get the job.

Reading & Writing

Writing Tip

Letters/Emails of application are formal in style. We usually use:

- **full verb forms:** *I am studying ...*
- **more polite language** *Thank you for taking time to read my letter.*

6 **Read the email and replace the informal phrases (1-8) with their equivalent formal ones (a-h) below to correct the style.**

a ☐ I am available to work
b ☐ I am particularly interested in
c ☐ Yours faithfully
d ☐ Dear Sir/Madam
e ☐ I am friendly and sociable
f ☐ I am writing to enquire
g ☐ I hope to hear from you soon.
h ☐ I am 20 years old and I am a student

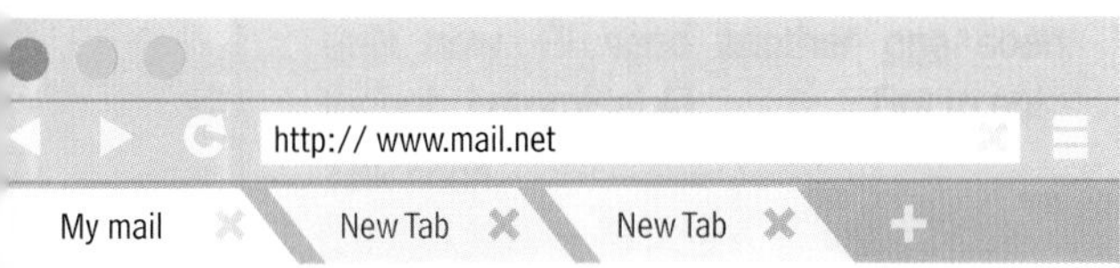

From: robin.gardner@mail.net
To: info@moah.mail.net
Subject: Part-time job

1) Hello,

2) I want to ask you about the part-time job at the Museum of Ancient History.
3) I'm 20 and I'm a student at the local university. I am studying History and **4) I love** ancient history. I know a lot about the subject.
I worked in the Foursquare Art Gallery last summer. I have excellent organisational skills, so I was responsible for listing and storing exhibits.
5) Everyone likes me, so I can talk to visitors and give them tours of the museum.
6) I can come to work in the evenings and at weekends. Thank you for taking time to read my application. **7) Send me a reply quickly.**

8) Love from,

Robin Gardner

Writing (an email applying for a job)

7 **Copy and complete the CV with the information in the text below.**

Name: Sarah Jones
Date of birth: _ _/_ _
Place of residence: 12 Cambridge Drive, ...
Contact number: ....
Email address: ....
Education: ....
Work experience: Bodley Library, assistant in the online reference section, last summer
Skills & Qualities: ....

Sarah Jones was born on 3rd July. She lives at 12 Cambridge Drive, Bodley. Her phone number is 0161 430 7873. Her email address is SarahJ_01@gmail.com. She is in her last year at Bodley Heath High School. Last summer, she worked as an assistant in Bodley Library in the online reference section. She is good with computers, has excellent communication skills and she is very sociable.

8 **You have seen this advert. Use the model in Ex. 6 and appropriate information from Ex. 7 to write Sarah's email applying for the post (100-120 words). Follow the plan.**

TECH SHACK
Sales assistant wanted for summer job
Hours: Mon-Fri, 9 am – 5 pm
Must be: friendly and sociable with excellent communication skills & knowledge of computers
Send your application to: techshack@live.co.uk

Plan

Dear Sir/Madam,
Para 1: reason for writing
Para 2: personal information (age, studies)
Para 3: work experience, skills & qualities
Para 4: availability & closing remarks
Yours faithfully,
(your full name)

VALUES

Productivity
Without hard work, nothing grows but weeds.
Gordon B. Hinckley

PART-TIME AMERICAN STUDENT JOBS

In the USA, like anywhere else, it can be expensive to be a college student. That's why a lot of students have part-time jobs. Working part-time helps pay the student's way through college and also develops valuable work skills. Let's take a look at two part-time jobs.

A. Cashiers

Jobs for part-time cashiers can be in supermarkets, fast food restaurants or even college campus bookshops. It's an easy job: scan the item, bag it, take the money and give the **customer** a receipt. Obviously, you need to have a head for figures as well as a friendly, polite manner. **Wages** are not very high, but they are regular, and depending on the store, there's a chance of promotion to a higher position. But some students find it a bit boring sitting down all day handling money and go for something a bit more active instead!

B. Car wash attendants

The world's first car wash opened in the American city of Detroit in 1914. Now it's a huge national industry and there are plenty of jobs for car wash attendants. Students can do this job in the evenings or at weekends, so it doesn't clash with their studies. Another good thing is that you don't need any special **qualifications** to do this job. And working as part of a car wash team can make the job more sociable than doing it alone. But it's low-paid work, often outdoors and attendants need to be physically **fit**.

Listening & Reading

1 **Read the title and look at the pictures. What is it like working as a cashier? a car wash attendant? Listen and read to find out.**

2 **a) Read the text again. Which people (A or B) ...**

1 don't get much exercise? ....
2 can find work easily? ....
3 work outside sometimes? ....
4 can find work in a number of different businesses? ....
5 need to be good at Maths? ....
6 do their job with the help of others? ....

b) Explain the words in bold.

Check these words

develop, scan, receipt, have a head for figures, promotion, industry, clash with, outdoors

Speaking & Writing

3 

Think of two part-time jobs for students in your country. Which one do you think is more difficult? Why? Tell your partner.

4 ICT **Research part-time jobs for students in your country. Write a short text about each one. Think about:** *name of job – what they do – earnings – advantages – disadvantages*. **Present the jobs to the class.**

Review 4

Vocabulary

1 Match the columns to form jobs.

1	☐ animal	a	tester
2	☐ app	b	specialist
3	☐ event	c	trainer
4	☐ fashion	d	editor
5	☐ video game	e	developer
6	☐ tour	f	planner
7	☐ social media	g	designer
8	☐ public relations	h	guide

(8 x 2 = 16)

2 Use: *make, do, work, pass, follow* **in the correct form to complete the sentences.**

1 Mike .... long hours, from 8 am until 6 pm.
2 I need to .... a phone call.
3 Just try to .... your best in your job interview.
4 He .... his dream and became a doctor.
5 She .... her tests and got her degree.

(5 x 2 = 10)

3 Read what the people say and fill in the quality.

1 "I'm not afraid of anything." **b**_ _ _ _
2 "I'm good at thinking of new ideas." **i**_ _ _ _ _ _ _ _ _ _
3 "I enjoy talking to people." **s**_ _ _ _ _ _ _
4 "I deal with some very rude customers." **p**_ _ _ _ _ _
5 "I try hard not to make mistakes." **c**_ _ _ _ _ _

(5 x 2 = 10)

Grammar

4 Choose the correct item.

1 Look out! You**'ll/'re going to** fall!
2 I think Amanda **will/is going to** study Biology.
3 I've decided I**'ll/'m going to** look for a new job.
4 This job looks great – I**'m going to/'ll** apply for it now!
5 After I finish work, I**'m going to/'ll** go to the gym.

(5 x 3 = 15)

5 Put the verbs in brackets into the correct tense.

1 We .... **(see)** John tonight after work.
2 I have no money, so I don't think I .... **(go)** on holiday next year.
3 The lecture .... **(start)** at 10:30 am.
4 I think John .... **(get)** the job.
5 Be careful. You .... **(break)** the laptop.

(5 x 3 = 15)

6 Choose the correct item.

1 If Laura **will pass/passes** the exam, she **becomes/will become** a lawyer.
2 If we **go/will go** now, we **catch/'ll catch** the train.
3 He **isn't/won't be** on time for his interview unless he **will wake/wakes** up soon.
4 If they **work/will work** an extra hour, they **earn/will earn** £10 more.
5 We **don't go/won't go** out if he **is/will be** late.

(5 x 3 = 15)

7 Fill in *if* **or** *when*.

1 I'll call you .... I can't come tonight.
2 We'll send you an email .... we get to Paris.
3 .... I get the job, I'll be very surprised!
4 I'll be at the bus stop .... she arrives.

(4 x 1 = 4)

Everyday English

8 Choose the correct response.

1 A: When can you start?
B: **a** On Saturdays. **b** Next Monday.
2 A: Please have a seat.
B: **a** Thank you. **b** Yes, that's fine.
3 A: Can you work at weekends?
B: **a** Yes, no problem. **b** I'm still a student.

(3 x 5 = 15)

Total 100

Competences

Lexical Competence

Understand words/phrases related to
- jobs
- job qualities

Reading Competence
- understand texts related to jobs (read for specific information – multiple matching)

Listening Competence
- listen to and understand monologues/a dialogue related to jobs (listen for detail – multiple matching, multiple choice)

Speaking Competence
- have a job interview

Writing Competence
- write an entry for a forum about a job I would like to do
- write a CV/an email applying for a job
- write short texts about part-time jobs for students

Vocabulary: food & drinks, fast food dishes & drinks
Grammar: countable/uncountable nouns; quantifiers; *some-any-no-every* & compounds; conditionals type 0
Everyday English: ordering a takeaway
Writing: an online review about a fast food restaurant

Food, glorious food!

fried rice with chicken and prawns
pizza and Buffalo wings
poached salmon
lamb & mashed potatoes
spaghetti Bolognese & garlic bread
steak with jacket potato
fried fish and chips with peas
lasagne
wholemeal bread
mussels
yoghurt
mayonnaise
bread rolls
doughnut
watermelon
melon
fruit salad
apple juice
carrot juice
cheesecake

Vocabulary

Food & Drinks

1 **Look at the pictures. Listen and learn. Which food and drinks are:** *healthy? low-fat foods? fatty foods? junk food?*

2 GAME **In one minute think of as many food items as you can that you can:** *bake, boil, poach, fry, roast, grill.*

3 **Act out dialogues, as in the example. Use:** *eggs, mushrooms, chicken, fish, rice, broccoli, prawns, salmon.*

A: *How do you like your eggs?*
B: *Fried. What about you?*
A: *I prefer them poached.*

Tasty Cuisine on a Submarine

Food writer Ben Hayes reports ...

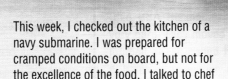

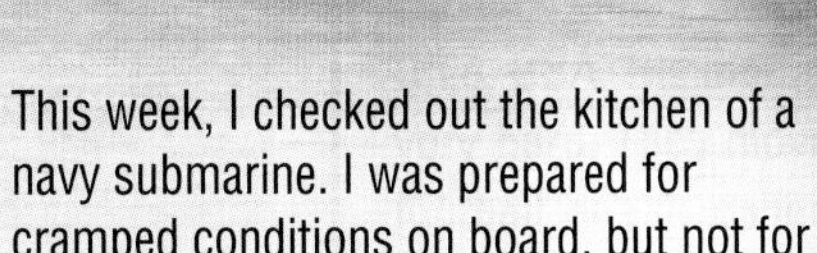

This week, I checked out the kitchen of a navy submarine. I was prepared for cramped conditions on board, but not for the excellence of the food. I talked to chef Tom Walsh ...

"Life down here can be difficult for everyone, so it's important to keep up the crew's spirits with good food! My kitchen team and I do our very best to create tasty meals with healthy **ingredients**.

"On a typical **mission**, the submarine store cupboard must be well stocked. Eighteen hundred pounds of frozen meat and twenty thousand pounds of tinned food can last 100 crew three months. Of course, we always carry fresh **produce**, too; I order crates of cabbages, potatoes, onions, carrots, apples and oranges before every **voyage**.

"Our team runs a 24-hour restaurant! Crew working night shifts can get hungry! In addition to breakfast, lunch and dinner, there's a midnight snack and we keep a big pot of soup boiling all day! Favourite dishes include lasagne, spaghetti Bolognese, steak and poached salmon, while the daily salad bar is especially **popular** with vegetarians. We usually make pizza and Buffalo wings on Saturday nights – no, not buffalo the animal! They're actually barbecued chicken wings!"

I found the menu impressive, but it also **made sense**. Life deep under the **waves** is not always easy. Sailors are often away for months and don't see much sunshine. If the food is great, though, everyone has something to keep them happy! That's why submarine cuisine is the best in the navy!

Check these words

submarine, on board, keep spirits up, well stocked, frozen, tinned, crew, vegetarian

Reading & Listening

4 **Read through the text quickly. Do you think the food on a submarine is good?**

5 **Read the text and for questions 1-4 decide which the best answer (A, B or C) is. Then, explain the words in bold.**

1 What does the writer say is good about being on a submarine?
A the space **B** the food **C** the company

2 How many people go on a typical mission?
A 18 **B** 20 **C** 100

3 Which meal is popular at the weekend?
A pizza **B** spaghetti **C** steak

4 What is the writer's main purpose?
A to give advice to people in the navy
B to explain why life is hard on a submarine
C to describe what people eat on a submarine

6 THINK **Listen to and read the text. How healthy is the food on the submarine? Is there anything you would like to change on the menu?**

7 **Fill in:** *healthy, fresh, salad, store, cramped, tinned, typical, well, midnight, frozen*. **Use five phrases and make sentences based on the text.**

1 .... conditions
2 .... ingredients
3 .... mission
4 .... cupboard
5 .... stocked
6 .... meat
7 .... food
8 .... produce
9 .... snack
10 .... bar

8 PREPOSITIONS **Fill in the correct preposition, then make sentences using the phrases.**

1 .... board
2 talk .... sb
3 .... a mission
4 popular .... vegetarians

Speaking & Writing

9 THINK **Imagine you work for an airline. Design a day's menu for the flights under the headings:** *breakfast – lunch – dinner – drinks*. **Present it to the class.**

Grammar in Use

A: *I've finished making the fish, Chef. Is there anything else to do?*

B: *You can help me with the prawn salads. Put some lettuce leaves and cucumber slices into glass bowls, and add a few small tomatoes to each.*

A: *OK, and how many prawns do I need?*

B: *Four big ones for each serving. Boil them and take off their shells before serving.*

A: *What about the dressing? How do I make that?*

B: *Mix two spoons of tomato ketchup with six spoons of mayonnaise and add a few drops of lemon juice.*

A: *Sorry, Chef, but I can't find any lemon juice. Can I use lime juice instead?*

B: *Yes, but don't add much. When you've mixed the dressing, pour it over the salads. Everyone's going to love them!*

1 **Read the theory. List all the countable and uncountable nouns in the dialogue.**

Countable/Uncountable nouns – Quantifiers

Countable nouns are nouns we can count *an apple – two apples*. **Uncountable** nouns are nouns we can't count *milk* (NOT: ~~a milk~~ – ~~two milks~~).

Countable nouns – Quantifiers

*We've got **an** apple and **some** berries.*
*There are **a lot of/lots of** mushrooms.* (plenty of)
*Are there **any** eggs? There aren't **many** eggs.* (not a lot)
*We haven't got **any** potatoes./We've got **no** potatoes.* (none at all)
*There are **a few** eggs.* (not many but enough)
*There are very **few** peppers.* (hardly any)
***How many** apples do you need? Not **many**.*

Uncountable nouns – Quantifiers

*We've got **some** milk.*
*We've got **a lot of/lots of** flour.* (plenty of)
*We haven't got **much** sugar.* (not a lot)
*We've only got **a little**.* (not much but enough)
*There is very **little** butter.* (almost none)
*Is there **any** orange juice? There isn't **any** orange juice./There's **no** orange juice.* (none at all)
***How much** milk is there? Not **much**.*

NOTE: We can use ***some*** in questions to make a request/offer. *Can I have **some** cake? Would you like **some** tea?*

2 **Which of the words in bold in the theory box in Ex. 1 do we use in:** ***affirmative sentences? negative sentences? questions?***

3 **Write** ***C*** **for countable or** ***U*** **for uncountable. Then write the corresponding plural forms.**

1	milk	*U*	—
2	melon	*C*	*melons*
3	honey	....	....
4	potato	....	....
5	salmon	....	....
6	yoghurt	....	....
7	lettuce	....	....
8	peach	....	....
9	tea	....	....
10	strawberry	....	....
11	grape	....	....
12	lamb	....	....
13	pea	....	....
14	burger	....	....

4 **a) Which of the words in the list go with:** ***a? an? some?***

• pasta • chips • apple • sweets • burger • orange juice • tea • banana • coffee • milk • chocolates • apricot • eggs • jacket potato • grapes • biscuit • peach • cheese

b) **Act out short dialogues, as in the example. Use words from Ex. 4a as well as your own ideas.**

*A: Would you like **some pasta**?*
*B: Yes, please. And can I have **some cheese**, too?*
*A: Of course. Do you want **an apple**?*
*B: No, thanks. I'd rather have **a peach**.*

5 **Find the odd word out. Check in your dictionary.**

1 **a packet of** biscuits – spaghetti – bread – peanuts
2 **a carton of** orange juice – lettuce – milk – cream
3 **a slice of** bread – cheese – butter – cake
4 **a cup of** coffee – meat – tea – hot chocolate
5 **a bowl of** salad – pizza – soup – cereal
6 **a glass of** milk – apple juice – salmon – cola
7 **a bottle of** ketchup – fish – water – lemonade
8 **a jar of** honey – jam – potatoes – mustard
9 **a bag of** flour – sugar – mayonnaise – crisps
10 **a box of** coffee – chocolates – eggs – tea bags

6 a) Fill in: *some (x3)*, *any (x4)*, *much (x2)*, *many*, *a few* or *a little (x2)*.

A: Have we got what we need for the cheeseburgers?
B: Let me see. Well, there are **1)** .... burgers, but there aren't **2)** .... buns at all.
A: How **3)** .... buns do you need?
B: Just **4)** .... I need **5)** .... cheese, too.
A: How **6)** .... cheese is there in the fridge?
B: Not **7)** .... , but I only need **8)** ....
A: Is there **9)** .... ketchup left?
B: Only **10)** .... , but we don't need much, so don't buy **11)** .... We haven't got **12)** .... mustard at all, though.
A: I'll buy **13)** .... , then.

b) Act out similar dialogues using the prompts below.

- **omelette:** eggs, onions, cheese, milk, butter
- **pizza:** mushrooms, tomatoes, chicken, olive oil, cheese

7 Read the theory. Complete the table with words from the examples. Find more examples in the dialogue on p. 40.

some/any/no/every & compounds

- We use ***some*** and its compounds in positive statements. *There is **someone** in the garden.*
- We use ***any*** and its compounds in negative sentences and questions. *There isn't **anything** left. Is there **anything** in the fridge?*
- We use ***no*** and its compounds instead of ***not any***. *There is **no one** in the room.* (= There isn't anyone in the room.)
- We use ***every*** and its compounds in affirmative and interrogative sentences. ***Everything's** ready. Is **everyone** here?*

	Things	People	Places
some	something	somebody/ **1)**	somewhere
any	**2)**	anybody/anyone	anywhere
no	nothing	nobody/ **3)**	nowhere
every	**4)**	everybody / **5)**	everywhere

8 Choose the correct item. Give reasons.

1 Is there **any/no** sugar?
2 I want to cook **something/everything** special for tonight.
3 There wasn't **no/any** milk left in the supermarket.
4 I want to go **everywhere/somewhere** exciting for Sunday lunch.
5 Sheila didn't know **no one/anyone** at the dinner.
6 I need to buy **some/every** biscuits for tea.
7 I'm hungry, but there is **something/nothing** to eat.
8 I can't find the salt **anywhere/everywhere**.
9 There is **nothing/anything** on the table.
10 **Everyone/No one** liked the cake; it was delicious.

9 Use *some*, *any*, *no*, *every* and their compounds to complete the exchanges, as in the example.

1 A: Does *anyone* know a good café?
B: *Someone* told me that Alberto's is great.
2 A: Why isn't .... ordering steak?
B: Because .... is a vegetarian.
3 A: Is there .... to eat?
B: There's only .... pizza in the fridge.
4 A: There's .... to eat for lunch.
B: Well, let's order .... from the takeaway then.
5 A: I'm looking for .... to buy a chocolate cake.
B: .... makes chocolate cakes as good as they do in the bakery.

10 Read the theory. Then, make *Type 0 conditional* sentences, as in the example.

Conditionals Type 0

- We can use conditionals Type 0 to talk about something which always happens as a result of something else. ***If** you **heat** water, it **boils**.*
- We can use ***when*** instead of ***if*** in conditionals Type 0. ***If/When** sharks **smell** meat, they **get** excited.*

1 you/boil/water → it/produce/steam
If/When you boil water, it produces steam.
2 you/heat/butter → it/melt
3 you/mix red and white → you/get/pink
4 it/rain/regularly → it/help/flowers/to grow
5 I/eat/a lot of chocolate → I/get/spots

Skills in Action

Vocabulary

Fast food dishes & drinks

1 **Look at the menu and fill in:** *Lemonade, Green, Apple, Chicken, Bread, Vanilla, Shake, Fish.*

HAPPY TIME
Fast Food

Main Meals

Fried **1)**	
4pcs	£4.20
Burger	£2.70
Kebab	£4.80
Cheeseburger	£2.90
2) .... & Chips	£4.50
Pizza	£5.50

Desserts

Ice Cream **5)** (................	
Chocolate, Strawberry)	£2.50
Cheesecake	£4.50
6) .... Pie	£3.80
Pancakes & Syrup	£3.90
Chocolate Brownie	£3.30

Side Dishes

Chips small	80p
Chips large	£2.00
Garlic **3)**	£1.90
4) .... Salad	£2.00
Onion Rings	£2.00

Drinks

Tea	£1.00
Milk **7)**	£1.80
Coffee	£1.20
Cola	80p
8)	80p
Water (still)	£1.20
Water (sparkling)	£1.30

2 **Which is your favourite fast food dish? How often do you eat:** *fast food*? *takeaways*?

Listening

3 **You will hear the first half of some short exchanges. Choose the best reply (A, B or C) to each.**

1 **A** That'll be £6.30, please. **B** I'll just check. **C** Would you like to see the menu?

2 **A** Is everything OK? **B** Thank you. Here's your change. **C** Thanks, you're welcome.

3 **A** I'm ready to order. **B** No, I don't. **C** No, thanks.

4 **A** Yes, of course. **B** Yes, I'd like some dessert. **C** Yes, right away!

5 **A** Certainly. **B** No, thanks. **C** Is that large or small?

Everyday English

Ordering a takeaway

4 **a) Complete the dialogue with sentences from the list.**

- Would you like anything else?
- I'd like a kebab, please.
- Would you like chips with it?
- Here you are. • How much is it?
- Anything to drink? • Is that to eat in or take away?

Waitress: Can I take your order?
Customer: Yes, **1)** ....
Waitress: **2)** ....
Customer: Just a small portion.
Waitress: **3)** ....
Customer: A diet cola.
Waitress: Fine. **4)** ....
Customer: No, thanks.
Waitress: **5)** ....
Customer: To take away, please. **6)** ....
Waitress: That's £6.40, please.
Customer: **7)** ....
Waitress: Thank you. Enjoy your meal.

b) Listen and check.

5 **Use the menu in Ex. 1 to act out similar dialogues. Use sentences from the Language box. You can use the dialogue in Ex. 4 as a model.**

Taking orders	Ordering
• Can I take your order? • Would you like ...? • What can I get you? • Anything else?	• Can/Could I have ...? • Have you got ...? • I'd like ... .
Asking about prices	**Stating prices**
• How much is it?	• That's (£5.50 – five pounds fifty), please.

Pronunciation *like – 'd like*

6 **Listen and repeat the sentences.**

1 I'd like some fresh orange juice, please.
2 I like eating vegetables.
3 We'd like to have dinner at Monty's.
4 We like eating low-fat foods.
5 They like healthy foods.
6 They'd like to have ice cream for dessert.

Reading & Writing

7 **Read the text and complete the gaps with:** *treat, heart, top, friendly, starter, high, disappointed, homemade.*

RESTAURANTS | HOTELS | DESTINATIONS

The Riverside Retreat

15 Reviews

#2 of 6 Restaurants in Tavistock,

££-£££,

British Restaurant

The Riverside Retreat

20 Reviews

3 weeks ago

Sophie D, London, UK

A great Sunday lunch!

This beautiful little restaurant is located on the banks of a small river in the **1)** .... of the English countryside. My friend and I went there for a quiet Sunday lunch last Sunday noon and we weren't **2)** ....!

We kicked off our meal with an excellent prawn **3)** .... For main course, I had fish and chips with peas. It was an absolute **4)** .... and a nice change from the ordinary Sunday roast. My friend chose the vegetarian lasagne. Everything was PERFECT! We rounded off our meal with **5)** .... apple pie, made with apples from the restaurant garden.

I gave the food **6)** .... marks. The only unpleasant surprise was the prices – they were a bit **7)** .... But you do get great food served by **8)** ...., professional staff in a beautiful setting.

I would definitely recommend the place! There's nowhere better for Sunday lunch!

★★★★½ Value ★★★★★ Service ★★★★★ Food

8 **Complete the sentences. Use phrases from the list. How does Sophia recommend the Riverside Retreat?**

• a thumbs down • highly recommend
• you'll love • worth visiting

1 If you like spicy food, ... Steve's.
2 I ....dinner at this place.
3 The Four Seasons Restaurant is well ....
4 I give it ....

9 **What good/bad points does Sophia mention in her review in Ex. 7?**

10 a) **Find the adjectives Sophia uses to describe the:** *restaurant, river, Sunday lunch, apple pie, prices, food, staff, setting.*

b) **Circle the adjective that does not match the noun. Check in your dictionary.**

1 varied – boring – friendly – interesting **menu**
2 homemade – great – spicy – beautiful **dishes**
3 unusual – sociable – tempting – disappointing **desserts**
4 delicious – polite – rude – helpful **staff**
5 slow – fast – friendly – popular **service**
6 soft – loud – tasty – annoying **music**
7 crowded – noisy – relaxing – unfriendly **atmosphere**
8 reasonable – high – affordable – daily **prices**

Writing Tip

Writing an online review about a place

When you write an online review about a place, state when you visited the place, then provide information based on your experience. Say what was good and/or bad about your experience and give examples/reasons. Use descriptive language. In the conclusion, recommend/don't recommend the place to others giving reasons.

Writing (an online review about a restaurant)

11 **Think of a fast food restaurant you have recently visited. Make notes under the headings in the plan. Use them to write your review (100-140 words). Follow the plan.**

Plan

Para 1: name, place, when you visited it
Para 2: what you liked (with examples/reasons)
Para 3: what you didn't like (with examples/reasons)
Para 4: recommendation

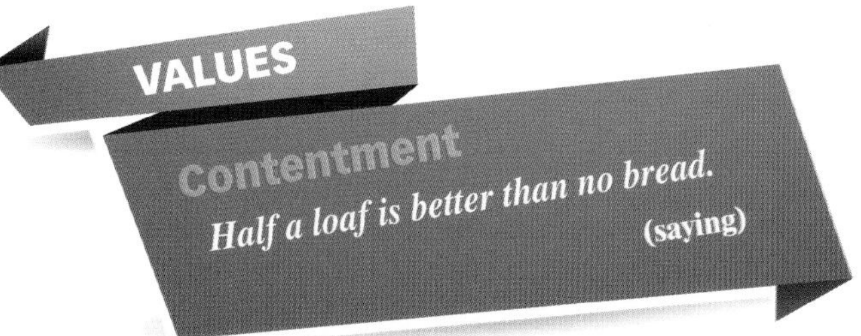

VALUES
Contentment
Half a loaf is better than no bread.
(saying)

5 Culture

VIDEO

Festive Sweets in the UK

A **Clootie dumpling** is a favourite festive dessert in Scotland. The Scots eat it on Burns Night every 25th January, when they celebrate their **national** poet, Robert Burns. It's got flour, suet*, dried fruit and spices in it. They make the **mixture** into a ball and wrap it in a cloth or 'clootie'. Then it goes into **a pan of** boiling water to cook. It's an old tradition that goes back to the days when the Scots had no ovens to cook in!

*suet = beef or mutton fat

B No Mother's Day in the UK is complete without **Simnel cake**. It's a dark, rich fruit cake with a yellow **topping** – the colour of many spring flowers! The topping is from ground nuts and honey. There are a few stories about how the cake got its name. One says that a man named Simon and his wife Nelly **invented** it. At first, it went by the name of Simon and Nelly's cake, but this was too long for people to say. In the end, they **shortened** the two names and called it 'Simnel' cake!

C English people **celebrate** Bonfire Night on 5th November. On this night in 1605, someone tried to blow up the Houses of Parliament in London, but failed. Nowadays, people eat squares of **parkin** while they watch fireworks displays. It's a spicy oatmeal cake – a perfect sweet **treat** to keep you warm on a cold November night outdoors!

Check these words

festive, dried, wrap, oven, ground nuts, blow up, fail, spicy, oatmeal

Listening & Reading

1 **Look at pictures A-C. When do the British eat these sweets?**

Listen and read to find out.

2 **Read the text again and answer the questions. Then explain the words in bold.**

1 When do the Scots celebrate Burns Night?
2 Why did the Scots cook clootie dumplings in boiling water?
3 When do people in the UK eat Simnel cake?
4 In the story about its name, who were Simon and Nelly?
5 What happened on 5th November, 1605?
6 How do people celebrate the event today?

Speaking & Writing

3 THINK **Think of a typical sweet people in your country eat at a festival and tell the class about it. If you like, you can make the sweet and video yourself explaining how to make it. Then show your video to the class.**

4 **Write a short text about the sweet you chose in Ex. 3 for an international cooking magazine.**
Write: *name – when you eat in – how you make it – the story behind it (if any).*

Vocabulary

1 Fill in: *low-fat*, *garlic*, *olive*, *poached*, *tinned*.

1 I always dress salads with .... oil.
2 I prefer fresh to .... tomatoes.
3 Eating .... foods helps you lose weight.
4 How about the .... salmon, sir?
5 I love eating .... bread.

(5 x 2 = 10)

2 Read the definitions and complete the words.

1 This water isn't still, it's fizzy. **s**_ _ _ _ _ _ _ _
2 Foods are this when you cook them in oil. **f**_ _ _ _
3 You pour this on pancakes. **s**_ _ _ _
4 It's bread that isn't white. **w**_ _ _ _ _ _ _ _
5 It's sweet and you eat it after the main course. **d**_ _ _ _ _ _

(5 x 4 = 20)

3 Choose the correct item.

1 **Bake/Steam** the cake in the oven for 40 minutes.
2 Fast food is **popular/cramped** with teenagers.
3 They **run/order** a 24-hour restaurant.
4 We had a great meal **on board/submarine** the yacht.
5 The restaurant had a **fast/cosy** atmosphere.

(5 x 2 = 10)

Grammar

4 Choose the correct item.

1 How **much/many** bananas are there?
2 There is only **a few/a little** coffee left.
3 We've got **a lot of/much** eggs.
4 We have **no/not much** ice cream in the freezer.
5 There isn't **any/no** milk in the fridge.
6 There are **very/too many** chips. I can't eat them all.
7 Can I have **a few/a little** biscuits with my tea?
8 Would you like **some/any** ice cream?

(8 x 2 = 16)

5 Fill in: *someone*, *anyone*, *everyone*, *no one*, *something*, *nothing*, *somewhere*, *anywhere*.

1 A: Is there .... I can get a Chinese meal near here?
B: Yes, I know .... in the town centre.
2 A: Does .... in your family like sushi?
B: Yes, ... does!
3 A: Don't order the lasagne here. .... recommends it!
B: OK, I'll try .... else, then.
4 A: .... has eaten all the cheese!
B: That means there's .... to make sandwiches with.

(4 x 3 = 12)

6 Put the words in the correct order.

1 If/boil/you/jam/get/sugar and fruit/you.
....
2 If/eat/too/stomach ache/get/much/I/I
....
3 If/people/put on/eat/weight/sweets/they/a lot of
....
4 If/they/don't water/die/we/plants
....

(4 x 3 = 12)

Everyday English

7 Match the exchanges.

1 ☐ Could I have the lasagne, please?
2 ☐ What can I get you?
3 ☐ How much is it?
4 ☐ Anything else?
5 ☐ Would you like onion rings with that?

A That's £7.20, please.
B No, thanks.
C Just a small portion.
D Certainly, madam.
E I'd like a burger, please.

(5 x 4 = 20)

Total 100

Competences

Lexical Competence
Understand words/phrases related to
- food & drinks
- fast food dishes & drinks

Reading Competence
- understand texts related to food/drinks (read for specific information – multiple choice)

Listening Competence
- listen to and understand dialogues related to food (listen for cohesion – multiple choice)

Speaking Competence
- order a takeaway

Writing Competence
- write a menu for an airline company
- write an online review about a fast food restaurant you've recently visited

Vocabulary: Illnesses & Remedies, Parts of the body & Injuries
Grammar: Present perfect simple & continuous
Everyday English: Going to the doctor's
Writing: An email about a health issue

6 Health

Vocabulary

Illnesses & Remedies

1 Listen and learn. Make sentences, as in the example.

1 Kim/a headache

2 Mike/a stomach ache

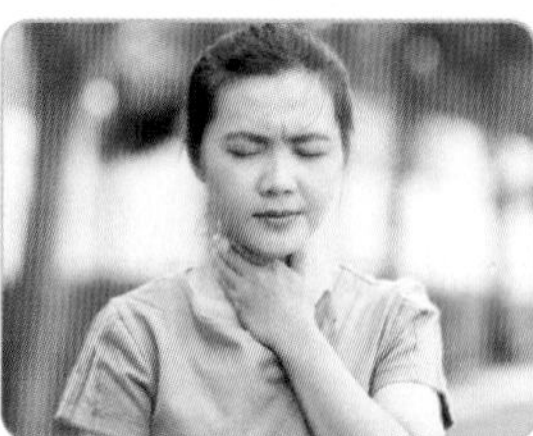

3 Jasmine/a sore throat

4 Sonia/a temperature

5 Trevor/a cough

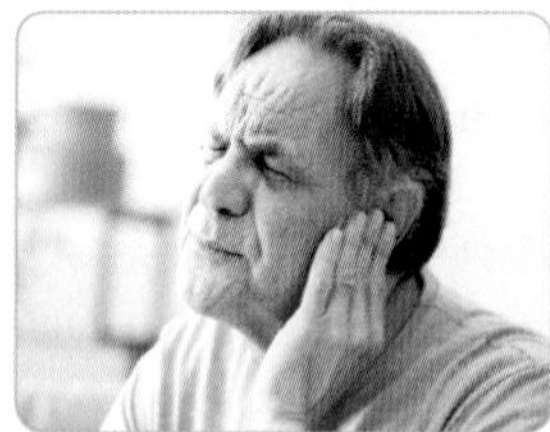

6 Jimmy/an earache

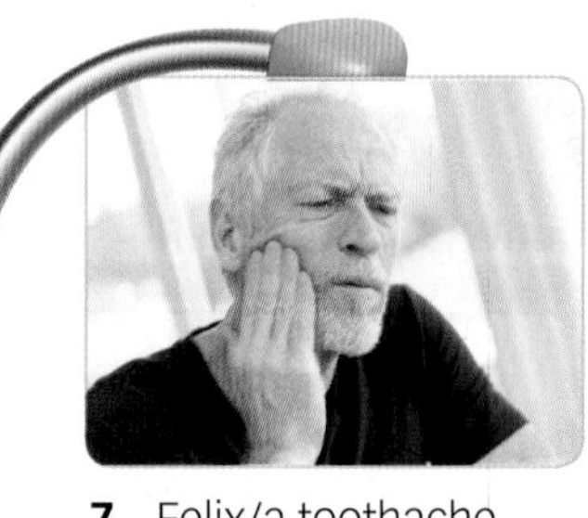

7 Felix/a toothache

8 Anne/a cold

1 *Kim has got a headache.*

Check these words

nettle, cure, fluid, fever, soak, vinegar, smelly, infection, medical, in doubt

Speaking

2 **Use the prompts to act out similar dialogues.**

- toothache – see the dentist
- a stomach ache – drink some ginger tea
- a cough – take some cough medicine
- a temperature – take an aspirin

A: *What's the matter?*
B: *I've got a headache.*
A: *Why don't you take an aspirin?*

Listening & Reading

3 **How are** *nettle tea*, *rice water* **and** *vinegar* **related to a cold? Guess.**

Listen and read to find out.

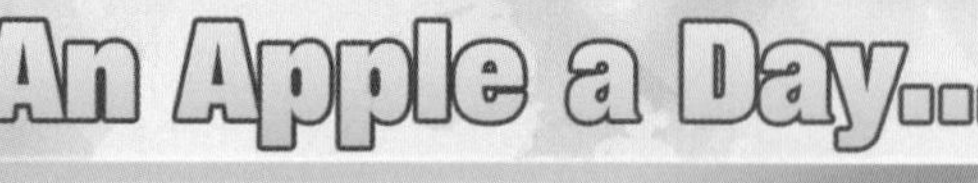

DrGreen
View my profile page

89	119	142
POSTS	FOLLOWING	FOLLOWERS

Cold Remedies

Posted by Betsy – 1 hour, 40 minutes ago
Help! I've got an awful cold. My exams are coming up and I really need to get rid of this one. Any ideas?

Posted by Brian – 1 hour, 30 minutes ago
I'm from Scotland. My grandma has always drunk nettle tea when she's had a cold. I've never tried it, but she says it works every time.

Posted by Betsy – 1 hour ago
Thanks, Brian! Amazingly, that's really done the trick for me. Any other reader with a cold – take Brian's grandmother's advice. It works!

Posted by DrGreen – 59 minutes ago
Glad that's worked for you, Betsy, but it's worth pointing out that there's no real cure for the cold – just get plenty of rest so your body can fight it, and drink lots of fluids.

4 **Read the text and for questions 1-4 choose the best answer, A, B or C. Then, explain the underlined words.**

1 Brian's cold remedy ...
 A is something he has not used.
 B doesn't work for Betsy.
 C came from a friend.

2 Dr Green thinks Betsy ...
 A should drink more tea.
 B shouldn't do much.
 C should go to a doctor.

3 'Kanji' is ...
 A a fever remedy.
 B rice with a little salt.
 C an Indian cure for the cold.

4 How does Dr Green feel about Maria's illness?
 A worried **B** relaxed **C** sad

Posted by Maria – 55 minutes ago
Does nettle tea bring down a fever too? I've had a temperature of 39°C for a couple of days now...

Posted by Sanjit – 50 minute ago
Have you tried rice water, Maria? Boil rice in water. Then take out the rice, add a little salt to the liquid and drink it. We've been using that here in India for years. We call it 'kanji'. It brings the temperature down and it's also good for a stomach ache!

Posted by Heidi – 48 minutes ago
Or try this: soak a pair of socks in vinegar, put them on, put plastic bags on top and keep on till the socks are dry. That's a <u>remedy</u> we've used in Switzerland for hundreds of years. Smelly, but it works!

Posted by DrGreen – 45 minute ago
Maria, if you've still got a temperature tomorrow, you need to see a doctor. This doesn't sound like a simple cough or cold. It's <u>probably</u> an infection.

Posted by Julie – 41 minutes ago
I've had a cold for a couple of days, but now I've got an earache too. Anything I can do for that?

Please log in to post.

Remember, the information on this site is not medical advice. If in doubt, please see your GP.

5 THINK **Why do people try home remedies instead of going straight to the doctor?**

> **Verbs of the senses + *like***
> We use verbs of the senses ***(smell, sound, feel, taste, look)*** with ***like*** to show how similar two things are.
> *It sounds **like** a cold to me.*

6 **Fill in *like* where necessary.**

1 This tea smells .... terrible.
2 It tastes .... ginger.
3 Ann looks .... exhausted.
4 The water feels .... warm.
5 It smells .... peppermint to me.
6 She sounds .... a doctor.

7 WORDS EASILY CONFUSED **Choose the correct word. Check in your dictionary.**

1 An aspirin will take away the **ache/pain**.
2 I've got a **sore/sick** throat.
3 Sally fell over and **ached/hurt** her leg.
4 The doctor wrote me a **recipe/prescription** for antibiotics.
5 Carl's getting **cure/treatment** for his bad leg.
6 He suffers from heart **disease/illness**.

8 PREPOSITIONS **Choose the correct preposition.**

1 Take this medicine and you'll soon get rid **from/of** that infection.
2 They haven't found a cure **for/to** this, yet.
3 Lemon tea is good **for/of** the common cold.
4 Ask your doctor if you're **under/in** any doubt.
5 There's lots of medical information **in/on** the site.

Speaking & Writing

9 ICT **Collect information about natural remedies people use in various countries to help relieve a cough. Tell the class.**

10 **Look at the final forum post from Julie again. Write a forum post giving her advice on her illness.**

Sorry you're so ill, Julie. I think ...

Grammar in Use

Dentist: *So, Larry, have you been taking the medicine twice a day since I last saw you?*
Larry: *Yes, I have. And the pain has gone.*
Dentist: *Let's have a quick look. Now, open wide. Well, the infection hasn't spread, so that's good.*
Larry: *Thank goodness. After all this pain, I've decided to look after my teeth.*
Dentist: *You've made a very wise decision. Your brother has had terrible trouble with his teeth. You don't want the same, do you?*
Larry: *Of course not!*
Dentist: *Where has he gone, anyway? I haven't seen him for ages!*
Larry: *He's gone to America. Harvard Medical School has given him a scholarship.*
Dentist: *Good for him!*

1 **Read the theory. When do we use the present perfect? Find examples in the dialogue.**

Present perfect *(have/has* + past participle)

Affirmative	Negative
I/You/We/They **have left**. He/She/It **has left**.	I/You/We/They **haven't left**. He/She/It **hasn't left**.
Interrogative	**Short answers**
Have I/you/we/they **left**? **Has** he/she/it **left**?	**Yes**, I/you/we/they **have**./ **No**, I/you/we/they **haven't**. **Yes**, he/she/it **has**./ **No**, he/she/it **hasn't**.

- to talk about an action which **started in the past and continues up to the present**. *Diane **has been** in hospital for the last two weeks.*
- to talk about a **recent action** whose **result is visible in the present**. *I**'ve broken** my leg, so I can't walk.*
- to talk about an experience. ***Have you ever had** an operation?*
- to talk about an **action** which happened at an **unstated time in the past**. The action is more important than the time. *He**'s been** to the dentist's four times this year.*

Time expressions used with the present perfect: ***just***, ***already***, ***yet***, ***for***, ***since***, ***recently***, ***lately***, ***so far***, ***ever***, etc.

Note: *They **have gone** to the hospital.* (They are on their way there or they are there now. They haven't come back yet.) *They **have been** to the hospital.* (They were there some time ago, but they have come back.)

2 **Put the verbs in brackets into the present perfect.**

1 A: How long .... **(it/be)** since you visited a dentist's?
B: I .... **(not/visit)** one for months, I'm afraid.

2 A: .... **(your husband/ have)** any pain since the last check-up, Mrs Vent?
B: He .... **(not/have)** the tiniest bit of pain, thank goodness!

3 A: My aunt and uncle .... **(just/ have)** a baby.
B: Congratulations! .... **(you/ see)** your new cousin yet?
A: No. I haven't. They .... **(not/ come)** home from the hospital.

4 A: Hello? I need an ambulance. My flatmate .... **(hit)** his head badly.
B: We'll send one right away. .... **(you/put)** something on the cut to stop the bleeding?

5 A: I .... **(not/be)** ill this year.
B: You're lucky! I .... **(be)** ill three times already!

3 **Fill in:** *have/has been* **or** *have/has gone*.

1 .... you .... to a specialist about your back problem?
2 The injured player .... to the USA for treatment – she'll be back next month.
3 Martina and Julie aren't home – they .... to the hospital to see their brother.
4 It's the first time my son .... to a football match.

4 **Choose the correct item. Give reasons.**

1 I've **just/yet** made an appointment to see Dr Graves.
2 Have you **never/ever** had a tooth taken out?
3 We haven't heard from Brandon **yet/already**.
4 I haven't had a temperature **since/for** 24 hours.
5 John hasn't been to the dentist's **since/for** last May.
6 Has the doctor called you in **just/yet**?
7 Pat has **never/ever** felt pain as bad as that in her life.
8 I've **yet/already** done my exercise for the day.

5 **Read the theory. Explain how the two tenses differ.**

Present perfect – Past simple

- We use the **present perfect** for an action which happened at an unstated time in the past or which started in the past and continues to the present.
  *I **have been** to Cairo.* (When? We don't know.)
  *He **has been** ill for a week.* (He was ill last week and he still is.)
- We use the **past simple** for a completed past action which happened at a stated or known time.
  *He **got** the flu last Monday.* (When? Last Monday.)

6 **Fill in** ***did(n't)***, ***have(n't)*** **or** ***has(n't)***.

1 .... you find the medical advice useful? Yes, I ....
2 .... she finished her studies? No, she ....
3 .... Tracy wash the cut by herself? No, she ....
4 .... anybody seen Dr Harris? No, we ....
5 .... Tom gone home? Yes, he ....

7 **Read the theory. How do we form the present perfect continuous? How does it differ from the present perfect? Find examples in the dialogue on p. 48.**

Present perfect continuous

Affirmative	Negative
I/You/We/They **have been working** since 9 o'clock. He/She/It **has been working** since 9 o'clock.	I/You/We/They **haven't been working** since 8 o'clock. He/She/It **hasn't been working** since 8 o'clock.
Interrogative	**Short answers**
Have I/you/we/they **been working** since 8 o'clock? **Has** he/she/it **been working** since 8 o'clock?	**Yes**, I/you/we/they **have**./ **No**, I/you/we/they **haven't**. **Yes**, he/she/it **has**./ **No**, he/she/it **hasn't**.

We use the **present perfect continuous** to talk about:
- an action which **started in the past** and **continues to the present** to give **emphasis to duration**.
  *The organisation **has been sending** medical teams and equipment to Angola since 1986.*
- a completed past action which has **visible results** in the **present**.
  *I'm dirty because **I've been working** in the garden.*

Time expressions used with the present perfect continuous: *for*, *since*, *how long*, *all day/morning* etc *lately*, *recently*

8 **Put the verbs in brackets into the present perfect continuous and complete the gaps with** ***for*** **or** ***since***.

1 I .... **(wait)** to see a doctor .... hours.
2 .... **(your aunt/work)** as a nurse .... 2002?
3 Bob .... **(not/feel)** well .... last Monday.
4 Chris .... **(talk)** with his patient .... an hour.
5 I can't believe it! It .... **(rain)** .... last Sunday!

9 **Use the prompts to ask and answer questions, as in the example.**

1 How long/you/study/French? – seven years
A: How long have you been studying French?
B: I've been studying French for seven years.
2 How long/you/live/in Japan? – last August
3 How long/you/work/here? – 2012
4 How long/you/wait/here? – a few minutes

10 **Put the verbs in brackets into the present perfect, present perfect continuous or the past simple. Give reasons.**

REPLY MAIL

Dear Aunt Kelly,
How are you and Uncle Pete? I hope you're both well.
Mum **1)** .... **(probably/tell)** you, but I **2)** .... **(start)** training at Mile Road Hospital a week ago. It **3)** .... **(be)** very hard so far. I **4)** .... **(work)** at the hospital 40 hours a week. Then I **5)** .... **(try)** to study at home. I **6)** .... **(not/have)** much sleep recently!
But of course you know all about that – you **7)** .... **(be)** a doctor for over thirty years! That's the reason I want to talk to you. You **8)** .... **(work)** as a GP for your whole career, and I want to ask you – **9)** .... **(you/ever regret)** your decision not to specialise? And when **10)** .... **(you/know)** that this was the kind of doctor you wanted to be? I **11)** .... **(start)** thinking about what to do after I finish my training, you see.
Any advice you can give me would be great! Write soon!
Love,
Kim

Skills in Action

Vocabulary

Parts of the body & Injuries

1 **Match the prompts (1-6) to the injuries (A-F). Then, act out dialogues, as in the example.**

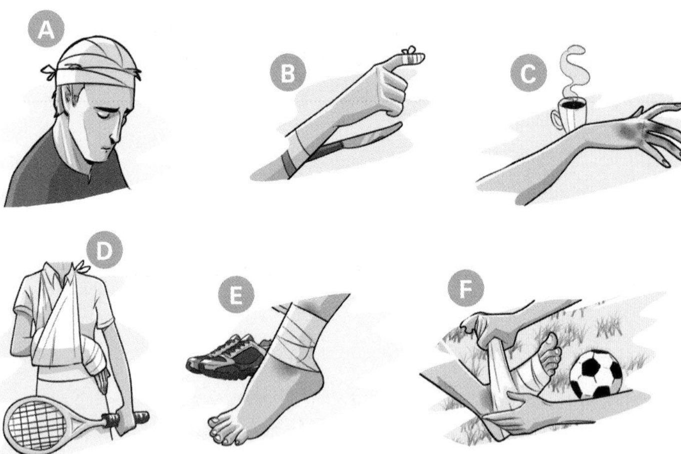

1	Tommy/cut/finger – slice some onions	*B*
2	Max/sprain/ankle – run	....
3	Sandy/break/wrist – play tennis	....
4	John/bump/head – clean up the garage	....
5	Carla/burn/hand – make coffee	....
6	Sam/bruise/foot – play football	....

A: What's wrong with Tommy?
B: He's cut his finger.
A: How did he do that?
B: He was slicing some onions.

Listening

2 **Listen to a doctor talking to some junior doctors and match the patients to their problems.**

	Patients		Problems
1	☐ Rita	**A**	broken leg
2	☐ Amanda	**B**	cut head
3	☐ Jane	**C**	temperature
4	☐ Sarah	**D**	stomach ache
5	☐ Kim	**E**	toothache
		F	headache

Everyday English

At the doctor's

3 **Read the first exchange. What is the patient's problem? What do you think the doctor will suggest?**
Listen and read to find out.

Doctor: Good afternoon, Mr Harris. What seems to be the problem?
Patient: I've got a terrible cough and a temperature that just won't go away.
Doctor: I see. How long have you had a temperature?
Patient: Today's the fourth day.
Doctor: Let me listen to your chest ... Yes, it sounds like you've got an infection. I'm going to give you a prescription for some antibiotics. I want you to take them twice a day for ten days.
Patient: Can I go to work?
Doctor: I don't think it's a good idea to go anywhere for a day or two. Wait until the temperature goes down. You need to stay warm, get lots of rest and drink plenty of fluids.
Patient: I will, doctor. Thank you so much.

4 **Act out similar dialogues. Use the prompts below and language from the box.**

- **earache and a temperature –** take antibiotics/take aspirin for the pain
- **a headache and a sore throat –** get rest/drink hot tea

<table>
<tr><th colspan="2">Asking about a problem</th></tr>
<tr><td>• What seems to be the matter/problem?</td><td>• What's wrong with you?
• What brings you to me?</td></tr>
<tr><th colspan="2">Explaining a problem</th></tr>
<tr><td colspan="2">I've got/I've developed/I'm suffering from .../ I've been having ... since/for ...</td></tr>
<tr><th colspan="2">Giving medical advice</th></tr>
<tr><td colspan="2">My advice is to .../The best thing to do is .../ I (don't) think it's a good idea to .../You need to .../I want you to ...</td></tr>
</table>

Pronunciation /ɪd/

5 **Listen and tick the words which end with the sound /ɪd/. Listen again and repeat. After which verb endings do we say /ɪd/?**

lik**ed**	liv**ed**	decid**ed**
want**ed**	work**ed**	succeed**ed**
treat**ed**	help**ed**	walk**ed**

Reading & Writing

6 **Read the email and complete the gaps with the sentences in the list. One sentence is extra.**

A I stopped in time, but Stuart didn't.
B Thank you for all your help with Stuart.
C Send one too with more news of Japan.
D Sounds like you've been enjoying your trip to Japan!
E I've been helping him.

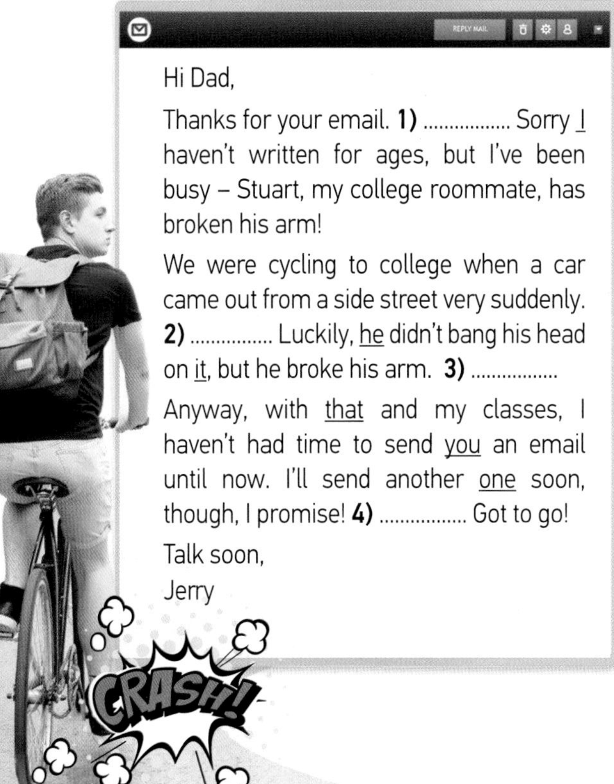

Hi Dad,

Thanks for your email. **1)** .... Sorry I haven't written for ages, but I've been busy – Stuart, my college roommate, has broken his arm!

We were cycling to college when a car came out from a side street very suddenly. **2)** .... Luckily, he didn't bang his head on it, but he broke his arm. **3)** ....

Anyway, with that and my classes, I haven't had time to send you an email until now. I'll send another one soon, though, I promise! **4)** .... Got to go!

Talk soon,
Jerry

7 **Read again. Match the underlined words into the text to the people/things below.**

1 Jerry	**3** Stuart	**5** email
2 Jerry's dad	**4** the car	**6** helping Stuart

Writing Tip

Proofreading
Check your piece of writing for grammar and spelling mistakes. Try to notice if there are any mistakes you often make. Make a list of mistakes and always check for those in your writing.

8 **Find the mistakes in the extract.**

Sorry I haven't writen for a while but I have broke my wrist.

I was playing tennis last Wednesday when I sliped and fell. They tooked me to hospital and the doctor put it in cast. It's really painfull. I don't think I'll be able to take part in the tennis tournament in this year.

Writing (an email about a health issue)

9 **a) Read the task. Who are you writing to? What are you going to write? How many words should you write?**

This is part of an email from an English relative of yours. Write an email in reply (100-120 words).

> I was in hospital with a chest infection! I'm feeling better now. Have you ever been very ill? What happened?

Write your email.

b) Imagine there was a time when you were very ill. Make notes under the headings: *when – where – what was wrong – how doctor treated you – how you felt after* **in your notebook.**

10 **Use your notes in Ex. 9 to write your email. Follow the plan. Proofread your piece of writing.**

Plan

Hi/Hey/Hello, (+ first name)!
Para 1: ask how he/she is; say when and where you were very sick
Para 2: narrate your experience of being sick, going to the doctor and getting treatment
Para 3: tell your relative of the results of the treatment and make a closing remark
Take care/Love/All the best,
(your first name)

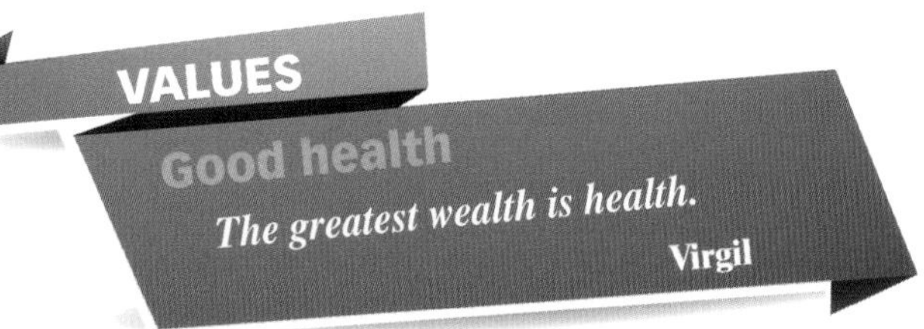

VALUES
Good health
The greatest wealth is health.
Virgil

6 Culture

A HUGE JOB

Imagine living in the middle of the outback in Australia, on a farm or in a small town or in an Aboriginal community. A snake has just bitten you, but the nearest hospital is hundreds of miles away. **1)** .... Call the Flying Doctors, of course!

IN CASE OF EMERGENCY

The Royal Flying Doctor Service of Australia has been providing emergency medical care in remote areas since the 1920s. **2)** .... Since then, it has grown to nearly 70 planes and a thousand people flying out of 20 airfields. They provide emergency services 24 hours a day, seven days a week and 365 days a year!

OTHER HEALTH SERVICES

But the organisation is not just for emergencies. It transports patients between hospitals, when a trip by road would be too hard on a patient. It runs clinics in remote communities, flying in every week or so and giving check-ups, shots and medical advice. **3)** ....

NOT-FOR-PROFIT

Every year, the planes of the Flying Doctors cover a distance equal to flying to the moon and back 25 times. The service is not-for-profit and gets some money from the state. **4)** .... The rest comes from donations. For more details, go to https://www.flyingdoctor.org.au

Check these words

outback, Aboriginal, community, remote, check-up, shot, donation

Listening & Reading

1 **Look at the pictures, the title and the sub-headings. What do you think the Royal Flying Doctor Service of Australia does?**

Read to find out.

2 **Read the text and complete the gaps with the sentences in the list. Pay attention to the beginning of each sentence. One sentence is extra.**

A And it gives out medical advice over the radio, telephone and Internet.

B The TV show *The Flying Doctors* has made it famous.

C However, it is not enough money to fund the service completely.

D What can you do to get treatment for the bite?

E In the beginning, there was one plane and one doctor.

Speaking & Writing

3 THINK **Listen to or read the text. What do you think are the good things about being a doctor in the Royal Flying Doctor Service of Australia? Can you think of any disadvantages?**

4 ICT **Find out about a service like the Royal Flying Doctor Service of Australia in your country or in another country. Collect information, then write a text for an international health magazine. Write about:** *name – history – services – funding*.

Review 6

Vocabulary

1 Fill in: *ache, infection, temperature, throat, toothache.*

1 I've got a really bad sore ....!
2 John went to the dentist about his ....
3 Her younger sister has got a(n) .... of 40°C.
4 You'll need antibiotics if you have a(n) ....
5 We ate too much and now we've both got a stomach ....!

(5 x 2 = 10)

2 Fill in: *do, get (x2), go, see, take* **in the correct form.**

1 That aspirin .... the trick – my headache's gone.
2 I .... your advice and stayed in bed yesterday – and I feel better.
3 You aren't .... enough rest, and so you're always tired.
4 You aren't well – .... to bed and I'll bring you some tea.
5 The doctor gave me medicine to .... rid of my cold.
6 You've got a fever – you need to .... a doctor!

(6 x 2 = 12)

3 Choose the correct item.

1 I **cut/burnt** my hand with hot tea yesterday.
2 He fell down the stairs and **broke/bumped** three bones.
3 Jo can't walk because she sprained her **wrist/ankle**.
4 I **bruised/cut** my finger while chopping an onion.
5 Carl ran into a tree and **burnt/bumped** his head.
6 He fell off his bike, but he only **bruised/broke** his knee.

(6 x 2 = 12)

Grammar

4 Choose the correct item.

1 Jodie has **been/gone** to LA – she's back tomorrow.
2 I **went/have gone** to the dentist's yesterday.
3 Don't worry – the ambulance has **just/yet** arrived.
4 Have you ever **been/gone** to London?
5 Ken's **yet/already** taken an aspirin for his earache.
6 I've **ever/never** been so sick in my life!
7 You've **coughed/been coughing** since Tuesday.
8 You haven't visited the dentist **for/since** a year!

(8 x 3 = 24)

5 Put the verbs in brackets into the present perfect or the present perfect continuous.

1 I .... **(visit)** John in hospital three times this week.
2 .... **(you ever/spend)** the night in hospital?
3 Don't worry – I .... **(not/wait)** for long.
4 Mandy .... **(read)** three books so far this weekend.
5 The doctor .... **(not/finish)** yet.
6 You look tired. .... **(you/sleep)** enough these days?

(6 x 5 = 30)

Everyday English

6 Match the exchanges.

1 ☐ I've got a headache, Jo.
2 ☐ What's wrong with you?
3 ☐ My advice is to stay in bed.
4 ☐ I don't think it's a good idea to go to work.

A I will, doctor.
B I won't.
C I've got a cold.
D Why don't you take an aspirin?

(4 x 3 = 12)

Total 100

Competences

Lexical Competence
Understand words/phrases related to
- illnesses & remedies
- parts of the body
- injuries

Reading Competence
- understand texts related to health (read for detail – multiple choice)/read for cohesion & coherence – missing sentences)

Listening Competence
- listen to and understand dialogues related to health (listen for specific information – multiple matching)

Speaking Competence
- go to the doctor's
- give health advice

Writing Competence
- write a forum post giving advice
- write an email about a health issue

Values: Volunteering

Home https://volunteer2day.co.uk/international _volunteer_day/volunesia Friends Blog Forum

Volunteer2day>internationalvolunteerday>volunesia

It sounds like an island in the South Pacific, but it's actually a new word to describe a life-changing moment. **1)** .... It's the word volunteers use for the moment when they **forget** they're trying to change other people's lives because their own life is changing.

Because, yes, we volunteer to help others, but we often forget that it **benefits** us, too. Studies have shown that people who volunteer are happier, healthier and less **stressed** than those who don't. They are better at making and keeping friends. **2)** ....

But why? One **simple** reason is that it gets you out of your room, out of your flat. You talk to new people, people who think like you do. You're doing something new, and that means you're learning new skills, finding out what you're good at. **3)** .... And of course, you are often helping people, which feels good.

A quarter of all young people in the UK are volunteering these days. **4)** .... A lot are just helping in their **local** communities. It doesn't matter what you do, because whatever kind of volunteer you are, it will change your life!

Join Now!

1 **Look at the title. Where do you think you can find such a text? What is its purpose:** *to entertain*? *to describe*? *to persuade*? **Read through and check.**

2 **Read the text again and complete the gaps with the sentences (A-E). One sentence is extra.**

A You keep busy, so you don't have time to worry about any problems you have.
B 'Volunesia' comes from the words 'volunteer' and 'amnesia'.
C Some are teaching in other countries, others are planting trees in national parks.
D Research has shown that children as young as two try to help other people.
E Most importantly, they feel like they have a purpose in life.

Listen and check. Then, explain the words in bold.

3 ICT **Research ways to volunteer in or near the place where you live.**

4 THINK **Imagine you have volunteered in your local community e.g. visiting an old people's home, helping out in a youth club or clearing up a park. Describe your experience. How has this changed your life?**

5 **Create a one-minute video promoting volunteering.**

Public Speaking Skills

1 **Read the task. What is the purpose of the presentation?**

Imagine International Volunteer Day is coming up. Your college has decided to hold an event to encourage people to volunteer. They asked you to present a famous person from your country who spends time helping others.

Study Skills

Using cue cards

Cue cards can help you remember what you want to tell the audience. Write the main idea on one side of each card. Use large fonts so that you can see what you have written. Number the cards so that you know their correct order.

2 **Listen to and read the model. Number the cue cards correctly.**

A ☐
- **Cleveland Cavaliers**
- **Miami Heat – 2 NBA**
- **Cleveland Cavaliers – 1 NBA**

B 1
- **born 30/12/1984**
- **Akron, Ohio**

C ☐ **2003 – LeBron James Family Foundation**

D ☐
- **Frank Walker**
- **age 9 – basketball**

E ☐
- **After-School All-Stars**
- **the Boys and Girls Club**

Hello, I'm Scott Sanders. The man I'm going to talk about is one of the best basketball players of all time – but he's much more than just that.

LeBron James was born on 30th December, 1984, in Akron, Ohio, USA. His mother was only 16 and his early years were very hard. They moved home often. When a local American football coach called Frank Walker offered to give James a home, his mother agreed. Walker introduced him to basketball at age 9 and his talent was clear from the start.

James' school basketball team rarely lost a game. After school, he joined the Cleveland Cavaliers, then the Miami Heat for three years, then back to the Cavaliers. He won two NBA championships with the Heat and one with the Cavaliers. LeBron James is one of the greatest basketball players of all time, because of his all-round ability as a scorer, passer and defender.

But there is more to Lebron James than just basketball. He has never forgotten his difficult childhood, and works to help children in a similar position today. He has donated money and volunteered a lot for a number of charities like After-School All-Stars and the Boys and Girls Club, which help poor children and teens.

In 2003, he set up the Lebron James Family Foundation. The goal of the Foundation is to stop kids from Akron dropping out of school, and James has spent a lot of time and money creating clubs, schools and even a programme to help hard-working students to go to the University of Akron.

As LeBron James said: "I'm just a kid from Akron." And even when he became the biggest basketball star in the world, he never forgot where he came from.

3 **ICT** **Think of a famous person from your country who helps others. Research him/her and make notes under the headings:** *Name – Early life – Fame – Volunteering*. **Then prepare your cue cards. Don't forget to number them. Use your cue cards to present the person to the class.**

Vocabulary:	Rules & Regulations, Chores
Grammar:	Modal verbs: present & past modals, the imperative
Everyday English:	Asking about/Explaining rules
Writing:	An advert about a flat for rent

Stick to the rules!

Vocabulary
Rules & Regulations

1 **Look at the sign.**
Listen and learn.

Campsite Regulations
1 Keep your dog on a lead.
2 Don't light fires.
3 Recycle your rubbish.
4 Do your washing-up in the area provided.
5 No loud music after 11 pm.
6 Use the campsite kitchen for cooking.
7 Keep your campsite clean. No litter.
8 Park your car near your tent.

Listening & Reading

2 **Look at the leaflet. What is its purpose?**
Listen and read to find out.

3 **Read the leaflet again and for questions 1-4, choose the best answer *A*, *B* or *C*. Then explain the words in bold.**

1 At the campsite, campers aren't allowed to
A light fires anywhere. **B** cook in their tents.
C eat food in their tents.

2 Campers don't need to pay for
A cleaning products. **B** hot showers.
C rubbish bags.

3 Campers with dogs have to
A exercise them every day.
B keep them on a lead when outdoors.
C keep them in a special tent.

4 At night, it is important for campers
A to respect that other people are sleeping.
B not to drive around the campsite.
C to keep their tents closed.

We want all our campers to enjoy a peaceful and relaxing stay, so here are a few simple rules and regulations to make sure that happens!

Cooking & Heating

In the interests of safety, please use the areas provided for cooking and washing-up. You mustn't light fires, except in places where there is a fire pit. You mustn't try to **light** a cooking fire inside your tent, as this can be **extremely** dangerous!

Keeping the campsite clean

A clean, **tidy** campsite makes life more pleasant for everyone. We ask you to keep showers and toilets clean, recycle your rubbish and **pick up** your litter after picnics, etc. You don't have to buy rubbish bags – we supply them free of **charge.**

Pets

Pets are allowed at the campsite, but they shouldn't run around **freely.** This may annoy fellow campers. Please keep your dog on a lead when it is outside your tent or caravan. There is a special outdoor area for pets where they can take their **daily** exercise off the lead.

Respecting fellow campers

From the hours of 11 pm to 8 am, you are not allowed to play loud music. This could disturb others who are sleeping. Also, don't park your car in the way of other campers. You should park next to your own tent or **caravan**.

Thank you for your kind cooperation. We wish you a very happy stay!

Check these words

safety, fire pit, litter, supply, annoy, lead, respect, disturb

4 **Use the words in the list to complete the gaps, then make sentences using the completed phrases.**

• daily • fellow • simple • loud • relaxing • rubbish • fire

1 .... stay
2 .... rules
3 .... pit
4 .... bag
5 .... camper
6 .... exercise
7 .... music

5 **Fill in:** *light, take, pick up, recycle, keep, play.*

1 Don't .... music after 11 pm.
2 Please use the special bins to .... rubbish.
3 Never .... a fire in the forest.
4 You should drink water when you .... exercise.
5 You have to .... any litter you drop in the countryside.
6 Always .... the camping area clean or it will attract wild animals.

6 PREPOSITIONS **Fill in the correct preposition, then make sentences using the completed phrases.**

• to • at • from • of (x2) • in • on

1 in the interests ....
2 .... the campsite
3 .... a lead
4 free .... charge
5 .... 11 pm to 8 am
6 .... the way of
7 next ....

7 **Underline the imperative forms in the leaflet. How do we form the imperative?**

Speaking & Writing

8 **Cover the leaflet, then use the pictures on p. 56 to talk about rules and regulations at Green Forest Campsite.**

9 THINK **Imagine you are a trekking guide. You are about to take a group of tourists up a mountain, where you will camp for the night. Create a leaflet with rules for them. Think about:** *fire safety, damaging trees/plants, litter, disturbing wildlife.*

Grammar in Use

Landlady: *Welcome to Clippers Apartments. You have to sign here please, and I'll give you the key.*
Mark: *OK, there you are. Do I have to pay the rent today?*
Landlady: *No, you don't need to pay rent until the first of each month.*
Mark: *Great. Am I allowed to have visitors stay with me?*
Landlady: *You must let me know if you're expecting a guest just so I know what's going on, but of course they can stay.*
Mark: *Right ... And one last thing – is it OK to get a dog when I've settled in?*
Landlady: *Sorry, you can't have pets here. I'm allergic to cats and dogs.*
Mark: *OK. No problem.*

1 **Read the theory. Find examples in the dialogue. Identify the uses.**

have/need to – don't have/need to – must/mustn't

We use ***have/need to*** to express:
- **necessity/lack of necessity.**
  *You **have/need to** leave early to catch the flight.* (It's necessary.)
  *You **don't have/need to** help me wash the car.* (It isn't necessary.)
- **obligation/duty coming from outside the speaker.**
  *Campers **have to** keep their pets on a lead.* (It's their duty. The campsite owner says so.)

We use ***must/mustn't*** to express:
- **very strong advice.**
  *You **must** stay away from the boats.* (It's very important that you do.)
  *You **mustn't** go near the rocks.* (It's very important that you don't.)
- **obligation/duty coming from the speaker.**
  *I **must** call Ann tonight.* (It's my duty. I say so.)
- **prohibition.**
  *You **mustn't** light a fire in the forest.* (It's forbidden.)

2 **Fill in:** *must (x2), doesn't have to, mustn't (x2), don't have to, have to, has to.*

1 Campers .... check out of the campsite by noon.
2 You .... forget to pay your rent today.
3 He .... take a special test to be a taxi driver.
4 You .... book our hotel room before it's too late.
5 We .... pay for Wi-Fi. It's free of charge.
6 Children .... swim in the pool without an adult present.
7 I .... thank Molly for helping me to find my new flat.
8 She .... buy a bus ticket. She's already got one.

3 **a)** **Listen to Ann and Chris talking about the colleges they go to. Put a tick (✓) or a dash (–) in each column.**

Who has to ...	**Chris**	**Ann**
1 get up early to catch the bus?	✓	–
2 go to a lesson on Saturday mornings?	....	....
3 help out at the Students' Union?	....	....
4 do housework on Sundays?	....	....
5 pay for college lunches?	....	....

b) **Now make sentences, as in the example.**

Chris has to get up early to catch the bus.
Ann doesn't have to get up early to catch the bus.

4 **Discuss chores, as in the example. Use these ideas as well as your own:** *wash the car/do the gardening, clean up my room/mop the floors, do the laundry/tidy the garage.*

A: *Tomorrow, I have to wash the car.*
B: *So do I, but I don't have to do the gardening.*
A: *Neither do I.*

may/might/could

We use ***may***, ***might*** or ***could*** to express **possibility in a specific situation**.
*Stay away from the dog. It **may/might/could** bite you.* (It's possible.)

5 **Match the advice to the results, then make sentences, as in the example.**

	Advice		**Results**
1	☐ Never play with matches.	A	the fire/spread
2	☐ Always be careful when cooking with hot oil.	B	you/start a fire
3	☐ Never throw water on an oil fire.	C	it/set on fire

Never play with matches. You might start a fire.

6 **Read the theory. Find examples in the dialogue on p. 58.**

can/can't – be allowed to – should/shouldn't

- We use ***can*** to ask for or give permission, and ***can't*** to refuse permission.
  *"**Can** I go out?"* (Is it OK if ...) *"Of course you can."*
  *I'm afraid you **can't** enter this room.*
- We use ***be allowed to*** to talk about rules and regulations:
  ***Am I allowed to** use the pool?* (What is the rule?)
- We use ***should/shouldn't*** to give advice – i.e. to say it is a good/bad idea for someone to do sth.
  *You **should** drink a lot of water daily.* (It's a good idea.)
  *You **shouldn't** drink too much coffee.* (It isn't a good idea.)

7 **Read the theory in Ex. 6 again. Use the prompts to act out short dialogues, as in the example.**

1 I/park my car/here? (park somewhere else)
A: Can I park my car here?
B: No, I'm afraid you can't. You aren't allowed to park here. You have to park somewhere else.
2 my son/come to the hospital? (leave him at home)
3 we/eat/in here? (eat your food outside)
4 I/wear shorts/in this restaurant? (wear a suit and tie)
5 I/take this olive oil/on the plane with me? (leave it with airport security)

8 **Complete the sentences about going hiking with *should* or *shouldn't*.**

1 You .... wear strong, comfortable shoes.
2 You .... go hiking in bad weather.
3 You .... go hiking on your own.
4 You .... take some water with you.

9 **Read the theory. Then, fill in:** *didn't have to*, *could*, *couldn't*, *wasn't able to*, *had to (x2)*.

had to/didn't have to – could/couldn't – was/were(n't) able to

- ***Had to/didn't have to*** are the past forms of ***have to/ don't have to***.
  *When my father was a boy, he **had to** wear a uniform to school. He **didn't have to** learn ICT back then.*
- ***Could/couldn't*** are the past forms of ***can/can't***.
  *She **could** swim when she was five. I **could** go out when I was 16, but I **couldn't go** on my own; I **had to** go with my brother.*
- We use ***was/were able to*** to express **specific ability in the past**. *They **were able to** get there on time.* (They had the ability on that particular occasion. They managed to.)

BUT: We use ***could*** with ***hear***, ***see***, ***smell***, ***feel***, ***taste***, ***understand***, ***believe***, ***decide***, ***remember***. *He **could hear** the wind howling.* We use both ***couldn't*** and ***wasn't/ weren't able to*** to express **specific negative ability in the past**. *He **couldn't/wasn't able to** win the race.*

1 Thanks to his university job, Joe .... travel a lot.
2 He .... pay for his trips because the university did.
3 One year, he .... fly to Paris to give a lecture, but the weather that day was bad.
4 In those days, pilots .... take off in thick fog.
5 The passengers .... wait on the runway for three hours.
6 The flight arrived so late that Uncle Joe .... give his lecture!

10 **Fill in:** *must*, *should*, *need*, *may*, *shouldn't*, *don't have to*, *mustn't*, *can't*.

TRAVELLING ABOARD | the basics

When travelling to another country, you **1)** .... to have an up-to-date passport before you can enter. Also, in some countries, you **2)** .... enter without a visa. You **3)** .... know the language, but it does help! You **4)** .... also respect the customs of the place. Ignoring them **5)** .... offend the locals and that's something to avoid! And you **6)** .... break the law – you could end up in prison! When visiting countries, you **7)** .... try and support local businesses. Also, you **8)** .... buy souvenirs from just anyone – shops are safest.

Skills in Action

Vocabulary

Chores

1 **Look at the pictures.**
Listen and learn.

1 take out the rubbish

2 clean the bathroom

3 sweep the floors

4 clean the windows

5 dust the furniture

6 vacuum the carpets

7 do the laundry

8 do the washing-up

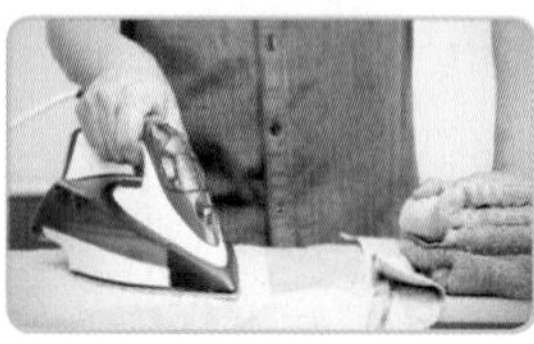
9 do the ironing

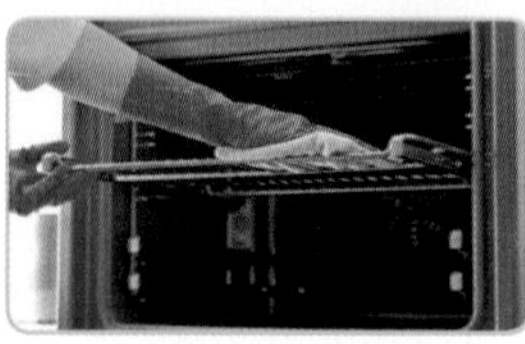
10 clean the oven

2 **Which of the chores do you have to do this weekend? Tell your partner.**

Listening

3 **Listen and match the people (1-5) to the chores (a-g). Two chores are extra.**

1 ☐ Chloe
2 ☐ Dave
3 ☐ Penny
4 ☐ Gale
5 ☐ Ricky

a vacuum the carpets
b do the washing-up
c clean the bathroom
d sweep the floors
e clean the windows
f dust the furniture
g take out the rubbish

Everyday English

Asking about/Explaining rules

4 **Colin has rented a holiday flat and is discussing the rules with its owner, Lydia. Read the dialogue and choose the correct item.**
Listen and check.

Lydia: Welcome! Here are the keys.
Colin: Thank you. What time do we **1) have to/must** check out on Sunday, please?
Lydia: By 11 am at the latest. You **2) may/should** leave the keys in the letterbox. Here's a full list of rules.
Colin: OK. Are there any rules about quiet hours?
Lydia: You **3) don't have to/mustn't** make any noise between 11 pm and 7:30 am.
Colin: Right. Is it OK to park on the street?
Lydia: Yes, you **4) could/can**. But you can also park in the garage.
Colin: Great!
Lydia: The main thing is you **5) can/have to** keep the flat clean and tidy.
Colin: No problem at all!
Lydia: You **6) can/are able to** use the cleaning products provided and there is a vacuum cleaner available.
Colin: Great!
Lydia: Enjoy your stay!
Colin: Thanks!

5 **Use the prompts to act out a dialogue between someone renting a holiday cottage and the landlord/landlady. Use the dialogue in Ex. 4 as a model.**

A	B
• Monday/check out? • cook in garden? • park my bike at the main entrance?	• 2 pm • use barbecue provided • not leave rubbish outside the bins

Pronunciation *can* /kæn/ – *can't* /kɑːnt/

6 **Listen and repeat.**

- We can't use the pool today.
- You can use our Wi-Fi – it's free.
- How many pets can we bring with us?
- Visitors can't stay overnight.

Reading & Writing

7 **Read the advert and fill in the appropriate headings. Where could you see such an advert?**

• Cancellations • House Rules • The Space • Facilities

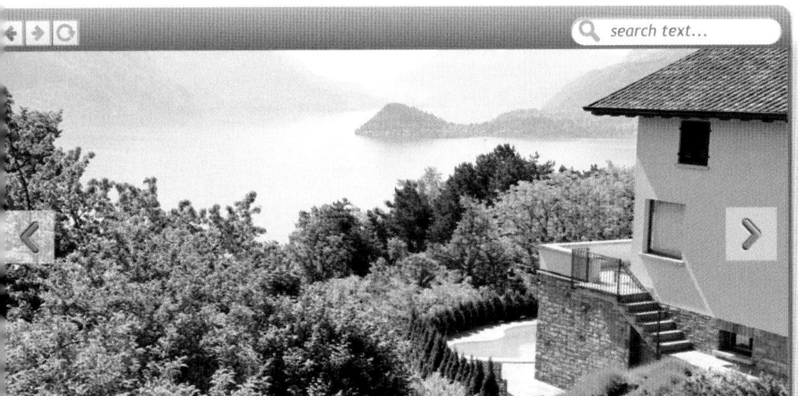

Italian holiday villa on Lake Como

6 guests | 3 bedrooms | 3 beds | 2 bathrooms

1) ....

This lovely villa near Lake Como can sleep six and is perfect for relaxing holidays. There are fantastic views of the lake and Milan is only a 2-hour drive away.

Read more ▾

2) ....

- fully equipped basement gym
- large garden with swimming pool
- laundry room
- Wi-Fi

Show all ▾

€150 per night
DATE
Check in → Check out
GUESTS
1 Guest
BOOK
You won't be charged yet.

42 Reviews ★★★★★
Search Reviews

3) ....

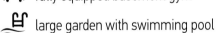

- Guests are not allowed to remove equipment from the gym.
- Guests must wear trainers in the gym.
- For garden meals, please cook on the barbecue provided.
- Young children mustn't use the pool without an adult present.
- Please do laundry in the laundry room only. Clothes dryer available.

Read more ▾

4) ....

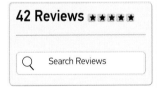

- Cancel up to 30 days before your trip for a full refund.

Read more ▾

Writing Tip

Presenting information in adverts

When we write an advert, it is important to present the information clearly. This catches the reader's attention and invites them to read more. Use headings to introduce each new section. You can also use bullet points to present separate ideas.

8 **Read the Writing Tip. Is the advert in Ex. 7 properly laid out? Give reasons.**

9 **List the items in the list below under the headings from Ex. 7.**

- report any damage to property
- laptop-friendly workspace
- fully air-conditioned
- lock all doors when leaving
- park in the garage, not on the street
- weekly cleaning service
- sort rubbish into recycling bins
- large balcony

Writing (an advert about a flat for rent)

10 **a) Read the rubric and underline the key words. What do you have to write? Who for?**

You own a flat in a block of flats in the city centre and you want to rent it for the summer. Write an advert for a holiday homes website giving full details (100-120 words).

b) BRAINSTORMING **Use the headings in Ex. 7 to brainstorm for ideas.**

c) **Use your ideas from Ex. 10b to write your advert. You can use the advert in Ex. 7 as a model.**

VALUES
Cleanliness
Leave a place as you would wish to find it.
saying

7 Culture

The Greatest Race in the Land Down Under

VIDEO

Australia – or the Land Down Under – is home to Ayers Rock, the Great Barrier Reef and one of the world's top yacht races: the Sydney to Hobart Yacht Race. People travel from all over the world to **take part**. They set sail from the capital city on Boxing Day (26th December) and finish over 1,000 kilometres away, in Hobart on the island of Tasmania.

The race is one of the oldest and most famous sailing competitions in the world. It first took place in 1945 and quickly became world-famous because it was so dangerous and difficult. It **lasts** six days and competitors have to sail against strong winds all the way to Tasmania. Even though it is summer, they can face storms and huge waves in the Tasman Sea.

To **join** the race, you have to have a yacht between 9 and 30 metres long, with between 6 and 24 crew members. Each member has to be over 18 years old, but there is no **limit** on how old competitors can be. In fact, in 2015, 88-year-old Syd Fischer competed and finished the race!

The Sydney to Hobart Yacht Race might be a challenge for competitors, but it's great fun for spectators! At the start, 600,000 people **gather** on the shores of Sydney Harbour, and more watch from cruise ships or the Manly ferry boat. Many bring a picnic and make it a Boxing Day tradition! At the finish line, there is the Hobart Race Village, where there are live bands, food stalls, face-painting and games. It's also the perfect **spot** to watch the New Year's fireworks display after the race is over. Visitors to Australia in December shouldn't miss it!

Listening & Reading

1 **Read the title. What type of race is the text about? Where does it take place? How long does it last?**

Listen and read to find out.

2 **Read the text and decide if the sentences are *T* (True), *F* (False) or *DS* (Doesn't say). Then explain the words in bold.**

1 You must be Australian to compete in the race. ....
2 The summer weather is perfect for sailing. ....
3 Competitors pay to participate. ....
4 More than half a million people watch the start. ....
5 There are fireworks in Hobart on 31st December. ....

Check these words

yacht, set sail, competitor, face, wave, crew member, challenge, spectator

Speaking & Writing

3  **Would you like to take part in the Sydney to Hobart Yacht Race? Why/Why not?**

4 ICT **Collect information about a race in your country. Make notes under these headings:** *Where/When is it? – What is it? – What are the rules? – Why go?* **Present the event to the class.**

Review 7

Vocabulary

1 **Fill in**: *charge, area, pit, litter, fire, lead, rubbish, ironing*.

1 Please do your washing-up in the .... provided.
2 Do not leave .... behind after your picnic; take it home with you.
3 We supply rubbish bags free of ....
4 It's your turn to do the ....
5 Only use the campsite's fire .... to cook meals.
6 We had to light a(n) .... to keep warm.
7 You have to keep your dog on a(n) .... in this park.
8 Please recycle .... like glass and plastic.

(8 x 2 = 16)

2 **Match to form collocations.**

1	☐ do	A	the floors
2	☐ dust	B	the windows
3	☐ clean	C	the carpets
4	☐ sweep	D	the laundry
5	☐ vacuum	E	the rubbish
6	☐ take out	F	the furniture

(6 x 4 = 24)

Grammar

3 **Choose the correct item.**

Swimming pool rules

1 You **have to/mustn't** have a medical check.
2 You **might/need to** take off your jewellery.
3 You **mustn't/don't have to** wear a swimming cap.
4 You **mustn't/could** push other swimmers.

(4 x 3 = 12)

4 **Fill in:** *mustn't, may, can't, have to, should*.

1 We .... have a party in the garden. (aren't allowed to)
2 You .... bring insect repellent to the campsite. (It's a good idea.)
3 It .... stop raining soon. (It's possible.)
4 We .... play loud music at night. (It's forbidden.)
5 You .... check out by 12 noon. (It's your duty.)

(5 x 2 = 10)

5 **Fill in:** *had to, didn't have to, could, couldn't, was able to* **or** *wasn't able to*.

1 A: I .... go to the cinema with friends when I was 14.
B: Oh really? I .... I .... go with my parents.
2 A: I always brought lunch to school.
B: We .... do that. We had a canteen.
3 A: I .... book the hotel. It was full!
B: Never mind. I .... find a nice guest house instead.

(3 x 6 = 18)

Everyday English

6 **Match the exchanges.**

1 ☐ What time do I need to check out?
2 ☐ Is it OK to leave my bicycle here?
3 ☐ Here are your keys.
4 ☐ Are there any rules about music?
5 ☐ You have to buy your own cleaning products.

A You mustn't make any noise after 11 pm.
B Thank you.
C OK, I'll do that.
D Yes, you can.
E By 12 noon.

(5 x 4 = 20)

Total 100

Competences

Lexical Competence
Understand words/phrases related to:
- rules & regulations
- chores

Reading Competence
- Understand texts about accommodation, rules and regulations, events (read for specific information and gist – multiple choice; match headings to paragraphs; T/F/DS statements)

Listening Competence
- Listen to and understand dialogues about chores (listen for detail – multiple matching)

Speaking Competence
- ask about/explain rules

Writing Competence
- write a leaflet for camping rules
- write an advert about a flat for rent

Vocabulary: Geographical features, Man-made landmarks, Materials
Grammar: the passive
Everyday English: Ask for information
Writing: An article about a landmark

Landmarks

Vocabulary
Geographical features

1 a) **Look at the pictures of eight UNESCO World Heritage Sites and complete the gaps. Use:** *falls, lakes, mine, canyon, caves, mountains, rainforests, valley.*

Listen to a podcast about them and check.

1 Grand ...., National Park, USA

2 Plitvice ...., National Park, Croatia

3 Viñales ...., Cuba

4 .... of Atsinanana, Madagascar

5 Elephanta ...., India

6 The Greater Blue ...., Australia

7 Victoria ...., Zambia

8 Wieliczka Salt ...., Poland

VIDEO

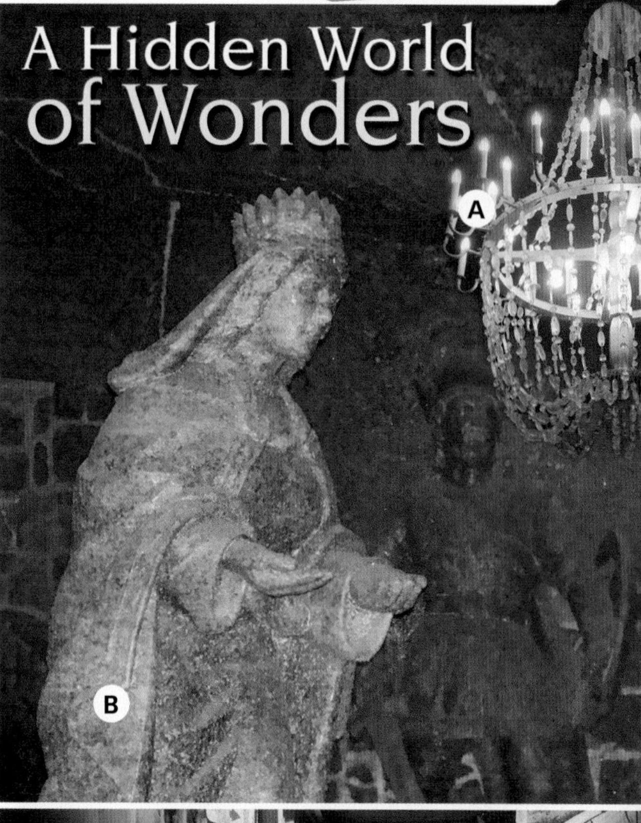

b) **Ask and answer questions about the places in Ex. 1a, as in the example.**

A: Where is Grand Canyon National Park?
B: It's in the USA.

2 **Pictures A-E show parts of the Wieliczka Salt Mine in Kraków, Poland. Which picture shows:**

1 a statue carved from rock salt?
2 an underground lake?
3 a mineshaft?
4 a light made out of huge salt crystals?
5 a model of a miner carrying salt up to the surface?

Listening & Reading

3 **What makes the Wieliczka Salt Mine unique? Listen, read and check.**

The Wieliczka Salt Mine near Kraków is one of Poland's most famous **attractions**. It is visited by 1.2 million people every year!

The mine was first opened in the 13th century. Today it is a museum. Visitors can see how salt was mined long ago. Miners dug it out by hand and then carried it along mineshafts and up to the surface. After 1620, horses were used to carry the salt out. Visitors can now admire huge **chambers**, green underground lakes and 250 kilometres of tunnels and caves. These are **decorated** with natural salt crystals in strange **shapes**. There are also many interesting statues the miners carved out of rock salt. Even the beautiful lights that hang from the high **ceiling** in the main chamber are made out of salt crystals!

According to an ancient **legend**, a Hungarian princess called Kinga was travelling from Hungary to Poland. On her way, she threw her ring into a salt mine at Marmaros! Later, when she visited Wieliczka, her **servants** were told to dig a well. Instead of water, salt was found – and **hidden** in the first lump was Kinga's ring!

Even if you don't believe this story, you will be amazed by the mine's unforgettable sights. If you ever go to Kraków, don't miss the **chance** to visit it.

Check these words

mine, dig, surface, carve, well, lump

4 **Read the article and complete the sentences in your notebook. Then, explain the words in bold.**

1 The Wieliczka Salt Mine is located ....
2 Nowadays, the mine is a ....
3 The tunnels are decorated with ....
4 The mine's statues were made by ....
5 Kinga's servants found her ring while they ....

5 **Fill in:** *strange, ancient, high, famous, huge, underground, salt, rock*. **Then, make sentences using the completed phrases.**

1 .... attractions
2 .... chambers
3 .... lakes
4 .... crystals
5 .... shapes
6 .... salt
7 .... ceiling
8 .... legend

There are a lot of famous attractions in Kraków.

Writing Tip

Learning new words

Learn new words together with their opposites. This helps you remember them.

6 **Fill in the opposites from the list:** *ugly, modern, boring, unknown, tiny, low*.

1 famous ≠ ....
2 huge ≠ ....
3 high ≠ ....
4 interesting ≠ ....
5 beautiful ≠ ....
6 ancient ≠ ....

7 PREPOSITIONS **Choose the correct prepositions. Then make sentences based on the text using the completed phrases.**

1 **on/in** the 13th century
2 dug out **with/by** hand
3 decorated **of/with** salt crystals
4 carve sth **out/in** of rock salt
5 hang **off/from** the ceiling
6 according **on/to** a legend
7 **at/on** her way
8 amazed **by/from** sth

Speaking & Writing

8 a) **List the phrases below under these headings:** *Place/Location – History – Things to see – Legend – Recommendation*.

- Wieliczka Salt Mine
- natural salt crystals
- servants dug well
- horses used after 1620
- Hungarian princess Kinga
- underground lakes
- opened in 13th century
- beautiful lights
- near Kraków in Poland
- interesting statues
- threw ring into mine
- huge chambers
- ring was found
- tunnels & caves
- salt dug out by hand
- should visit it

b) **Imagine you are a tour guide. Use your notes in Ex. 8a to tell visitors about the Wieliczka Salt Mine.**

Welcome to Wieliczka Salt Mine near Kraków in Poland.

9 THINK **Imagine you have visited the Wieliczka Salt Mine. Write a blog entry about your visit there. Use ideas from Ex. 8.**

Grammar in Use

NEW GALLERY FOR SHELBY MUSEUM

*Members of the public **are invited** to the opening of Shelby Museum's new Whittaker Gallery next Wednesday, 18th March, at 6 pm. The gallery, on the top floor of the museum, **was completed** in February and **will be opened** by the Mayor of Shelby. Opening hours at the museum are from 9 am to 6 pm daily. Admission is £2.50 for adults and £1.00 for children. Members of the Shelby Museum Society can enter free of charge. Please note that cameras **must not be used** inside the museum.*

1 **Read the theory How do we form the passive? When do we use it? Then use the passive verb forms in bold in the announcement to complete the table below.**

The passive (*to be* + past participle of the main verb)

We use the passive when **the action is more important than the agent** *(the person or thing doing the action). Salt was discovered. (We are more interested in the action than the person who did it.)*

Changing from active into passive

The object of an active verb becomes the subject of a passive verb. The subject of an active verb becomes the agent of a passive verb. We usually introduce the agent with ***by*** *(people)* or ***with*** *(objects, instruments)*. We omit the agent when the subject is *they*, *he*, *someone/somebody*, *people*, *one*, etc.

	subject	**verb**	**object**
Active:	*Horses*	*carried*	*coal.*

	subject	**verb**	**agent**
Passive:	*Coal*	*was carried*	*by horses.*

	Active	Passive
Present simple	invite	
Past simple	completed	
will	will open	
modals	must not use	

2 **Which sentences in the passive do not include an agent? Why?**

1 It **is visited** by 1.2 million people every year.
2 Visitors **are shown** how the salt was mined.
3 Salt **was carried** up to the surface.
4 You **will be amazed** by the mine's unforgettable sights.

3 **Fill in the missing active or passive forms.**

	Active	Passive
1	Visitors **should not touch** the exhibits.	The exhibits .... by visitors.
2	The ancient Egyptians .... the Pyramids.	The Pyramids **were built** by the ancient Egyptians.
3	Millions of tourists **will visit** the Louvre this year.	The Louvre .... by millions of tourists this year.
4	Gustave Eiffel **designed** a huge iron tower for Paris.	A huge iron tower .... for Paris by Gustave Eiffel.
5	You **can see** the Great Wall of China from space.	The Great Wall of China .... from space.
6	Tourists sometimes .... Tower Bridge with London Bridge.	Tower Bridge **is** sometimes **confused** with London Bridge by tourists.
7	The Romans **completed** the Colosseum in 82 CE.	The Colosseum .... by the Romans in 82 CE.
8	People **admire** Prague for its lovely buildings.	Prague .... for its lovely buildings.

4 **Ask and answer questions using the prompts, as in the example.**

• shoes – leather – Italy • ring – gold – France
• watch – silver – Switzerland • jacket – wool – Spain
• shirt – silk – China • skirts – cotton – England
• toy – plastic – Japan • desks – wood – Germany

A: What are these shoes made of?
B: They're made of leather.
A: Where were they made?
B: They were made in Italy.

5 **Complete each sentence using the word in bold, as in the example.**

1 Steven Spielberg directed the film *ET*.
BY *ET was directed by* Steven Spielberg.

2 Queen Elizabeth II owns the world's largest diamond.
IS The world's .... Queen Elizabeth II.

3 Millions of tourists visit London every year.
VISITED London .... every year.

4 They must repair the bridge immediately.
REPAIRED The bridge .... immediately.

5 The mayor will open the new gallery next Friday.
BE The new gallery .... next Friday.

6 Fleming didn't invent the TV.
INVENTED The TV .... Fleming.

6 **a) Choose the correct item.**
Listen to a quiz and check.

1 The cinematograph was invented by ...
a the Montgolfier brothers in 1783.
b the Lumière brothers in 1895.

2 The telephone was invented by ...
a Alexander Graham Bell in 1876.
b Thomas Edison in 1877.

3 The *Cafe Concert* was painted by ...
a Paul Gaugin in 1698.
b Édouard Manet in 1878.

4 The Gherkin was designed by ...
a Foster and Partners.
b Smith and Partners.

5 *Wuthering Heights* was written by ...
a Emily Brontë in 1845.
b Charlotte Brontë in 1845.

6 *The Blue Danube* was composed by ...
a Richard Strauss in 1876.
b Johann Strauss in 1867.

b) **Ask and answer questions using the passive voice, as in the example.**

A: Who was the cinematograph invented by?
B: It was invented by the Lumiére brothers.
A: When was it invented?
B: It was invented in 1895. Who was the telephone invented by?

7 **Put the verbs into the correct passive tense, then use the prompts (a-e) to ask and answer questions in pairs.**

The Louvre is the national museum and art gallery of France. In 1546, work on the Louvre **1)** .... **(start)** by King Francis I. The Louvre **2)** .... **(use)** as a royal palace until 1682. It **3)** .... **(open)** to the public as a museum and art gallery in 1793. Today many of the world's most famous paintings **4)** .... **(keep)** in the Louvre, as well as sculptures, jewellery and other forms of art. It **5)** .... **(visit)** by millions of people every year.

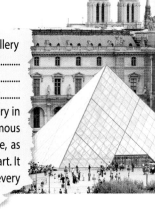

a When / work / the Louvre / start?
A: When was work on the Louvre started?
B: Work on the Louvre was started in 1546.
b What / it / use as / until 1682?
c When / the Louvre / open / to the public?
d What / keep / in the Louvre?
e How many people / it / visit / by / every year?

8 **SPEAKING** **Ask and answer questions, then present each place, as in the example.**

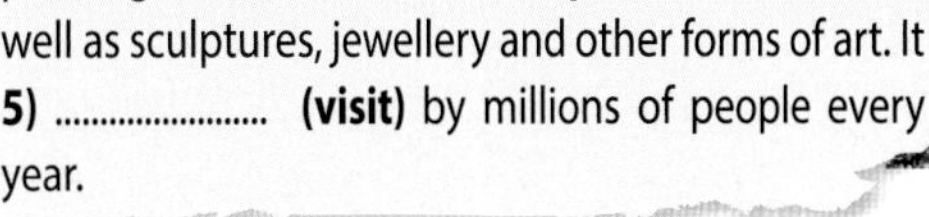

A
Name: Burj Khalifa, Dubai, United Arab Emirates
Designer: Adrian Smith
Completed: 2010
Material: steel, glass and concrete
Built as: a place both to live and work in

A: This landmark is ....
B: Where is it ... located?
A: It is located in ... .
B: Who was it ... by?
A: It ... by ... .
B: When ... completed?
A: It ... in ...
B: What ... made of?
A: It is ... .
B: Why ... built?
A: It was built as ...

The Burj Khalifa is located in ... . It was designed by ... and ...

B
Name: Sydney Opera House, Australia
Designer: Jørn Utzon
Completed: 1973
Material: concrete
Built as: performing arts centre

9 **ICT** **Collect information about a landmark and write a fact file about it. Use a photo as well. Present the landmark to the class. The class votes for the top landmark.**

Skills in Action

Vocabulary

Man-made landmarks & Materials

1 What is each landmark made of? Make sentences.

1 The Shard / glass

2 The Guggenheim Museum / concrete

3 The Parthenon / marble

4 The Golden Gate Bridge / steel

5 Stonehenge / stone

6 The Royal Albert Hall / brick

7 Trojan Horse statue / wood

8 The ancient city of Chan Chan / clay

1 *The Shard is made of glass.*

Listening

2 Listen to the recorded message. Fill in the missing information.

Opening times: 10 am to **1)** .... pm
Main attractions: horse-drawn **2)** .... & steam-powered underground train
Special events: Hidden London **3)** .... that explore the London Underground
Museum tickets: 4) £.......... for adults – under-18s free
Photography: Not allowed in the **5)** .... of the museum

Everyday English

Asking for information

3 Read the dialogue between a tour guide and a tourist and fill in the missing words.
Listen and check.

A: Welcome to the Tower of London. Please feel free to ask me anything.
B: Could you **1)** .... me what part of London we are in?
A: Certainly. The Tower of London is **2)** .... in the borough of Tower Hamlets.
B: When was it built?
A: Well, the White Tower was built in 1078 and it was expanded over the years. It was completed in 1399.
B: Right. **3)** .... was it built by?
A: It was originally built by William the Conqueror.
B: Thanks. Oh, and one more thing – can we **4)** .... photographs?
A: Yes, in most areas, but cameras are not allowed in the Jewel House, I'm **5)** ....
B: I see. Thank **6)** .... for your help.
A: You're welcome!

4 Imagine you are visiting Buckingham Palace in London. Act out a similar dialogue, using the prompts and the language from the box.

Location: City of Westminster
Built: 1703 (main house)
By: Duke of Buckingham
Completed: 1913
Photography: not allowed – only in the palace garden

Asking for information	Giving information
• Could you tell me ...? • Could give me some information about ...?	• Certainly. • Of course. • It's ... . Well, you can ... .

Intonation in passive questions

5 Listen and underline the stressed word. Then repeat the sentences.

1 What was it made of?
2 Who was it written by?
3 How was it discovered?
4 Where was it found?
5 When was it built?
6 Why was it chosen?

Reading & Writing

6 **Read the article and put the verbs in brackets into the correct passive form.**

Are you planning to visit Peru? Then, don't miss out on the ancient Inca city of Machu Picchu. It **1)** .... **(locate)** in Cusco, high up in the Andes Mountains. There are over 150 buildings. All **2)** .... **(make)** of stone and **3)** .... **(connect)** by an amazing network of terraces and steps.

The city **4)** .... **(build)** in the 15th century, but people lived there for only a hundred years before they abandoned it. One theory is that they **5)** .... **(kill)** off by disease, but no one knows what happened for sure.

In the summer, Machu Picchu **6)** .... **(visit)** by 2,500 tourists a day, who **7)** .... **(amaze)** by the magnificent ruins of temples and palaces. One of the top attractions, the Intihuatana Stone, **8)** .... **(use)** by the Incas to study the stars.

You **9)** .... **(thrill)** by the mysterious beauty of Machu Picchu. As Peru's most famous landmark, it is a must-see.

Writing Tip

Writing titles

A catchy title attracts the reader's attention and helps them predict the content of the article. Titles should be short and simple. You can use interesting adjectives, numbers or the imperative.

7 **Which two of the titles (A-D) are suitable for the article in Ex. 6? Why?**

A Magical Machu Picchu
B A thrilling place that you should go and see
C Head for Machu Picchu
D 5 reasons to visit Machu Picchu

Writing Tip

Writing an article describing a famous landmark

Articles describing a famous landmark can appear in magazines, newspapers, websites, etc. We normally use **present** tenses to describe the landmark and **past** tenses to write about the historical facts.

Writing (an article about a landmark)

8 **Read the task. What does it ask you to write about? Who for?**

An international online travel magazine has asked its readers to send in articles describing a famous landmark. Write your article for the magazine (100-120 words).

9 **Listen and complete the missing information.**

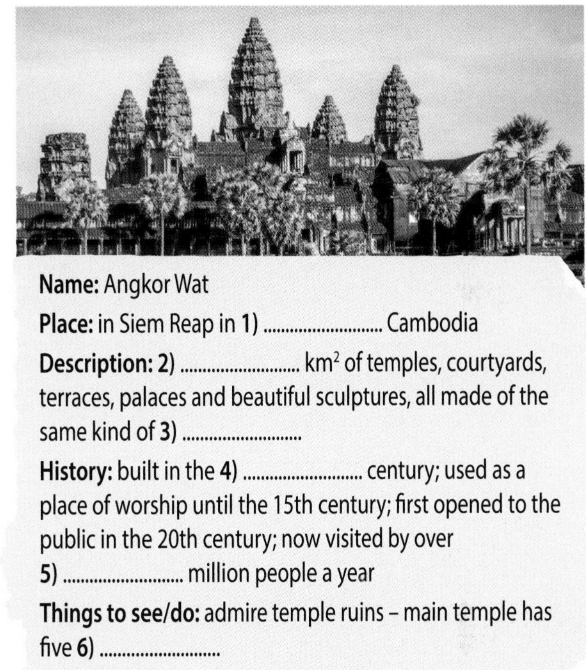

Name: Angkor Wat
Place: in Siem Reap in **1)** .... Cambodia
Description: **2)** .... km² of temples, courtyards, terraces, palaces and beautiful sculptures, all made of the same kind of **3)** ....
History: built in the **4)** .... century; used as a place of worship until the 15th century; first opened to the public in the 20th century; now visited by over **5)** .... million people a year
Things to see/do: admire temple ruins – main temple has five **6)** ....

10 **Use the notes in Ex. 9 and the plan below to write an article about Angkor Wat. You can use the article in Ex. 6 as a model.**

Plan

Title
Introduction
Para 1: name, place, description
Main Body
Para 2: historical facts
Para 3: what visitors can see/do there
Conclusion
Para 4: recommendation

VALUES
Inspiration
Good architecture lets nature in.
Mario Pei

8 Culture

VIDEO

Man-made LANDMARKS in the UK

A

The Kelpies are Scotland's hot new landmark! This pair of 30-metre high horse-head sculptures were designed by sculptor Andy Scott and completed in 2013. The heads are made of steel and decorate the entrance of the Forth and Clyde Canal. In Scottish mythology, Kelpies were water spirits with the strength of 10 ordinary horses. The modern sculptures symbolise how important the horse was in Scottish trade and transport.

B

The Uffington White Horse in Oxfordshire is one of England's most famous hillside figures. It is a huge 110-metre long horse and dates back to prehistoric times. It was dug into the chalk, a metre deep in some places. Looking like a piece of modern art, it's hard to believe it is 3,000 years old! It is thought it was an emblem of an ancient tribe, or it symbolised a Celtic horse goddess.

D

The Big Fish of Belfast in Northern Ireland is 10 metres long and covered in blue and white ceramic tiles. It was created by sculptor John Kindness in 1999. Each tile tells a story of Belfast's past. A time capsule was also placed inside the fish. It contains pictures, poems and other information about the city. That's why this landmark is also called the Salmon of Knowledge, after the legendary wise fish in Irish mythology!

C

The Marquess of Bute of Cardiff Castle, Wales, wanted to make his garden more exciting. It was the 19th century – the age of explorers, when wild animals were seen as mysterious and exotic – so he created the **Animal Wall**. Fifteen stone sculptures were carved, starting in 1890, and they can still be seen today. Lions, bears, hyenas and other wild beasts look down at you from the top of the garden wall, many with the glass eyes they were originally given!

Check these words

trade, figure, chalk, emblem, tribe, explorer, beast, ceramic tile, time capsule

Listening & Reading

1 **Find two things all the landmarks in the pictures have in common. What do they symbolise?**
Listen and read to find out.

2 **Read the texts again. Which of the landmarks (A, B, C or D) ...**

1 is near the water? ....
2 was made for a private home? ....
3 is part of the countryside? ....
4 has something hidden inside? ....

Speaking & Writing

3 THINK **Tell your partner one thing that you find interesting about each landmark.**

4 ICT **In groups of four collect information about four interesting landmarks in your country or other countries. Prepare a poster. Use pictures.**

Vocabulary

1 **Fill in:** *carved, dug, amazed, hang, made, decorated.*

1 The room is .... with crystals.
2 We were .... by the sights.
3 They .... the statue out of rock.
4 The Parthenon is .... of marble.
5 Beautiful lights .... from the ceiling.
6 Miners .... out salt by hand.

(6 x 3 = 18)

2 **Choose the correct word.**

1 Homes built of **wood/steel** are a fire risk.
2 The **glass/clay** roof lets you see the sky.
3 A river runs through the **lake/canyon**.
4 Inside the **valley/cave** it was very dark.
5 The village homes are made of **steel/stone** from the nearby mountain.
6 There are tall trees in a **mine/rainforest**.

(6 x 3 = 18)

Grammar

3 **Choose the correct item.**

1 The museum was opened **by/with** the mayor.
2 Photos shouldn't **take/be taken** with a flash inside the exhibition hall.
3 The Tower of London **is/was** once used as a prison.
4 Gold is carried out of the mine **with/by** machines.
5 Plays in ancient Greece **aren't/weren't** performed indoors.
6 Visitors are kindly **ask/asked** not to touch the exhibits.
7 Dinner is **serve/served** on the terrace.
8 The museum **will/will be** opened next Sunday.

(8 x 3 = 24)

4 **Put the verbs in brackets into the correct passive form.**

The awe-inspiring Segovia Aqueduct **1)** .... **(situate)** in Central Spain. It **2)** .... **(build)** by the Romans in the first century CE and **3)** .... **(design)** to bring water to the town centre. Today, the aqueduct is still an amazing piece of architecture and **4)** .... **(visit)** by tourists from all over the world. Standing at 28.5 metres high, it's got two rows of arches which **5)** .... **(support)** by pillars. The entire structure **6)** .... **(make)** of granite. Day trips from Madrid can easily **7)** .... **(arrange)** with Golden Travel. You will **8)** .... **(drive)** there by coach and then you will **9)** .... **(take)** on a tour of the town and the aqueduct with a guide. This magical experience really mustn't **10)** .... **(miss)**! Book your tour here.

(10 x 2 = 20)

Everyday English

5 **Match the exchanges.**

1 ☐ Could you tell me when it was built?
2 ☐ Who was it built by?
3 ☐ Thank you for your help.
4 ☐ Can I take photographs there?

A I'm afraid cameras are not allowed.
B William the Conqueror.
C You're welcome.
D It was completed in 1399.

(4 x 5 = 20)
Total 100

Competences

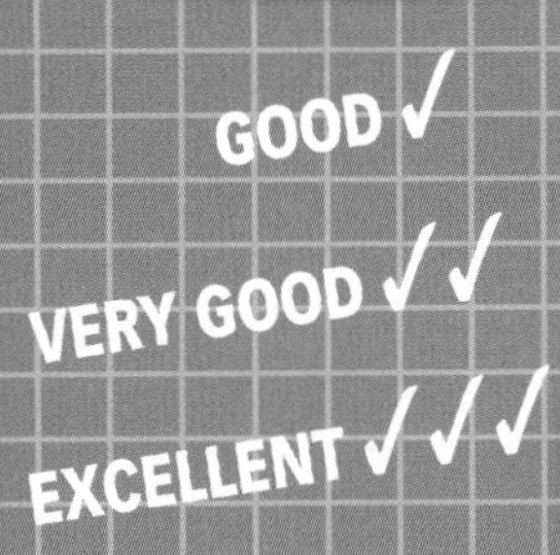

Lexical Competence
Understand words/phrases related to:
- geographical features
- man-made landmarks & materials

Reading Competence
- Understand texts about landmarks (read for specific information – complete sentences)

Listening Competence
- Listen to and understand a monologue about landmarks/ attractions (listen for detail – gap-fill)

Speaking Competence
- present famous landmarks
- ask for information

Writing Competence
- write a blog entry about a visit to a salt mine
- write an article about a landmark

Vocabulary: Endangered animals, Green activities
Grammar: past perfect; conditionals type 2; reflexive pronouns
Everyday English: Making suggestions – Agreeing/Disagreeing
Writing: An article providing solutions to a problem

9 Live and let live

Vocabulary
Endangered animals

1 **Label the pictures. Use:** *gorilla, bear, elephant, penguin, dolphin, rhino, eagle, tiger.*
Listen and check.

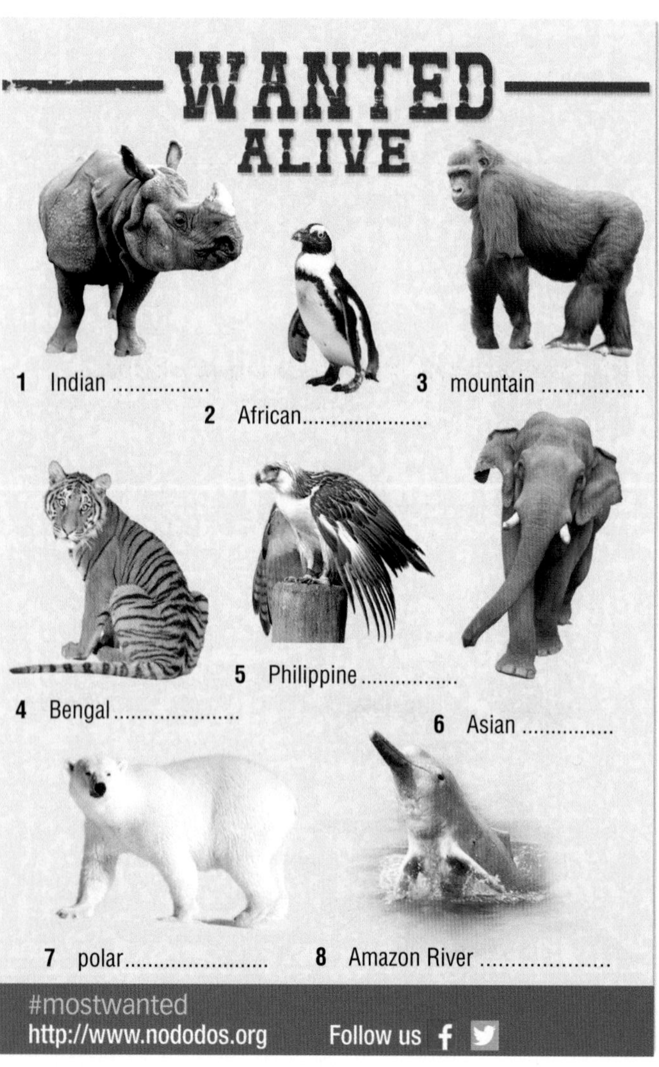

WANTED
ALIVE
1 Indian ....
2 African.....................
3 mountain ....
4 Bengal.....................
5 Philippine ....
6 Asian ....
7 polar........................
8 Amazon River ....
#mostwanted
http://www.nododos.org
Follow us

2 **Check the words in bold in your dictionary. Which of the animals in Ex. 1:**

A ☐ has got a **horn** and four **hooves**?
B ☐ has got black **stripes** and **whiskers**?
C ☐ has got black skin, thick white **fur** and huge **paws**?
D ☐ has got **feathers**, a **hooked beak** and sharp **claws**?
E ☐ has got smooth skin, a long nose and **fins**?
F ☐ has got wings and **webbed feet**?
G ☐ has got two **tusks** and a long **trunk**?
H ☐ has got thick black **fur** and no **tail**?

twitter Home Notification

NoDodos
An animal protection organisation
http://www.nododos.org

Following

Tweet to **@NoDodos**

Latest tweets

It's Earth Day so we're going to tweet about the most endangered species on Earth. We call them 'most wanted' because we really WANT to keep these animals on our planet! Find us on social media to see how you can **take action** to help them – they can't help themselves! #mostwanted 5 hours ago

There are only 55,000 African penguins left, all on the south-west coast of Africa. An oil spill in 2000 put 40,000 of them in danger, but a quick response from green groups and lots of **volunteers** saved them. If there's another spill, will we act as quickly as before? #mostwanted
4 hours ago

Check these words

oil spill, response, hunt, ivory, seal, source, treetops, logger

Reading

3 a) **Read the tweets quickly. Which of the animals in Ex. 1 are they about?**

b) **Match the animals in the tweets to the reasons they are facing extinction. Choose from:** *water, pollution, melting ice, hunting, disappearing forests.*
Listen, read and check.

4 **Read the text and answer the questions. Then, explain the words in bold.**

1 What is the purpose of this series of tweets?
2 What nearly killed many African penguins in 2000?
3 How many Asian elephants are there in the wild?
4 What does the polar bear usually eat?
5 When did the Philippine eagle become the national bird of the country?

Messages

The 50,000 Asian elephants in South and South-East Asia are still hunted for the ivory in their tusks. That means people are still buying things made from ivory. If there were no buyers, **hunters** would stop killing elephants. It's as simple as that. Don't buy ivory. #mostwanted 3 hours ago

Polar bears hunt seals, their biggest food source, on the Arctic ice. But as the Earth gets warmer, this ice starts melting earlier each spring so the bears have less time to **fatten** up for the winter. If a bear doesn't gain enough weight, it won't survive the cold months. #mostwanted 2 hours ago

The Philippine eagle was made the national bird of the Philippines in 1995, but its numbers had already **dropped** to 500 by then. It hunts monkeys in the treetops, but loggers are cutting down the Philippine rainforest fast. No trees, no monkeys. No monkeys, no eagles. #mostwanted 1 hour ago

5 PREPOSITIONS **Fill in *on* or *in*.**

1 Polar bears live longer .... the wild than in zoos.
2 The tallest tree in the world, the coastal redwood, now grows only .... the coast of California and Oregon.
3 There are no penguins .... the Arctic – they only live ...... and around the Antarctic.
4 There are 3,740 species of birds .... Asia – and 1,330 .... India alone.
5 One of the most endangered species .... Earth is the Javan rhino – with fewer than 100 still alive.

6 **Complete the text. Use:** *action*, *source*, *endangered*, *national*, *numbers*.

the bald eagle

The American bald eagle isn't really bald. Its head is covered in white feathers! It has been the **1)** .... bird of the USA since 1782, but by 1967, its **2)** .... had dropped to under 1,000. That's when the Americans took **3)** ...., putting it on the **4)** .... species list and protecting it from loggers, hunters and farmers. Cleaner rivers and lakes also protected its biggest food **5)** .... , fish. In 1995, it was taken off the list and today there are over 70,000 eagles in North America.

Similes with animals

7 **Use the animals in the list to complete the similes. Check in your dictionary. Explain their meaning.**

mouse	lion	bat	peacock
bird	kitten	dog	bee

1 Help me find my glasses. I'm **as blind as a** .... without them.
2 The park ranger was **as brave as a** .... to stop those hunters.
3 Sue's exhausted – she's been **as busy as a** .... all day.
4 Let me just finish this email – then I'm **as free as a** ....
5 My cousin was **as proud as a** .... when he passed his exams.
6 Jo is **as weak as a** .... after her illness.
7 The baby is sleeping, so I want you to be **as quiet as a** ....
8 I can't come out tonight. I'm **as sick as a** ....

Speaking

8 THINK **What problem(s) do you think the other animals from Ex. 1 are facing? Discuss with your partner.**

Writing

9 ICT **Research another endangered animal from the list in Ex. 1. Write a tweet for the '#mostwanted' list. Use the tweets in Ex. 3 as models.**

Grammar in Use

International College forum

FORUM | WHAT'S NEW? | SUPPORT | MEMBERS

Question of the day:

What would you do … if you were the leader of your country for a day?

I'm from the Philippines. If I were the leader of my country, I would stop loggers from cutting down the forests. Or I'd make them plant a new tree for each one they cut down.

I'm from Mauritius. Before people arrived on Mauritius at the end of the 16th century, a bird called the dodo had already lived there happily for thousands of years. By the end of the 17th century, they had all disappeared! If I were the president, I would create national parks where animals could live safely.

I'm from Brazil, and I agree with you both. A tree can't protect itself. Animals can't protect themselves. With 7 billion people on the planet, animals and plants need special places to live.

1 **Read the theory. When do we use the past perfect? Find examples in the forum discussion.**

Past perfect (*had* + past participle)

Affirmative	Negative
I/You/He, etc **had left**.	I/You/He, etc **hadn't left**.
Interrogative	**Short answers**
Had I/you/he, etc **left**?	**Yes**, I/you/he, etc **had**./ **No**, I/you/he, etc **hadn't**.

We use the **past perfect** for an action which **had finished** in the **past before another past action**. *He **had left** before we arrived.*

Time expressions used with the past perfect: *just, already, yet, for, since,* etc.

2 **Put the verbs in brackets into the past perfect.**

1 After he .... **(clean)** the cages, he prepared food for the animals.

2 She realised someone .... **(injure)** the animal.

3 He .... **(not/notice)** any signs of illness until the monkey stopped eating.

4 .... **(he/book)** tickets before he went to the aquarium?

3 **Put the verbs in brackets into the past perfect or the past simple.**

REPLY MAIL

Hi Jane,

I have something incredible to tell you about! Simon and I were deep in the rainforest. We **1)** .... **(leave)** at dawn that day and by midday, Simon **2)** .... **(fall)** behind, so I **3)** .... **(stop)** to let him catch up when I saw the tiger. I **4)** .... **(not see)** it before because it was lying in the shade. I **5)** .... **(hear)** how dangerous tigers were, but for some reason, I **6)** .... **(feel)** no fear. The tiger was just watching me. I **7)** .... **(take)** my camera out of its case earlier, to take a photo of an elephant in the river, so I **8)** .... **(raise)** it slowly. But I **9)** .... **(not manage)** more than one shot before Simon arrived, asking if I **10)** .... **(ever/see)** an elephant before. I turned round, but when I **11)** .... **(turn)** back, the tiger **12)** .... **(go)**.

What an experience!

Tim

4 **Match to form sentences, then say which action happened first.**

1 ☐ Tracy started her speech
2 ☐ I had read the text several times
3 ☐ When they arrived at the beach,
4 ☐ After the lecture had ended,
5 ☐ Kim had finished her work

a the clean-up had already started.
b after the people had sat down.
c by the time her flatmate got home.
d the students left the hall.
e before I understood it.

5 **Read the theory. When do we use Conditionals type 2? Find examples in the forum discussion.**

Conditionals type 2

If-clause	Main clause
If **+ past simple,** →	**... *would/could/might* + infinitive without *to***

We use **conditionals type 2** to talk about unreal, imaginary or highly unlikely situations in the present or future.
NOTE: We can use ***were*** in all persons
If *I* ***were*** *the president, I* ***would not allow*** *hunting.*
I ***wouldn't allow*** *hunting* ***if*** *I* ***were*** *the president.*

6 **Put the verbs in brackets into the correct form. Add commas where necessary.**

1 If you .... **(take)** your bicycle you would get there faster.

2 If he had showers rather than baths he .... **(save)** on water.

3 Our beaches would be much cleaner if people .... **(not/drop)** litter.

4 You'd save on electricity if you .... **(turn)** off lights you don't need.

5 If hunters stopped killing Bengal tigers they .... **(not/be)** an endangered species.

6 The air .... **(be)** cleaner if we all planted more trees.

7 There would be more forests if people .... **(not/cut)** down trees.

8 If people used public transport instead of driving their cars there .... **(be)** less air pollution in big cities.

7 **Make sentences using the prompts.**

1 we all/use/bicycles/instead of cars → there/not be/ so much air pollution

If we all used bicycles instead of cars, there wouldn't be so much air pollution.

2 there/be/more bins in towns and cities → there/not be/so much litter on our streets ....
....

3 we/not pollute/our lakes and rivers → we/have/ clean drinking water ....
....

4 we/recycle/all of our waste → there/be/no rubbish
....
....

5 we/stop/cutting down rainforests → animals/not lose/their homes ....
....

8 **Ask and answer questions, as in the example.**

1 find/a spider on you

A: What would you do if you found a spider on you?

B: If I found a spider on me, I'd scream.

2 find a sick cat

3 you/be able to travel back in time

4 you/have one wish for the environment

5 your friend/throw litter onto the ground

9 SPEAKING **Look at the example sentences, then use the prompts below to act out a similar sequence.**

1 If I had enough money ...

S1: If I had enough money, I'd open a new shop.

S2: If I opened a new shop, I'd sell recycled products.

S3: If I sold recycled products, I'd ... .

2 If I won £1,000,000, ...

3 If I saw a stray animal, ...

4 If I saw a bear, ...

10 **Read the theory. Underline the reflexive pronouns in the forum discussion on p. 74.**

Reflexive pronouns

myself	yourself	himself/herself/itself
ourselves	yourselves	themselves

We use reflexive pronouns when the subject and the object of the verb refer to the same person or thing.

***They** might cut **themselves**.*

We also use reflexive pronouns in these phrases: ***behave yourself***, ***help yourself***, ***be yourself***, ***by yourself*** (= on your own)

11 **Fill in the correct reflexive pronoun.**

1 A: Are the dogs still swimming in the river?
B: No, they're drying .... in the sun.

2 A: What happened to the cat?
B: It hurt .... when it fell out of a tree.

3 A: Shall I pick up this broken glass?
B: No, you'll cut .... I'll get gloves.

4 A: How was the beach clean-up?
B: I found it tiring, but we enjoyed ....

5 A: Shall I make you something to eat?
B: No, I can make a sandwich by ....

12 THINK **What would you do for the environment if you were the leader of your country? Write a few sentences. Tell the class.**

Skills in Action

Vocabulary

Green activities

1 **Do the quiz. Find out how green you are.**

1. If you finished a can of cola, would you ...
   a drop it? b find a bin? c recycle it?
2. If you lived 3km from work or college, how would you get there?
   a by car b on public transport c by bike
3. Where do you get your fruit and vegetables?
   a the supermarket b the market c my garden
4. How much rubbish do you throw out every day?
   a one bagful b most is recycled
   c everything is recycled
5. If you had £10,000 to spend on something eco-friendly, what would you spend it on?
   a I'd buy a car that doesn't create much air pollution.
   b I'd buy a really good bicycle to get around on.
   c I'd plant some trees – more greenery equals more fresh air.

Mostly a's: You're not very green, are you?
Mostly b's: You try to be green, but you don't always get it right.
Mostly c's: Well done! You're really green!

Listening

2 **You will hear three short conversations. For each conversation, choose the correct answer, A, B or C.**

1 How many litter bins will they need?

A  B  C 

2 What is the advert for?

A  B  C 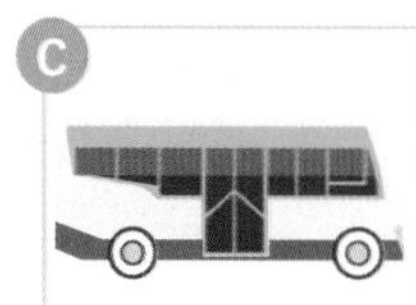

3 What environmental problem are they talking about?

A  B  C 

Everyday English

Making suggestions – Agreeing/Disagreeing

3 **Al and Jo are talking about making their college greener. With a partner, think of three suggestions they might make.**

Listen and check. Do they make any of them

Al: Shall we discuss the Green College programme?
Jo: Yes, let's. First, a campus bus would encourage us not to drive.
Al: I see your point, but that would cost money. How about hiring bikes?
Jo: What a good idea! Then the air pollution would be much lower! Now, litter. Why don't we put a bin on every corner?
Al: I couldn't agree more. If there were bins everywhere, nobody would drop litter.

4 **Replace the underlined phrases/sentences with phrases/sentences from the language box.**

Suggesting	
• Let's ... • Why not ...? • Why don't we ...? • Shall we ...? • What/How about ...? • We can ...	
Agreeing	**Disagreeing**
• Yes, let's. • All right. • I couldn't agree more. • (What/That's a) Good idea!	• I see your point, but ... • I don't think so because ... • I'm afraid I don't agree because ...

5 **Use phrases from the language box and the prompts to act out a dialogue similar to the one in Ex. 3 about how to make the place where you live greener.**

- more public transport → fewer cars
- plant more trees → improve air quality
- recycle more → produce less rubbish

Intonation: identifying feelings

6 **Listen and circle how the speaker sounds. Listen again and repeat.**

1 Really? That's so easy! pleased-shocked
2 Really? That's so easy! excited-sarcastic
3 What's the matter? sad-annoyed
4 What's the matter? worried-angry
5 Oh, no! Not again! scared-angry
6 Oh, no! Not again! bored-puzzled

Reading & Writing

7 **a) Read the article quickly and choose the best title.**

a Good Times for the Hedgehog
b How to Help the Hedgehog
c The UK's Endangered Species

We all want to save tigers and elephants, but what about the UK's endangered species? Hedgehog numbers have fallen by 30% in the last 10 years and there are now less than 1 million left.

One problem for these cute creatures is new roads. This is because they are often killed by cars when they are crossing them. Another problem is all the new houses. This means fewer places for the hedgehogs to live and less for them to eat.

The solution is to make our gardens 'hedgehog-friendly'. Make sure hedgehogs can get in and out easily. Some sticks in one corner make a great hedgehog home! You can leave out water, but not milk, because milk is bad for them. Then, our gardens would be good places for hedgehogs to live and a safe way to get around.

If we all took these simple steps, hedgehog numbers would quickly go back up.

b) Read the article again and complete the table.

Problem	
Causes & effects	
Solutions & results	

8 **How does the writer support his/her solutions in the article in Ex. 7a?**

Writing (an article providing solutions to a problem)

Writing Tip

When we write **an article providing solutions to a problem**, we need to support our solutions with the results they will have. We can use:

- ***then/as a result/so.*** *We could put more bins in the park.* ***Then/As a result****, people would have somewhere to put their litter. One idea is building cycle paths,* ***so*** *people have somewhere to cycle safely.*
- **type 2 conditionals.** *We could have more buses. If we did that, people would leave their cars at home.*

9 **Read the task. What are you going to write? Who for? How many words should you write?**

Your teacher has asked you to write an article for the college magazine providing solutions on how to make our cities better places. Write your article (100-120 words).

10 **a) Match the causes with the effects.**

1 ▢ no cycle paths
2 ▢ nowhere to put litter
3 ▢ many people drive cars
4 ▢ not enough trees
5 ▢ few parks

a air pollution
b litter on the streets
c nobody uses bicycles
d children don't go out to play
e no fresh air

b) Match the solutions with the results.

1 ▢ improve public transport
2 ▢ put bins everywhere
3 ▢ create cycle paths
4 ▢ create more parks
5 ▢ plant more trees

a people use their bicycles
b people put litter in them
c people have more fresh air
d fewer cars and less air pollution
e children have somewhere to play

11 **Use some ideas from Ex. 10 to write your article. Follow the plan.**

Plan

Title *(Think of a good title)*
Para 1: state the problem
Para 2: explain problems and causes
Para 3: provide solutions & expected results

VALUES

Moderation

Earth provides enough to satisfy every man's needs, but not every man's greed.
Mahatma Gandhi

Culture

Home | News | Contact | search... | Follow us

Festivals > Green Festivals

Footprints Eco Festival

The Footprints Eco Festival is a popular event that teaches visitors about the environment and celebrates our natural world.

Learning to be green!

Every year in August, crowds **gather** for a day of eco-friendly fun. Apart from musicians, face-painting and market stalls selling organic food and crafts, there are **workshops** for both children and adults. Kids can learn how to turn rubbish into art, while adults can learn about bee-keeping or finding food in the wild.

You are what you wear!

The festival has its own 'eco fashion' show with clothes from recycled materials. Visitors can also take part in the Footprints Clothes Swap. You can bring six pieces of clothing that you don't wear anymore and **swap** them for clothes you want. You can get a whole new outfit for free!

On your bike!

Visitors are encouraged to travel to the festival in an eco-friendly way, so there's a 'bike park' instead of a car park, and a place where your bike will be serviced free of charge! And the cinema at the Footprints Film Festival gets clean electricity from cyclists who **pedal** as they watch the films!

Join us at Whites Creek Valley Park in the heart of Sydney, Australia. click here

Check these words

celebrate, outfit, service, free of charge, in the heart of

Listening & Reading

1 **Look at the name of the festival and the sub-headings. What do you think you can do at the Footprints Eco Festival?**

Listen and read to find out.

2 **Read the text and answer the questions.**

1 When does the festival take place?
2 What can children learn about at the festival?
3 How many pieces of clothing can you swap in the Footprints Clothes Swap?
4 If you go by bike, what can you get without paying?
5 Where does the festival take place?

3 **Explain the words in bold.**

Speaking & Writing

4 THINK **Why do people need to go to festivals like this? Share your ideas with your partner.**

5 ICT **Collect information about an eco festival in your country. Make notes under the headings:** *name of festival – where & when it takes place – what you can do there – why people enjoy going.* **Present your festival to the class.**

Review 9

Vocabulary

1 **Fill in:** *hooked, sharp, thick, webbed.*

1 The bear had .... brown fur.
2 This kind of fish has very .... teeth.
3 The eagle has got a .... beak.
4 Ducks swim fast as they have .... feet.

(4 x 1 = 4)

2 **Match the words.**

1	☐ fresh	a	spill
2	☐ air	b	air
3	☐ oil	c	species
4	☐ public	d	pollution
5	☐ endangered	e	transport

(5 x 2 = 10)

3 **Fill in:** *drop, plant, recycle, save, take, throw.*

1 Don't .... litter on the street!
2 Let's .... action to save the Earth!
3 What are you doing to .... the planet?
4 You can .... cans here.
5 Don't .... out those old clothes – give them to charity.
6 Why not .... some trees in the park?

(6 x 3 = 18)

Grammar

4 **Fill in the correct reflexive pronouns.**

1 I made this photo frame by ....
2 Be careful not to burn ....
3 Tell Jane to help .... to some coffee.
4 We really enjoyed .... at the eco-festival
5 Animals can't protect .... from hunters.

(5 x 2 = 10)

5 **Put the verbs in brackets into the past perfect.**

1 I .... **(not see)** such a beautiful animal before.
2 Michael .... **(just/finish)** clearing up the rubbish when the rain started.
3 .... **(you/know)** Sylvia long before I met her?
4 I .... **(be)** to Peru five times before that trip.
5 Sammy and Jo .... **(not/go)** to the Amazon until 2014.
6 .... **(Penny/ever/cycle)** to college before yesterday?

(6 x 3 = 18)

6 **Choose the correct item.**

1 Jodie **planted/would plant** lots of flowers if she **had/would have** a bigger garden.
2 If you **found/would find** a plastic bag on the beach, what **did/would** you do?
3 If ivory **wasn't/wouldn't be** so expensive, hunters **didn't/wouldn't** kill elephants for it.
4 More fish **lived/could live** in this lake if we **didn't/wouldn't** pollute it.
5 **Did/Would** your friends help with the recycling project if I **asked/would ask** them?
6 If I **didn't/couldn't** do it, I **did/would** ask for help!

(6 x 4 = 24)

Everyday English

7 **Match the columns.**

1	☐ I'm afraid	A	agree more.
2	☐ I couldn't	B	I don't agree.
3	☐ Why not	C	recycling more?
4	☐ How about	D	go green?

(4 x 4 = 16)

Total 100

Competences

Lexical Competence
understand words/phrases related to
- endangered animals
- green activities

Reading Competence
- understand texts related to animals & the environment (read for specific information – comprehension questions)

Listening Competence
- listen to and understand dialogues related to the environment (listen for specific information/gist – multiple choice)

Speaking Competence
- make suggestions – agree/disagree

Writing Competence
- write a tweet about an endangered animal
- write an article providing solutions to a problem

Values: Good citizenship

About Us | Services | Solutions | Support | Contacts

Circles of citizenship

Our responsibilities as a citizen start with ourselves and spread out to cover the whole world. You need to hit every circle of the target to be a good citizen.

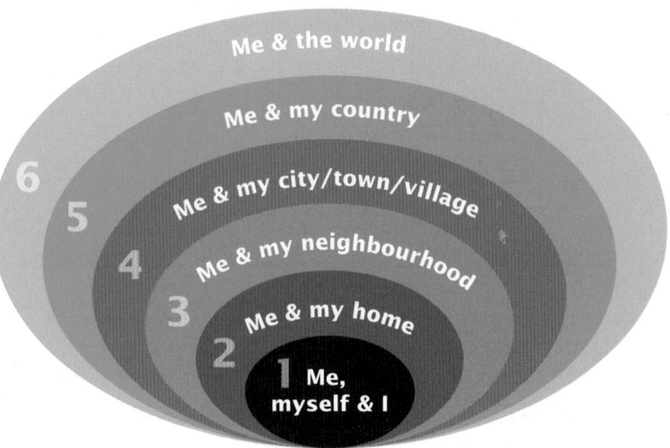

A Do you **obey the law**? We've all heard those words: 'Stop! You're **under arrest**!' The difference is that the good citizen has only heard them on TV!

B Do you know the people in your street? It's **impossible** to know everyone, but what about the ones you see every day? Do you know your next-door neighbours' names, jobs or where they come from?

C Do you look after your own health? We need to eat healthily and take exercise, so we can look after ourselves properly.

D Do you have a green lifestyle? Good citizens are green citizens because they understand that their actions have an **impact** on the whole planet. They can't stand litter, wasting water and electricity or pollution.

E Do you do your fair share of housework? There's no point in being the perfect citizen **in public** but avoiding responsibilities at home! Draw up a schedule with the people you live with and **stick** to it.

F Do you volunteer in the place where you live? Whether it's **coaching** a kids' football team, reading at an old people's home or clearing up a park after a festival – good citizens **gift** their time to the community.

1 **Look at the title of the text and the introductory paragraph. What do you think the 'circles of citizenship' are? Read through to find out.**

2 **Read the text and match the paragraphs (A-F) with the circles (1-6) they talk about. Then explain the words in bold.**

3 THINK **Listen to and read the text. With your partner, think of one more activity to put under each circle of citizenship. Share your ideas with the class.**

Public Speaking Skills

1 **a) Read the task.**

Imagine you are a representative of an organisation that helps the environment. Give a presentation about how to save water at home to a group of students.

b) Listen to and read the model. What techniques has the speaker used to start/end his presentation?

Study Skills

Transition phrases

We can make a smooth transition from one point to the next or from one paragraph to the next using transition phrases *(e.g. But there's more.)*. This helps keep the audience's attention.

2 **Find the transition phrases the speaker has used in his presentation. Replace them with the transition phrases below.**

- Don't forget ...
- To begin with, there's ...
- But that's not all.

3 ICT **Collect information on how to save electricity. Use your notes to prepare and give a presentation. Use transition phrases.**

Good evening everyone! My name's Gun Seung and I'm from Precious Green, the environmental organisation.

Thank you for the introduction and the warm welcome.

Can you believe that 1 in 9 people in the world have no clean water near their home? We have running water in our homes, but instead of feeling lucky, we pour it down the drain. It's time to stop wasting water.

Let's start with brushing your teeth. Do you know how much water you use if you leave the tap running the whole time? 19 litres! Just wet your brush and fill a glass for rinsing your mouth at the end. Another way to cut down on water use is to turn off the shower while you're using the soap, then turn it back on to rinse.

But there's more. While you are waiting for tap water to get warm – when you're washing a cup in the kitchen sink, for example – water is pouring down the drain. Why not catch it in a bowl instead? That way, you can use it to water your plants! The dishwasher also uses a lot of water, so if you have one, make sure it's full every time you use it, and put it on a short wash.

Then there's outdoors. We use about a quarter of our water outdoors, but a few simple steps can greatly reduce your use. First, water the plants in the evening, not under the midday sun! Make sure your garden really needs water – lots of people overwater their gardens, which is both wasteful and bad for the plants. Finally, fix any leaking taps and you save up to three litres of water a day.

As you can see, you can save water by doing these simple things. It's not difficult at all, is it? So what are you waiting for? Start saving water today! Are there any questions? ....

Thank you for listening.

Vocabulary: Types of holidays, Weather, Hotel services & facilities
Grammar: *(to)* infinitive/*-ing* form; relative pronouns/adverbs, defining relative clauses; *the*
Everyday English: Checking in at a hotel
Writing: An online hotel review

Holiday time

VIDEO

Top Travellers

On a budget? Check out our springtime deals and get your holiday for less!

HOME | ABOUT US | OUR HOLIDAYS | CONTACT US | FAQ

Package holidays

If April showers and freezing cold mornings are **getting you down**, book a break with us on this exotic island! For just €699 – with meals, flights and hotel all included – you can spend a fortnight swimming in the warm blue sea and sunbathing on the soft white sand of Phu Quoc Island in Vietnam. In the evenings, stroll back to your five-star hotel, where helpful staff will take care of your every need.

Show more ▼

City breaks

The UK's capital city is huge, and that can get a bit much for visitors. There's so much sightseeing to do, so where do you start? That's where we come in! For just €250, our three-day city break, staying at a comfortable city-centre hotel, ticks every box. The London Eye, Buckingham Palace, Madame Tussauds – see all the **sights** without the stress!

Show more ▼

Cruises

Ahoy there! If you liked the look of the tropical islands in the 'Pirates of the Caribbean' films, why not see them for yourself? Our 9-day, 9-island, €999 cruise is the best way to do it. When you're not relaxing on a sandy beach, swimming in crystal waters, or dining on delicious Caribbean cuisine in beachside restaurants, you'll be **on board** our luxury cruise ship, travelling in style.

Show more ▼

Adventure holidays

Adventurers, look no further! Let's go hiking through the High Tatra Mountains in Slovakia. This one-week **expedition** is perfect for you – and for just €550! We have local guides who'll **look after** you, but it's not a walk in the park – you'll cover long distances every day and the weather in the mountains can go from bright sunshine to clouds to thunderstorms in no time. But it will be a memorable experience.

Show more ▼

Vocabulary

Types of holidays

1 Look at the types of holidays in the adverts. Which is your favourite? Use the adjectives in the list to discuss.

• cheap • tiring • boring • exciting • relaxing • interesting • expensive • close to nature

A: I prefer … because … . What about you?
B: Well, I prefer … to … . They are … .

Check these words

budget, deal, fortnight, stroll, tick every box, dine, thunderstorm

Reading

2 **Read the text quickly and find seven words or phrases describing holiday activities and five words or phrases describing weather.**

3 🎧 **Listen to and read the text and decide if the statements (1-5) are *T* (true), *F* (false) or *DS* (doesn't say). Then explain the words in bold.**

1 The best time to visit Phu Quoc Island is spring. ....
2 Tourists in London sometimes feel lost. ....
3 On the cruise around the Caribbean all the meals are eaten on the ship. ....
4 The adventure holiday is tough on the body. ....
5 All of the holidays last more than ten days. ....

4 THINK **What other types of holidays can you think of? Do you prefer them to the holidays in the adverts? Why?**

5 **Use the words from the list to fill in the gaps. Then use the phrases to make sentences based on the text.**

• delicious • capital • crystal • five-star • warm • local • sandy • tropical

1	.... sea	5	.... beach
2	.... hotel	6	.... waters
3	.... city	7	.... cuisine
4	.... island	8	.... guide

6 PREPOSITIONS **Choose the correct item.**

1 The family stayed in a house **at/in** the mountains.
2 The hotel is **in/on** a small Caribbean island.
3 All the passengers were **on/in** board, so the ship left.
4 We're **on/with** a budget, so no 5-star hotels!
5 I'll be on holiday **from/at** 26th June to 2nd July.
6 Let's hire a limousine and arrive at the hotel **in/on** style!

7 **Match the highlighted adjectives in the text to their opposites. Check in your dictionary.**

1	tasteless ≠	5	dark ≠ ....
2	cool ≠	6	small ≠ ....
3	short ≠	7	forgettable ≠ ....
4	hot ≠	8	worst ≠ ....

Vocabulary

Weather

8 **Complete the weather forecast with the adjectives in the list.**
🎧 **Listen and check.**

• bright • fine • heavy • high • strong • thick • wet

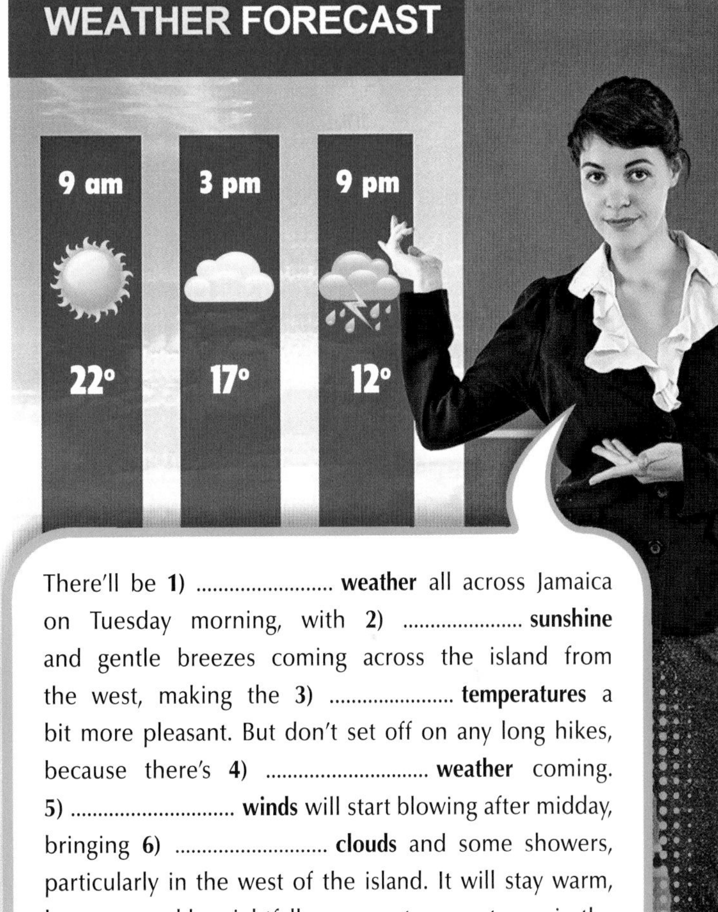

There'll be 1) .... **weather** all across Jamaica on Tuesday morning, with 2) .... **sunshine** and gentle breezes coming across the island from the west, making the 3) .... **temperatures** a bit more pleasant. But don't set off on any long hikes, because there's 4) .... **weather** coming. 5) .... **winds** will start blowing after midday, bringing 6) .... **clouds** and some showers, particularly in the west of the island. It will stay warm, however, and by nightfall we expect some storms in the mountains, with 7) .... **rain**.

Speaking

9 **What is the weather like in your country in spring? What about in summer, autumn and winter? Discuss in pairs.**

Writing

10 **Write a weather forecast for your country for tomorrow. Use the weather forecast in Ex. 8 as a model. Read it to the class.**

Grammar in Use

Would you like to spend a night in an igloo? Then come to the Icehotel in north Sweden. Every year, the owners use 30,000 tonnes of snow to build it. Of course, the weather has to be cold enough, so they avoid building until November. You can stay there from December to April – after that, the hotel melts and building starts all over again! Everything inside is made of ice and the temperature is -5°C. But there's no point bringing a sleeping bag – the hotel provides thermal ones! Most guests who stay there go skiing and dog sledding. And if you enjoy watching the night sky, this is definitely the place for you!

1 **Read the theory. Find examples in the advert.**

(to) infinitive / *-ing* form

- We use ***to*-infinitive**:
  - after ***would love***, ***would like***, ***would prefer***. *I'd love to visit Vietnam one day.*
  - after the verbs ***agree***, ***ask***, ***decide***, ***expect***, ***forget*** (= not remember), ***hope***, ***manage***, ***need***, ***offer***, ***promise***, ***refuse***, ***seem***, ***want***, etc. *We decided to go to Italy.*
  - after ***too/enough***. *The tickets are too expensive for us to buy. They aren't cheap enough for us to buy.*
  - to express **purpose**. *We went to the travel agent's to get the tickets.*
- We use **infinitive without *to*** after **modals** (***can***, ***could***, ***should***, ***may***, ***might***, ***must***, ***will***, ***would*** etc.) **BUT**: ***have/ need to*** *She may come with us to the beach.*
- We use the ***-ing*** form:
  - after the verbs ***like***, ***love***, ***dislike***, ***fancy***, ***hate***, ***enjoy***, ***prefer***, etc. *I enjoy travelling by boat.*
  - (often with the verb ***go***) to talk about activities. *Terry goes windsurfing every year.*
  - after the verbs ***avoid***, ***admit***, ***deny***, ***finish***, ***forget*** (= not recall), ***keep***, ***mind***, ***miss***, ***remember*** (= recall), ***risk***, ***stop*** etc. *He avoids telling us where he is planning to go.*
  - after the phrases ***be busy***, ***it's no use***, ***it's (not) worth***, ***look forward to***, ***there's no point (in)***, ***can't stand*** etc. *There's no point trying to get the files back. They're lost.*

2 **Choose the correct item.**

1 Oh no! I forgot **to make/make** a reservation.
2 Tom's busy **pack/packing** his suitcase.
3 She can't stand **to camp/camping**.
4 Will he **let/to let** us go to the pool?
5 I would like **staying/to stay** in a B&B.
6 Josh wants **buy/to buy** some souvenirs.

3 **a) Put the verbs in brackets into the correct form**

A: Do you remember me **1)** .... **(tell)** you about the Icehotel in Sweden? I'd love **2)** .... **(spend)** a week there in April.

B: I want **3)** .... **(go)** too, but April is too late **4)** .... **(visit)**. The hotel melts every spring.

A: That's a shame! I was looking forward to **5)** .... **(do)** something exciting after all our hard work on the project.

B: We can still **6)** .... **(take)** a trip somewhere. We should **7)** .... **(book)** soon, though, or the flights will be too expensive.

A: We don't have to fly somewhere **8)** .... **(have)** a good time. We could book a cottage in the mountains here in Scotland and go **9)** .... **(hike)**.

B: Yes, that sounds nice. Another idea is a city break in London. I really enjoy **10)** .... **(visit)** big cities.

b) **Continue the dialogue in Ex. 3a. Use:** ***can***, ***would prefer***, ***need***, ***go***, ***dislike***, ***should***, ***decide***, ***love***, ***too***.

4 **Read the theory. Find an example in the advert.**

Relatives – Defining relative clauses

We use **relative pronouns/adverbs** to **introduce relative clauses**.

People: *That's the man **who/that** showed us the way.*

Things/Animals: *The leaflets **which/that** are on the table are about Thailand.* **Possession** (people, things & animals): *That's the woman **whose** son works at the hotel.*

Place: *This is the cottage **where** we spent our holiday.*

A **defining relative clause** gives essential information about someone or something. We cannot omit it and we do not use a comma to separate it from the main clause. *This is the hotel **which/that we've booked for you**.*

5 Make sentences, as in the example.

• carry luggage • serve meals • welcome guests
• make meals • clean rooms

1 chef
2 hotel receptionist

3 porter 4 waiter 5 chambermaid

A chef is someone who/that makes meals.

6 Listen to Barry and Sandra talking to Tom about their trip to London and match the two columns. Then, make sentences, as in the example.

1 [b] The Piccadilly Theatre
2 [ ] Trafalgar Square
3 [ ] The National Gallery
4 [ ] The Savoy Hotel
5 [ ] Wembley Stadium

a see Nelson's Column
b see *Romeo and Juliet*
c watch a football match
d admire paintings
e have afternoon tea

The Piccadilly Theatre is where they saw 'Romeo and Juliet'.

7 Make sentences, as in the example.

• open bottles • keep food & drinks cool
• cook food • light up dark places

1 camping stove 2 torch 3 cool box 4 bottle opener

A camping stove is something which/that we use to cook food.

8 Fill in: *who/that*, *which/that*, *whose* or *where*.

1 The girls .... travelled all the way to Canada with Molly were French.
2 The bags .... are in the hall are Mark's.
3 That's the guest .... sent his meal back.
4 The guidebook .... was published in 1964 belongs to Pat.
5 That's the man .... uncle owns a hotel.
6 That's the restaurant .... they serve delicious seafood.

9 Read the theory. Find examples in the advert on p. 84. Then fill in *the* or – . Give reasons.

the

• We use ***the*** with the names of: rivers *(the Amazon)*, oceans *(the Pacific Ocean)*, seas *(the Adriatic Sea)*, deserts *(the Kalahari Desert)*, hotels *(the Ritz)*, museums *(the Louvre)*, cinemas *(the Odeon)*, mountain ranges *(the Andes)*, groups of islands *(the Hebrides)*, unique objects *(the Moon, the Parthenon)*.
• We don't use ***the*** with the names of: people *(John)*, continents *(Africa)*, countries *(Brazil* **BUT:** *the UK, the USA, the Netherlands, etc.)*, cities *(Edinburgh)*, streets *(Regent Street)*, squares *(Times Square)*, parks *(Central Park)*, single mountains *(Mount Fuji)*, lakes *(Lake Victoria)*, single islands *(Capri)*, months *(January)*, days of the week *(Sunday)*.

Did you know that ...

1 .... Oxford Street in .... London, in .... UK, is .... Europe's busiest shopping street?
2 .... Canary Islands are named after the Latin word for dog?
3 there are no snakes in .... Ireland?
4 .... Mount Kilimanjaro is the world's tallest free-standing mountain?
5 .... Danube flows through ten countries?
6 .... tomatoes and potatoes originally came from .... Andes?
7 .... Ritz was the first London hotel to have bathrooms in every guest room?
8 .... Pyramids of Giza are just 18 kilometres from .... Cairo city centre?
9 the shore of .... Dead Sea is the lowest dry land on .... Earth, at 413 m below sea level?
10 .... Lake Hillier in .... Australia is naturally bright pink in colour?

10 ICT In groups, collect information about various geographical features. Prepare a quiz.

Skills in Action

Vocabulary

Hotel services & facilities

1 **Look at the symbols. Which of these hotel services/facilities would you use? Why?**

Listening

2 **Listen to Robert telling his friend Penny about his last holiday. For questions 1-4, choose the best answer A, B or C.**

1 How long did Robert stay at the hotel?
A two days **B** two weeks **C** one month

2 What did the hotel NOT have?
A a gym **B** a lift **C** a porter

3 What was the weather like most of the time?
A rainy **B** windy **C** warm

4 Which activity could Robert NOT do?
A scuba diving **B** snorkelling **C** kayaking

Everyday English

Checking in at a hotel

3 **Which room will Mr and Mrs Smith be staying in? What services/facilities does the hotel provide? Listen and read to find out.**

A: Hello. How may I help you?
B: Hi! My wife and I have a reservation for a double room under the name of Smith.
A: Let me see … Ah, yes, for two nights. Would you please fill in your name and email, and sign here?
B: Certainly …
A: And could I see your passport, please?
B: Sure ... here you are.
A: Thank you. How are you paying for your stay?
B: By credit card.
A: May I take your credit card details, please?
B: Yes, I've got it right here. Here it is.
A: Thank you. So, this is your room key – you're in Room 308. The porter will help you with your bags.
B: Thanks. Is there a Wi-Fi password?
A: Of course. Here it is. If you need anything, just dial zero.
B: Thanks. Oh, and we'd like a 7:30 wake-up call tomorrow, please.
A: Certainly. Have a pleasant stay.

4 **Use the ideas below and the language box to act out a dialogue similar to the one in Ex. 3.**

- single room • 3 nights • Room 426
- room service • 8 o'clock wake-up call

Receptionist	Hotel guest
• Please fill in your name, …. • May I take your …? • This is your room key. • You're in Room …. • I hope you enjoy your stay!	• I've made a reservation. The name's … . • Here you are. / Here it is. • Can you give me a(n) *(8:30)* wake-up call, please?

Pronunciation: rhyming words

5 **Match the words which rhyme, then listen and check. Listen again and repeat.**

sea	him	heart	well
guest	three	fun	hot
gym	pretty	yacht	start
city	west	hotel	one

Reading & Writing

Search

A hotel that ticks nearly every box

Star rating: ★★★★☆

I spent three days in July at the Green Cove Hotel in Wales and I had a really enjoyable stay. Though it's not the most luxurious hotel on the seafront, it suited me just fine.

This modern, four-storey hotel has only got 20 rooms, but there's a swimming pool, a small gym and a pretty little restaurant on the roof with tasty food. My hotel room was large, clean and very comfortable. The Wi-Fi was quite fast, too.

Green Cove's only problem? No hotel parking. I had to leave my car on the street, and that was worrying. I also had to carry my suitcase to and from the hotel because there was no porter – which was tiring.

Despite these small inconveniences, I would definitely recommend the Green Cove Hotel. For a quiet stay by the sea at a good price, you couldn't ask for more.

6 Read the review and answer the questions.

1 How long was the guest's stay at the hotel?
2 Where is the hotel located?
3 What services & facilities did the hotel offer?
4 What did the writer like about her room?
5 What did the writer dislike about the hotel?
6 What is the writer's general opinion of the hotel?

Writing Tip

Informal style

When you write an online hotel guest review, you should use informal language. That is:

- short verb forms *It's ...*
- first-person point of view *I was in Hawaii.*
- simple linking words *and*, *but*, *or*, etc.

You should avoid *extremely* informal language, however.

7 Read the hotel guest review again. Find examples of informal style.

Study Skills

Expanding vocabulary

Learn words together with their opposites. This helps you remember them.

8 Read the two extracts from hotel guest reviews. Replace the adjectives in bold with their opposites in the list.

A • enjoyable • fast • modern • quiet • tasty

My stay was really **1) terrible**! The hotel is located on a road that is very **2) noisy** night and day. The decoration of the whole place is **3) old-fashioned** and the food in the restaurant was **4) tasteless**. Also, the Wi-Fi was **5) slow**.

B • dirty • rude • uncomfortable • unpleasant • small

It was an **1) enjoyable** stay. The staff were **2) polite** to the guests and the room that I stayed in was **3) large** and **4) clean**. And on top of that, the bed was really **5) comfortable**!

Writing (a hotel review)

9 You recently stayed at the hotel in the advert below. Write a guest review of your stay for an online travel website (100-120 words). Follow the plan.

Beachside Hotel, Sandy Bay ★★★★

- **Small friendly family hotel**
- **Just 25 metres from the sea**
- **Free Wi-Fi**
- **Hotel parking**
- **Breakfast served (no lunch or dinner)**

Plan

Para 1: name, place, when and how long your stay was
Para 2: what you liked with examples/reasons
Para 3: what you didn't like with examples/reasons
Para 4: recommendation

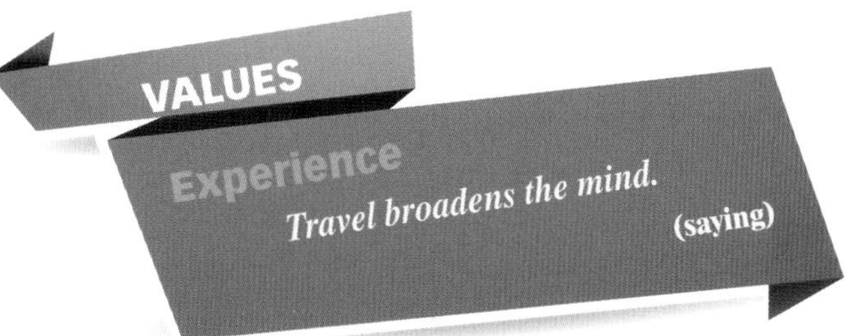
VALUES
Experience
Travel broadens the mind.
(saying)

10 Culture

DISCOVER Scotland

Scotland is full of exciting places to visit, whatever kind of holiday you choose!

A Edinburgh

VIDEO

Historic Edinburgh Castle and Holyrood Palace in Scotland's capital are perfect for those who like going sightseeing. Enjoy some shopping down the Royal Mile and there's also the Edinburgh Festival if you go there in August.

B Mallaig

If you enjoy spending time around boats, it's worth visiting the village of Mallaig. Here you can go fishing and kayaking, or simply wander around the fascinating old harbour. So peaceful!

C Mull

Planning to see Scottish wildlife? Then you couldn't do better than the Isle of Mull. From there you can take an organised tour to see eagles, otters, puffins and even whales. If whale-watching is your thing, this is the place for you!

D Fort William

Fort William, just seven miles from the UK's highest mountain Ben Nevis, is a great base for activities like skiing, snowboarding, ice-climbing and more! Don't forget to bring your skis with you – or you can hire a pair!

E Glasgow

Scotland's biggest city is waiting for you. Take a hop-on hop-off bus tour and see famous city landmarks like George Square and Glasgow Cathedral. Perfect for a weekend city break!

Check these words

capital, wander, eagle, otter, puffin

Reading & Listening

1 **Listen to and read the texts. In which of the places in Scotland (A-E) can someone:**
learn about animals? .... *enjoy a short stay?* .... *visit old buildings?* .... *do winter sports?* .... *be near water?* ....

2 **Look at the map and correct the statements (1-5). Then talk about the location of each place.**

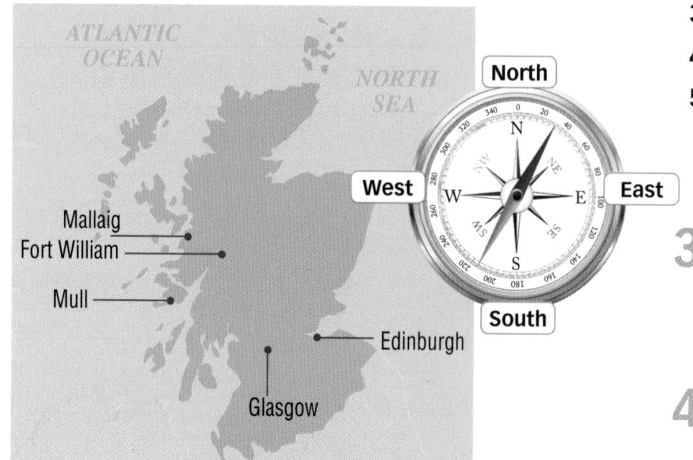

Describing the location of a place:
- ... is situated/located/etc. in the east/west/south-east/etc. of ...
- ... on the north/south/south-west/etc. coast of ...
- ... in the heart/centre of ...

1 Fort William is situated in the south-east of Scotland.
Fort William isn't situated in the south-east of Scotland. It's in the west of Scotland.
2 Mallaig is situated on the east coast of Scotland.
3 Glasgow is located in the north of Scotland.
4 Edinburgh is situated on the west coast of Scotland.
5 Mull is located in the centre of Scotland.

Speaking & Writing

3 THINK **What did you know about Scotland before you read the text? What did you learn? What else would you like to know?**

4 ICT **Collect information about different places and types of holidays in your country. Create a brochure.**

Vocabulary

1 Match the words to make collocations.

1 ☐ bright — a rain
2 ☐ crystal — b clouds
3 ☐ heavy — c temperatures
4 ☐ high — d sunshine
5 ☐ strong — e winds
6 ☐ thick — f waters

(6 x 2 = 12)

2 Fill in: *cruise*, *break*, *adventure*, *package*.

1 We're going to Paris this weekend on a city ....
2 Are all your meals included in your .... holiday?
3 Climbing in the Himalayas – now that's a(n) .... holiday!
4 The .... around the Mediterranean Sea costs £900, all included.

(4 x 2 = 8)

3 Fill in: *shuttle*, *call*, *pool*, *service*.

1 room ....
2 wake-up ....
3 airport ....
4 swimming ....

(4 x 2 = 8)

Grammar

4 Choose the correct item.

1 I would love **to go/going** to Dublin with you.
2 This restaurant is too crowded **to eat/eating** in.
3 The porter stood back **letting/to let** the guests in.
4 Paul might **to book/book** this bus tour.
5 Angie hates **to travel/travelling** by plane.
6 Let's go **swimming/to swim** tomorrow.

(6 x 2 = 12)

5 Join the sentences. Use the words in brackets.

1 This is a five-star restaurant. Its chef has won many awards. **(whose)**
2 Maggie lives in the north of Scotland. The summers are often wet there. **(where)**
3 This is the tour. It's on special offer this month. **(which)**
4 What's the name of the guest? You spoke to her just now. **(who)**
5 These are the keys. Lucy was looking for them. **(that)**.
6 This is the boy. His father works as a tour guide. **(whose)**

(6 x 4 = 24)

6 Fill in: *the* **or** — .

1 .... Atlantic Ocean
2 .... February
3 .... Cayman Islands
4 .... Hyde Park
5 .... Sphinx
6 .... Asia
7 .... Gobi Desert
8 .... Leicester Square

(8 x 2 = 16)

Everyday English

7 Match the exchanges.

1 ☐ May I see your passport?
2 ☐ I have a reservation.
3 ☐ I'd like an 8 am wake-up call.
4 ☐ How are you paying?
5 ☐ How may I help you?

A I've made a reservation.
B Certainly. Enjoy your stay!
C By credit card.
D What name, please?
E Here you are.

(5 x 4 = 20)
Total 100

Competences

GOOD ✓
VERY GOOD ✓✓
EXCELLENT ✓✓✓

Lexical Competence
Understand words/phrases related to:
- types of holidays
- weather
- hotel services & facilities

Reading Competence
- understand texts about holidays (read for specific information – T/F/DS statements; multiple matching)

Listening Competence
- listen & understand a dialogue about holidays (listen for specific information – multiple matching; multiple choice)

Speaking Competence
- compare types of holidays
- check in at a hotel
- identify locations on a map

Writing Competence
- write a weather forecast
- write a hotel guest review

Vocabulary: Festival activities, Types of entertainment
Grammar: reported speech (statements, questions); gradable/non-gradable adjectives
Everyday English: Describing an event
Writing: An email describing an event you attended

Join in the Fun!

VIDEO

Travel news Europe | Asia Thailand

Travel News > Home > Asia > Thailand

Two Festivals for the Price of One!

The city of Chiang Mai in northern Thailand is fascinating any time of year, with its 300 ancient temples and **histor** streets. The city truly comes alive in November, howeve when it's the place to go to make all your wishes come true!

I arrived in Chiang Mai last November, on the night before the fu moon. Preparations were already in full swing for not one, b two important festivals: Loy Krathong and Yi Peng. People all ov southeast Asia celebrate Loy Krathong to give **thanks** for th rain and the harvest. It's also a chance to feel sorry for the wror things they have done and make wishes for the future.

On the days before the festival, people make krathongs slices of banana tree trunk, **decorated** with leaves, flowe and a candle on top. On the night of the full moon, they lig the candle and place the krathong into the Ping River, makir a wish as they do so. If the candle stays lit until the krathor floats out of sight, their wish will **come true**.

E

Vocabulary
Festival activities

1 **Look at the pictures (A-E). Which shows:** *floating sky lanterns, a street parade, a local dish, a floating basket with a candle in it, a traditional dance performance.*

Study Skills

Predicting content

Read the title and the first sentence in each paragraph. They help you predict the content of a text.

Reading & Listening

2 **Read the title and the first sentence in each paragraph. What is the text about?**
Listen and read to find out.

3 **Look at the text. What type is it? Where could you see it?**

Antarctica	Australia/Oceania	North America	South America

Peng – the Festival of Lanterns – is only celebrated in northern ıailand. People make or buy lanterns and then, at night, they light em and **release** them into the sky to welcome a bright future. the same way as with the krathong, if the lantern stays lit, hatever the person wished for will happen.

ere are traditional music, theatre and dance performances during e festivals, a huge street parade and lots of delicious Thai food eat. I enjoyed every minute of the celebrations, which happen ter dark over three days, but my favourite moment was on the cond night, the night of the full moon. I'll never forget standing on awarat Bridge, the Ping River below me, on fire with krathongs. ousands of lanterns were floating above me and I stood, caught the moment, as tourists and **locals** sent their wishes across the ater and into the sky. Moments like these are what the traveller me lives for – to really see the world, instead of just looking at it.

Samuel Dixon

Samuel Dixon is a travel writer with Travel News. He has been all over the world – but he especially likes the sights, sounds, culture and tastes of Asia.

Check these words

come alive, full moon, in full swing, give thanks, harvest, tree trunk, out of sight, caught in the moment

4 **Read the text and for questions 1-4 choose A, B or C. Then explain the words in bold.**

1 Loy Krathong is celebrated
  - **A** in Chiang Mai only.
  - **B** in several different countries.
  - **C** on the last day of the year.

2 Krathongs are
  - **A** floating decorations. **B** small boats.
  - **C** lights to guide people to the river.

3 The lanterns and the krathongs are similar because
  - **A** they both float on water.
  - **B** they're both made of tree trunks.
  - **C** people believe they grant wishes.

4 The writer found the night of the full moon memorable because of the
  - **A** city lights. **B** event he attended.
  - **C** way the people worked together.

5 **Fill in the gaps with the verbs:** *celebrate*, *enjoy*, *come*, *make*, *light*, *give*, *float*, *feel* **in the correct form.**

1 We .... every minute of the festival last year.
2 I watched as my lantern .... out of sight.
3 We had to .... candles to see in the dark.
4 He .... lucky that he had such a special experience.
5 I hope all your wishes .... true.
6 In November, the people of Chiang Mai .... two festivals at once!
7 Every year, the villagers .... thanks for the harvest.
8 Don't blow out the candles on the birthday cake before you .... a wish.

6 **Fill in:** *parade*, *alive*, *in the moment*, *Asia*, *moon*, *temples*, *trunk*, *dark*. **Use the completed phrases to make sentences based on the text.**

1 southeast ....
2 ancient ....
3 come ....
4 full ....
5 tree ....
6 after ....
7 be caught ....
8 street ....

7 PREPOSITIONS **Choose the correct prepositions. Check in your dictionary.**

1 Come in! The party is **in/at** full swing!
2 Malta is beautiful **in/at** any time of year.
3 They're staying in a village **on/in** northern Thailand.
4 We arrived **on/in** the day before the competition.
5 We released lots of coloured balloons **into/on** the sky.
6 The festival takes place **at/over** three days.

8 THINK ICT **Is there a festival around the world you would like to go to? Why?**

Speaking & Writing

9 **Read the text in Ex. 2 again and make notes under these headings:** *Name of festival – Place – Date – Reason – Activities*. **Imagine you are a tour guide in Chiang Mai. Use your notes to present the festivals to some tourists.**

Grammar in Use

Kate: *Hi Wendy. Sorry I'm late. Has Alice arrived yet?*
Wendy: *No, she hasn't. She said that she would meet us outside the theatre at 7, right?*
Kate: *Yes, she called me an hour ago. She told me that she was just leaving her house. I wonder where she is.*
Wendy: *Well, I hope everything is OK. She said that she really wanted to see this play.*
Kate: *Oh, look! There she is! You tell her where we are, and I'm going to buy us some snacks.*

1 Read the theory. Find statements in the dialogue which are in reported speech. Which verbs have been used to introduce them?

Reported speech (statements)

Direct speech is the exact words someone said. We use quotation marks in direct speech. *Kate said, "The film is great."*
Reported speech is the exact meaning of what someone said, but not their exact words. *Kate said that the film was great.*

- We introduce a sentence in **direct speech** with: ***said, said to*** **+ object pronoun/name** or ***told*** **+ object pronoun/name.** *John **said**, "The event is great." Alice **said to me**, "We can go together." Tim **told us**, "I don't like horror films."*
- We introduce a sentence in **reported speech** with: ***said (that), said to*** **+ object pronoun/name *(that)*** or ***told*** **+ object pronoun/name *(that)*** *John **said (that)** the event was great. Alice **said to me (that)** we could go together. Tim **told us (that)** he didn't like horror films.*

2 Fill in *said* or *told*.

1 "I've never been to a food festival," Sam .... to them.
2 Kate .... her parents that she enjoyed the concert.
3 "I didn't see the parade," Alan .... us.
4 The children .... they wanted some popcorn.
5 Rachael .... me that she wouldn't attend the festival.
6 Peter .... to his friend, "I'll meet you outside the cinema."

3 Study the examples, then answer the questions.

Direct Speech

*"I want to help," she **says**.* *"I want to help," she **said**.*

Reported Speech

*She **says** (that) she **wants** to help.* *She **said** (that) she **wanted** to help.*

1 What tense is the verb in bold in the direct speech sentences?
2 Which is the reporting verb? What tense is it in?
3 Are the tenses in reported speech the same as in direct speech?
4 How has the pronoun 'I' changed in reported speech?
5 Why is 'that' in brackets?

Changing from direct to reported speech

Present simple → Past simple *"I'**m** thrilled," he said. → He said (that) he **was** thrilled.*

Present continuous → Past continuous *"John **is decorating** the house," he said → He said (that) John **was decorating** the house.*

Present perfect → Past perfect *"Ann **has gone** to India," Paul said. → Paul said (that) Ann **had gone** to India.*

Past simple → Past simple or past perfect *"I tried some exotic food at the festival," Dad said. Dad said (that) he **tried/had tried** some exotic food at the festival.*

am/is/are going to* → *was/were going to *He said, "I'**m going to** leave." → He said (that) he **was going to** leave.*

will* → *would *"I'**ll buy** her a present," he said. → He said (that) he **would buy** her a present.*

can* → *could *"We **can** buy tickets at the door," he said. → He said (that) we **could** buy tickets at the door.*

Note:
- The past perfect remains the same in reported speech. *"I **hadn't been** to a food festival before," he said. He said (that) he **hadn't been** to a food festival before.*
- Tenses do not change in reported speech if the **verb that introduces the speech** is in the **present simple**. *"I **don't have** the address," Tony says. Tony says (that) he **doesn't have** the address.*
- When we report **general truths the verb tense** is the same as in **direct speech**. *"Green-cheeked parrots **live** in Mexico," He said that green-cheeked parrots **live** in Mexico.* (general truth)

4 Complete the gaps with the verbs in the correct form.

1 "Lots of people are wearing costumes," he said to us. He told us that lots of people .... costumes.

2 "We can go to the museum," they said. They said that they .... go to the museum.

3 "I'll meet you at the opera house," Ann said to me. Ann told me that she .... me at the opera house.

4 Alex said, "Everyone has left." Alex said that everybody ....

5 "Hedgehogs sleep during the winter," she said. She said that hedgehogs .... during the winter.

Personal pronouns & Possessive adjectives – Time expressions in reported speech

Personal subject pronouns: *I → he/she; we → they*
Personal object pronouns: *me → him/her; us → them*
Possessive adjectives: *my → his/her; our → their*
You/Your changes according to the person it refers to in the direct speech.
Direct speech: *Ann said to Jane, "**You** look great in **my** dress."*
Reported speech: *Ann told Jane (that) **she** looked great in **her** dress.*
Time expressions change as follows: *now → then; this morning/evening, etc. → that morning/evening, etc.; today/tonight → that day/that night; yesterday → the day before/the previous day; tomorrow → the next/following day; next week/month, etc. → the following week/month, etc.*
Other words/expressions: *this/these → that/those; here → there*
Direct speech: *"She'll be **here tomorrow**," John said.*
Reported speech: *John said that she would be **there the following day**.*

5 Read the theory. Then, complete the gaps in the second sentence with the missing words/phrases.

1 They said, "We are in New York today." They said that .... were in New York ....

2 Kate said to us, "I will go camping next weekend." Kate told us that .... would go camping .... weekend.

3 Ben said, "I'm searching for information about this festival now." Ben said that .... was searching for information about .... festival ....

6 Rewrite the sentences in reported speech, as in the example.

1 Mandy said, "My cousin is marching in the parade this evening." *Mandy said that her cousin was marching in the parade that evening.*

2 They said, "We'll meet you here tomorrow." ....

3 She said, "We haven't heard this band before." ....

4 James said to me, "I went there yesterday." ....

5 We said to Mary, "We hadn't expected to see you here." ....

Reported questions

- In reported questions, the word order is the same as in statements. We do not use a question mark in reported speech. We use a full stop instead. Verb tenses, pronouns, possessive adjectives and time expressions change as in statements.
- ***Wh*-questions:** In reported speech the word order is: subject pronoun/name + ***asked/wanted to know*** (+ object pronoun/name) + question word + question in statement order
  Direct speech: *"Where do you live?" he asked me.*
  Reported speech: *He **asked me where I lived**.*
- ***Yes/No* questions:** In reported speech the word order is: subject pronoun/name + ***asked/wanted to know*** (+ object pronoun/name) + ***if/whether*** + question in statement order
  Direct speech: *"Do you like food festivals?" she asked me.*
  Reported speech: *She **asked if/whether I liked** food festivals.*

7 Read the theory. How do we report *wh*-questions? *Yes/No* questions?

8 Max is planning to attend a book fair. Read his questions to Andy. Then, rewrite the questions in reported speech in your notebook as in the example.

1 Where does the book fair take place?
Max asked where the book fair took place.

2 Which bus do we need to take to get there?

3 When does the event start?

4 Will there be any famous authors there?

5 Have you ever been to a book fair before?

6 Do you want to eat out afterwards?

7 What kind of restaurant do you like?

Skills in Action

Vocabulary

Types of entertainment

1 Match the pictures (A-F) to the comments (1-6).

A ice show

B opera

C fashion show

D escape room

E concert

F circus

1 ☐ Some of the designer's new dresses were stunning.
2 ☐ We managed to solve the final puzzle and open the door with only seconds left.
3 ☐ The clowns were hilarious and the acrobats were amazing.
4 ☐ Even though I couldn't follow the story, I admired the lead singers' voices.
5 ☐ It was awesome to listen to my favourite band perform live.
6 ☐ I loved watching the skaters glide across the rink.

2 Imagine you went to one of the events in Ex. 1 yesterday evening. Discuss with your partner, using the adjectives in the list.

• fun • enjoyable • interesting • fascinating
• boring • terrible • awful • disappointing

Listening

3 Listen to an advert and fill in the missing information.

Name of venue: The **0)** Blue Arena
Name of performance: 1) .... on Ice
Dancers from: 2) ....
Admission: adults: £15; children and disabled: £ **3)** ....
Dates: from 5th to **4)** .... March
Location of venue: 5) .... Street

Everyday English

Describing an event

4 Ann went to the theatre yesterday. Read the dialogue and fill in the missing words. Listen and check.

Jenny: Did you have a good **1)** .... at the play yesterday?
Ann: Yes, I really enjoyed it.
Jenny: **2)** .... theatre was it at?
Ann: It was at the Ladle Theatre. It's in Kent Road in the city centre.
Jenny: Oh, I know that one. How **3)** .... were the tickets?
Ann: Just £20 for adults and children were free.
Jenny: I see. And what was the play **4)** ....?
Ann: It was a science-fiction play about the world in 100 years. You'd like it.
Jenny: Hmm, maybe I'll go and see **5)** .... too, then.
Ann: I think performances are about to end so book your **6)** .... soon.
Jenny: OK, I'll try to go tomorrow!

5 Imagine you visited the ice show in Ex. 3. Use phrases from the Useful Language box to describe it to your partner. You can use the dialogue in Ex. 4 as a model.

Asking about an event
• Did you have a(n) good/enjoyable time at ...? • Did you enjoy yourself at ...? • Which gallery/theatre/arena, etc. was it at? • Where was it held? • How much was/were the tickets/admission? • What was the play/film/show, etc. about?
Describing an event
• It was a(n) interesting/boring play/show, etc. • I (really) enjoyed/loved it. • It was (held) at ... • It took place at ... • Tickets were (just) ... • It cost ... • It was about ...

Pronunciation: stressed syllables

6 Listen and underline the stressed syllable, as in the example. Listen again and repeat.

<u>pho</u>-to-graph → pho-<u>to</u>-gra-pher
mu-sic → mu-si-cian
pre-pare → prep-a-ra-tion
his-to-ry → his-to-ri-an
cel-e-brate → cel-e-bra-tion

Reading & Writing

7 Read the email. What tenses does the writer mostly use? Why?

REPLY MAIL

Hi Kate,

Hope you're well! Sorry I haven't written for so long. I'm having a great time here in Hanoi in Vietnam. We've visited some really amazing sights but the highlight was a performance we saw yesterday evening.

It was in the Thang Long Water Puppet Theatre in the city centre. It's a unique theatre because the stage is covered in waist-deep water! Wooden puppets are controlled by puppeteers who hide behind a bamboo screen. The strings are under the water, so it looks like the puppets are moving on their own! The whole thing was absolutely magical!

We were all very glad we went. If you're ever in Vietnam, you should check it out, too! Write back when you get the chance.

Lots of love,

Laura

8 a) Read the sentences below. Which are: opening *(O)*, closing *(C)* remarks?

1 Looking forward to seeing you soon. ....
2 Drop me a line when you can. ....
3 What's up? I've just read your email. ....
4 Thanks for your email – it was great to hear from you. ....
5 Keep me posted about what's going on. ....
6 Glad to hear everything is OK. ....

b) Underline the opening and closing remarks in the model email in Ex. 7 and replace them with appropriate ones from those in Ex. 8a.

9 a) Read the theory. Find examples in the email in Ex. 7.

Gradable/Non-gradable adjectives

Using adverbs with gradable/non-gradable adjectives
Gradable adjectives are adjectives which can have comparative and superlative degrees. We can use *a bit*, *extremely*, *quite*, *really*, *very* with these adjectives in their base form. e.g. *very expensive tickets*
Non-gradable adjectives do not have different degrees. We can use *absolutely*, *completely*, *really* with these adjectives. e.g. *an absolutely amazing experience*

b) Read the text and choose the correct adverbs.

The weather was **1) absolutely/very** terrible in Kraków, Poland that morning, but that didn't stop thousands of people coming out to see the Lajkonik parade. The band played traditional music and there was a **2) quite/really** fantastic atmosphere as Lajkonik moved his hobby horse through the streets towards the city's main square. On his way, he collected a 'ransom' in the form of food from local shopkeepers and stopped to perform dances for the public! It was **3) a bit/absolutely** strange to see a man on a hobby horse, but it was **4) completely/really** exciting, too!

Writing (an email describing an event you attended)

10 Read the task and make notes under the headings in your notebook.

This is part of an email from your English-speaking friend.

> *I remember you planned to go to a concert at the weekend. Did you enjoy yourself there? Where and when was it? Who was performing? Drop me a line when you can.*

Reply to your friend's email answering his/her questions (100-120 words).

WHERE – WHEN – WHO PERFORMED – DESCRIPTION – FEELINGS – RECOMMENDATION

11 Use your notes in Ex. 10 to write an email to your friend (100-120 words). Follow the plan.

Plan

Hi + *(your friend's first name),*
Para 1: opening remarks; reason for writing
Para 2: description of the event
Para 3: feelings; recommendation; closing remarks
All the best,
(your first name)

VALUES
Entertainment
"All the world's a stage. And all the men and women merely players."
William Shakespeare

11 Culture

VIDEO

Tjungu Festival

Do you fancy visiting a **famous** Australian landmark while learning about one of the **oldest** cultures on our planet? Then come to the Tjungu Festival! This annual festival **began** in 2014 and takes place in late April in the Ayers Rock Resort. Ayers Rock (or 'Uluru') is a huge sandstone rock that is sacred to the country's original inhabitants – the Aboriginal people – so it's the perfect place to experience their culture!

There is a lot for visitors to see and do during the festival. On the **opening** day, you can watch a group of local Aborigines perform the Inma dance. This is a traditional dance which welcomes visitors to the event. Dancing continues throughout the festival while you can also enjoy traditional Aboriginal music with instruments such as the didgeridoo. Another highlight is the Tastes of Tjungu section. Here you can sample traditional Aboriginal bushfood which **includes** various fruits, nuts and even insects! And don't **leave** without picking up some souvenirs from the art and crafts stalls. You can buy beautifully decorated boomerangs and other arts and crafts for **reasonable** prices.

All in all, there's a reason why 'tjungu' means 'coming together' in the local Aboriginal language. This festival is a gathering of Aboriginal people from across Australia, but it is also a way for people of all backgrounds to come **together** to celebrate Aboriginal traditions.

Check these words

sandstone rock, original, inhabitant, sample, bushfood, gathering

Listening & Reading

1 How are these words related to the Tjungu Festival?

- Ayers Rock Resort • Aboriginal people
- Inma dance • didgeridoo • Aboriginal bushfood
- boomerangs

Listen to and read the text to find out.

2 Read again and answer the questions.

1 When was the first Tjungu Festival?
2 What is the purpose of the Inma dance?
3 What can visitors do at the Tastes of Tjungu section?
4 What does 'tjungu' mean in an Aboriginal language?

3 Match the words in bold to their opposites.

- come • finished • earliest • last • separate
- unknown • excludes • high

Speaking & Writing

4 THINK **Is there an annual festival in your country? Why should people go to it?**

5 ICT **Collect information about an annual cultural festival in your country. Make notes under the headings:** *Name – Place – Date – Reason – Activities*. **Write a short text about it for a website's culture column.**

Vocabulary

1 Fill in: *floating*, *street*, *full*, *musical*, *local*.

When we arrived, there was a **1)** .... moon in the sky, and the celebrations were beginning. First, a **2)** .... parade passed through the city, and then people pushed **3)** .... baskets out onto the river. We also got the chance to try the **4)** .... cuisine and we listened to a band playing traditional **5)** .... instruments.

(5 x 2 = 10)

2 Choose the correct preposition.

1 We took a trip to a city **in/on** the north.
2 We need to prepare **to/for** the event tomorrow.
3 At the festival they release lanterns **into/from** the sky.
4 The market was filled **with/of** people.
5 The party was **on/in** full swing.

(5 x 2 = 10)

3 Fill in: *play*, *circus*, *escape*, *concert*, *opera*.

1 The .... room included many difficult puzzles.
2 Brian's favourite band is playing in a(n) ....
3 We have tickets for a(n) .... at the Bravo Theatre.
4 The acrobats in the .... were amazing.
5 I couldn't understand the singers in the ....

(5 x 2 = 10)

Grammar

4 Fill in *said* **or** *told*.

1 "I enjoyed the performance," Kate .... to them.
2 They .... us they were going to a concert.
3 Kate ....,"I'm not a big fan of art exhibitions."
4 James .... her that he had met the actor.
5 "We won't attend the festival," Alan .... to me.

(5 x 3 = 15)

5 Rewrite the sentences in reported speech.

1 "The play was excellent," Tim said.
....
2 "I will see you at the concert," she said to me.
....
3 "We can book tickets online," he said.
....
4 "I have turned off my smartphone," she said.
....
5 "We are listening to music now," they said.
....

(5 x 4 = 20)

6 Rewrite the questions in reported speech.

1 "Is Frank coming to the cinema?" he asked.
2 "When does the exhibition start?" John asked.
3 "Did they attend the ballet performance?" Mary asked.
4 "Have you ever seen an opera performance?" Steve asked them.

(4 x 5 = 20)

Everyday English

7 Match the exchanges.

1 ☐ Did you enjoy yourself at the art gallery?
2 ☐ Where was it?
3 ☐ How much was admission?
4 ☐ When does it end?
5 ☐ What is it about?

A At the Fine Art Gallery.
B Yes, it was an interesting exhibition.
C It cost £5 for adults.
D It features paintings of the artist's hometown.
E The last day is 15th March.

(5 x 3 = 15)

Total 100

Competences

GOOD ✓
VERY GOOD ✓✓
EXCELLENT ✓✓✓

Lexical Competence

Understand words/ phrases related to:

- festival activities
- types of entertainment
- adjectives describing entertainment

Reading Competence

- understand texts related to festivals & cultural events (read for specific information – multiple choice; answer questions)

Listening Competence

- listen to and understand adverts related to entertainment (listen for specific information – note taking)

Speaking Competence

- describe an event

Writing Competence

- write an email describing an event I attended
- write a text about an annual cultural festival in my country

Vocabulary: Computer parts, Using a smartphone
Grammar: reported orders/instructions/ commands, question tags, exclamations
Everyday English: Giving instructions
Writing: A for-and-against essay

Going online!

Vocabulary
Computer parts

1 **Label the pictures. Use:** *screen, tower, mouse, scanner, speakers, webcam, USB cable, printer, keyboard, flash drive, router, headset, hard drive.*

1 ....
2 ....
3 ....
4 ....
5 ....
6 ....
7 ....
8 ....
9 ....
10 ....
11 ....
12 ....
13 ....

2 **Match the computer parts (1-13) to their uses (a-m).**

a ☐ to protect the working parts of the computer
b ☐ to listen to music/sound
c ☐ to see each other in a video chat
d ☐ to connect to the Internet
e ☐ to move around the screen and click on things
f ☐ to scan documents/photos
g ☐ to see documents/watch videos
h ☐ to type with
i ☐ to talk and listen at the same time (e.g. webchat)
j ☐ to connect other devices to your computer
k ☐ to print a document/photo
l ☐ to store and save lots of information
m ☐ to store and move small amounts of information

Better Safe than Sorry!

1 e Why safety is a problem

The Internet is a very valuable tool, isn't it? But did you know it can also be dangerous? Hackers can access personal information like users' names, addresses and bank card details and use them to steal money. It's such a big problem that we need to protect ourselves. Here are five simple ways to do that.

2 ....

Don't use a simple password – use a **complex** one. Passwords should be long and include capital letters and special characters. Hackers can guess if you use something easy like '1234'. Also, don't use details someone might know already, like your date of birth or the name of your pet.

3 ....

If you see a link or an attachment that is not **familiar** to you, do NOT **click** on it! It might be a way for hackers to upload viruses to your computer. Beware of unknown emails too. They may claim to be from a well-known company or organisation and be well-written, but in fact they can be just another hacker's **trick**. They should be deleted immediately.

4 ....

Some people like buying things online but the thing to watch for here is the pop-up adverts. If you click on one when making a **purchase**, you could be **exposed** to viruses like ransomware. This is a special code that gets into your computer when you click on the advert and it locks all your data.

Listening & Reading

3 **Read the text about Internet safety and match the headings (a-f) to the numbered spaces (1-6), as in the example.**

a Watch out for fake websites
b Protect your computer
c Make things difficult for hackers
d Avoid strange messages
e Why safety is a problem
f Be careful when shopping

VIDEO

5 ....

Hackers can create a webpage that looks similar to the ones you use regularly. If it's a bank account, for instance, they can set up a page that looks the same as your banking page. Then, when you enter your name and password, the hacker **records** them to steal your money!

6 ....

Install an anti-virus program to protect your computer. The software can **detect** and delete viruses already on your computer and stop your computer from downloading others.

hacker, access, link, attachment, upload, virus, pop-up advert, anti-virus program, download

4 a) **Listen to or read the text. Then, complete the sentences.**

1 Hackers try to steal personal information such as users' ....

2 Passwords should not include details ....

3 Hackers sometimes send emails that appear to be from ....

4 Hackers can make a website look ....

5 If you want to avoid computer viruses, you should install ....

b) Explain the words in bold.

5 Fill in the words from the list. Then make sentences using the completed phrases.

• create • user's • access • enter • install • valuable • pop-up • bank

1 a .... tool
2 to .... personal information
3 .... name
4 to .... a webpage
5 a .... advert
6 to .... your password
7 .... account
8 to .... a program

Study Skills

Learning prepositions

Learn verbs, nouns, adjectives together with the preposition each goes with. This helps you remember them.

6 PREPOSITIONS Choose the correct prepositions, then make sentences using the completed phrases based on the text.

1 date **at/of** birth
2 familiar **to/of** sb
3 click **on/in** sth
4 upload **to/on** your computer
5 similar **with/to** sth else
6 a virus **at/on** your computer
7 stop your computer **in/from** doing sth

Speaking

7 Which of the pieces of advice in the text do you follow when you use the Internet? Discuss with your partner.

8 THINK Imagine a week in your life without Internet. What would it be like?

Writing

9 ICT Collect information about how to stay safe when using your social media accounts. Write a short information leaflet.

Grammar in Use

Commonroom Chat

12:24:30 **Christy:** *My laptop keeps crashing. It's so annoying!* ☹

12:24:45 **Josh:** *It's brand new, isn't it? I wonder why you have so many problems.*

12:25:30 **Christy:** *I don't know! I called the shop I got it from, but the guy just told me not to keep too much on the hard drive.*

12:25:45 **Josh:** *What nonsense! You haven't put many programs on there, have you?*

12:26:30 **Christy:** *No, hardly anything. I asked him to be there when I bring it to the shop tomorrow at nine. If he can't fix it, I want a new one! I'm not wrong, am I?*

12:26:45 **Josh:** *Of course not. You've just bought it, so it should work perfectly.*

Christy: *I know! Anyway, I'm going AFK for a bit. TTYL!!!!*

1 **Read the theory. Find examples in the chat. What were the actual words?**

Reported orders, instructions, commands

To report orders, instructions & commands we use: ***asked/told*** + object pronoun/name ***(+ not)*** + ***to*-infinitive**

Direct Speech: *"**Check** the manual, please," said Liam to me.*

Reported Speech: *Liam **asked me to check** the manual.*

Direct Speech: *"**Don't touch the wire, please,**" said Andy to me.*

Reported Speech: *Andy **told me not to touch** the wire.*

2 **Last Monday, Jeff had his first lesson on computer security. His instructor, Mr Smith, gave his class some basic tips. Rewrite the tips into reported speech.**

1 Don't click on any unknown links.

2 Use strong passwords.

3 Don't open strange email attachments.

4 Change your password regularly.

5 Don't give out personal information online.

6 Keep your antivirus software up to date.

1 ....

2 ....

3 ....

4 ....

5 ....

6 ....

3 **Phil cannot go to work this week, so he has sent Janet these instructions.**

Hi Janet,

I can't come to work this week – something's come up. Please:

Forward all the CVs for the computer technician position to Ms Connors.

Don't make the payment to Crown Computer Supplies yet.

Call Gordon Robinson to move my meeting with him to next Friday.

Don't book tickets for Madrid – call Ms Connors instead.

Thanks a million.

Phil

Now he is sending an email to his manager, Ms Connors, to explain what he has done. Complete his email to her.

http:// www.mymail.com

From: Phil_Crawley@noror.co.uk
To: KimConnors@noror.co.uk
Cc: JanetMcQueen@noror.co.uk
Subject: unavoidable absence

Dear Ms Connors,

Just a quick email to say that I am unable to come in this week. I have given my assistant, Janet McQueen, instructions on what to do in my absence.

Firstly, I told her **1)** .... Next, I asked her **2)** ....

I also asked her **3)** ....

Lastly, I told her **4)** .... I told her **5)** .... instead.

Please feel free to email me or text me. Once again, I apologise for my absence. I hope I will be back as soon as possible.

Phil

4 **Read the email. Turn the reported instructions into direct speech.**

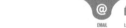

Dear Frank,

Just a quick note to check that I gave Tom Billings the correct instructions about the new offices.

I told him to make sure there are phone lines in each office. I asked him to order new desktop computers for all the offices. I also told him to finish the decorating by next week.

Hope I didn't forget anything.

Karen Briggs

5 **Read the theory. Find examples in the chat on p. 100.**

Question tags

- Question tags are short questions at the **end** of statements. They are formed with the auxiliary verb from the main sentence and the appropriate subject **pronoun**. *This laptop **is** too expensive, **isn't it**?* When there is no auxiliary verb in the main sentence, we use *do(n't)* or *does(n't)* in the question tag for the present simple, and *did(n't)* for the past simple. *He **bought** a camera yesterday, **didn't he**?*
- A positive statement takes a **negative** question tag. *I **can** delete the files, **can't I**?* A negative statement takes a **positive** question tag. *You **haven't sent** the email, **have you**?*
- When we are sure of the answer, our voice goes down in the question tag (↘). When we are not sure of the answer, our voice goes up in the question tag (↗).

Note: ***You have got*** (= possess) → ***haven't you***? *You**'ve got** a laptop, **haven't you**?*
You have (= other meaning) → ***don't you***? *You **have** dinner at about 8 pm, **don't you**?*

6 **Fill in the correct question tag.**

1 You've used the Internet before, ... ?
2 I can't use email without an email address, ... ?
3 My mouse isn't working, ... ?
4 He doesn't like this CD, ... ?
5 AFK means 'away from keyboard', ... ?
6 Strong passwords are hard to crack, ... ?
7 The keyboard was broken, ... ?
8 You won't use the computer, ... ?

7 a) **Fill in the missing question tags.**

	↘	↗
1 You're from France, *aren't you*?	✓	☐
2 You will be here tomorrow, ...?	☐	☐
3 I've made a mistake, ...?	☐	☐
4 You don't know my name, ...?	☐	☐
5 He has got a smartphone, ...?	☐	☐
6 This information isn't right, ...?	☐	☐

b) **Listen and tick (✓) each sentence ↘ (sure) or ↗ (not sure). Listen again and repeat.**

8 **Ask and answer questions, as in the example.**

A: You can .... , can't you?
B: Yes/No, ...
A: You've got .... , haven't you?
B: Yes/No, ... etc.

9 **Read the theory. Find examples in the chat on p. 100.**

Exclamations

Exclamations are words or sentences used to express admiration, surprise, etc. To form exclamatory sentences, we can use ***how***, ***what (a/an)***, ***so*** or ***such (a/an)***.

- ***how*** + adjective/adverb *How clever he is! How fast he types!*
- ***what a/an*** (+ adjective) + singular countable noun *What an expensive laptop!*
- ***what*** (+ adjective) + plural/uncountable noun *What fantastic speakers!*
- ***so*** + adjective/adverb *I'm so sorry! He speaks so fast!*
- ***such a/an*** (+adjective) + singular countable noun *It is such a fast connection!*
- ***such*** (+ adjective) + plural/uncountable noun *She makes such nice paintings! They gave us such useful advice!*

Note: *so + much/many, such + a lot of*

10 **Fill in *what*, *such*, *how* or *so*.**

1 A: Guess what my parents bought me – a new tablet!
B: Really? .... a nice present!
A: Yes – and I already use it more than my laptop.
B: .... exciting!

2 A: I dropped my new smartphone and the screen's cracked.
B: Oh, no. .... a pity!
A: I saved up for it for .... a long time.
B: I feel .... sorry for you!

11 SPEAKING **Respond to each statement. Use: *how*, *what*, *so* or *such*.**

1 I'm afraid I can't go online.
2 Guess what — I got a new laptop!
3 There's no Internet connection.
4 My computer broke down last week.
5 I lost all my files.

Skills in Action

Vocabulary

Using a smartphone

1 a) **Look at the icons. Which of these would someone tap to ...**

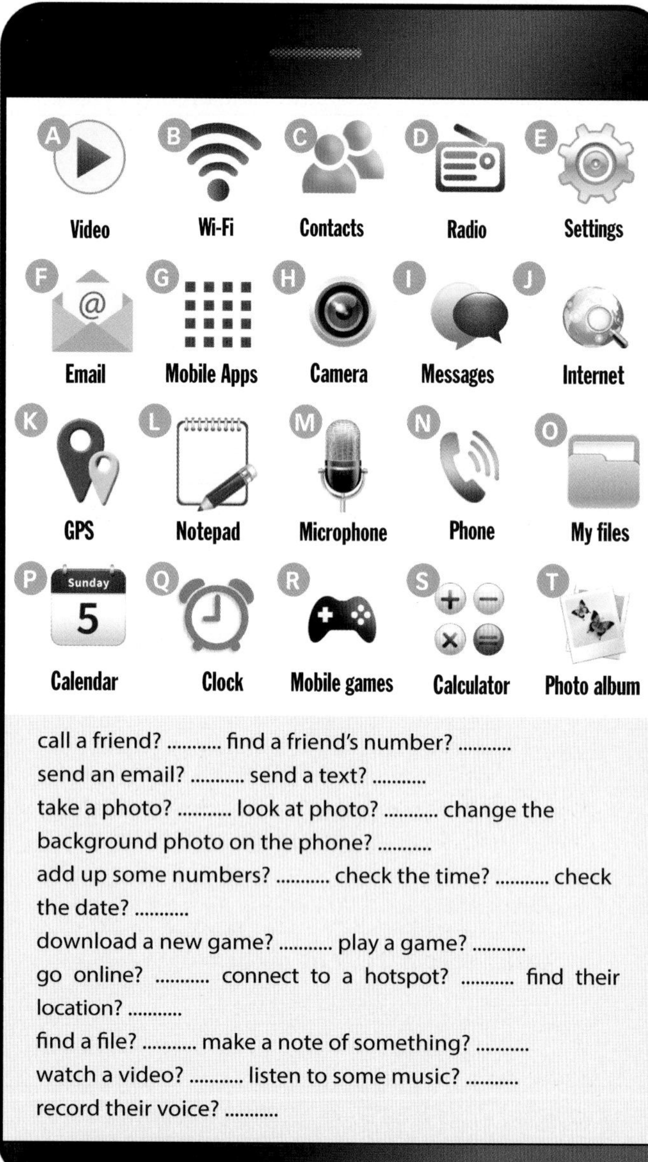

call a friend? .... find a friend's number? ....
send an email? .... send a text? ....
take a photo? .... look at photo? .... change the background photo on the phone? ....
add up some numbers? .... check the time? .... check the date? ....
download a new game? .... play a game? ....
go online? .... connect to a hotspot? .... find their location? ....
find a file? .... make a note of something? ....
watch a video? .... listen to some music? ....
record their voice? ....

b) **Which of these do you use every day? What for?**

I use the radio to listen to music while I walk to school.

Listening

2 **Listen to a dialogue and match the people to their favourite gadgets. Two are extra.**

Speaker 1 ☐
Speaker 2 ☐
Speaker 3 ☐
Speaker 4 ☐

a desktop computer
b laptop
c tablet
d smartphone
e smart watch
f flash drive

Everyday English

Giving instructions

3 **Listen to and read the dialogue and put the images in the correct order.**

A 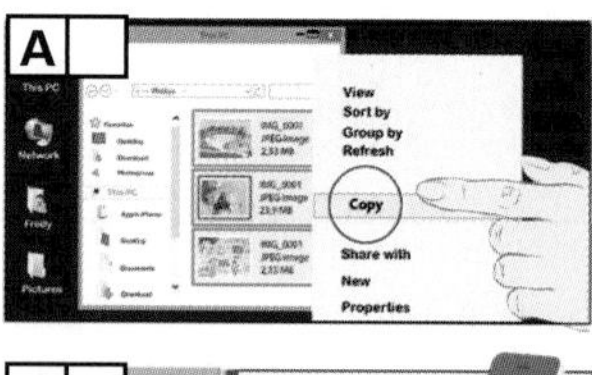

B 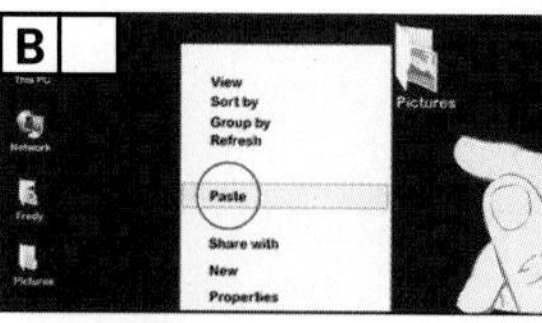

C 

D 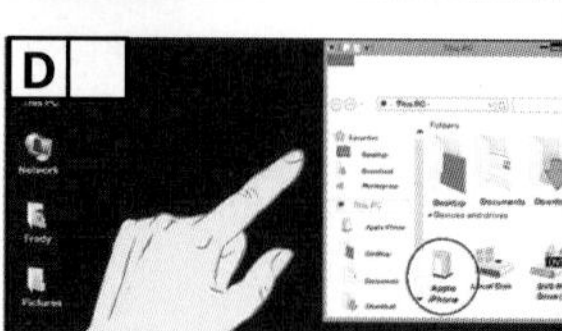

Anna: Hey, Uncle Phil. What's the matter?
Phil: I've got this new smartphone and I've been taking all kinds of photos, but I don't know how to transfer them onto my PC.
Anna: Let me show you. First, you connect the phone to the PC using a USB cable.
Phil: OK. What's next?
Anna: Next, look at the window that just popped up and click on the icon for your phone. Then open the photos folder.
Phil: Right. Now what?
Anna: Select the pictures you want and right click. This gives you a number of options. One of them is 'copy'. Click on that one.
Phil: But where do I put them?
Anna: Create a folder on your desktop. Then you right click on the folder and click on 'paste' and your photos are on your computer.
Phil: Really? That's so easy! And do I just disconnect the USB cable now?
Anna: Well, close the window first. Then click on 'Safely remove hardware' down here. Once the computer says it's OK, pull it out.

4 **Use the ideas from the dialogue to explain to your partner how to upload songs from a smartphone to a computer.**

Intonation in exclamations

5 **Fill in:** *what, what a, how.*
Listen and check, then repeat.

1 .... interesting!
2 .... nonsense!
3 .... great smartphone!
4 .... little he knows!

Reading & Writing

6 Read John's essay and fill in the gaps with: *Firstly, This is because, For example, However, In conclusion, What is more, On the other, As a result.*

Stephen Hawking once said, "We are all now connected by the Internet, like neurons in a giant brain." The Internet has changed the way we think, communicate and entertain ourselves. **1)** ...., it is not all perfect.

Using the Internet offers a lot of advantages. **2)** ...., you can get information easily. For example, you can read newspapers from all over the world for free, watch videos or learn about things you want in detail. **3)** ...., you can join a social networking site. **4)** ...., you can make new friends and stay in touch with old ones.

5) .... hand, the Internet has some disadvantages. To start with, it can become addictive. **6)** ...., social media and online games make people spend more time in their virtual life than in their real one. Also, online 'friends' can be dangerous. **7)** .... they can pretend to be someone else and steal your personal information.

8) ...., the Internet obviously has positives and negatives. I think it is important to use it wisely, because it is here to stay.

7 Copy and complete the table with ideas from the text in your notebook.

Advantages	Justifications
Disadvantages	**Justifications**

Writing Tip

Topic sentences
Topic sentences introduce the main idea of the paragraph. They are followed by supporting sentences that further expand the main idea. Topic sentences help the reader follow your essay.

8 Find the topic sentences in the essay in Ex. 6.

Writing (a for-and-against essay)

9 Read the task. Then read the sentences (1-4) and decide which are *A* **(advantages) and which are** *D* **(disadvantages).**

Listen and check your answers.

Your lecturer has asked you to write an essay discussing the advantages and disadvantages of online shopping. Write your essay (100-140 words).

1 Delivery of goods can take time. ....
2 It is a very convenient way to shop. ....
3 Shopping on the Internet is often cheaper than in shops. ....
4 Shoppers can't try on what they buy. ....

10 Read the sentences. Which: *introduces points for? states the topic? sums up the topic? introduces points against?*

1 On the other hand, some people are against Internet shopping.
2 Online shopping is part of our lives.
3 A lot of people are in favour of online shopping.
4 All in all, online shopping offers both advantages and disadvantages.

11 Use the ideas in Exs 9 and 10 to write your essay. Follow the plan.

Plan

Introduction
Para 1: state the topic & main viewpoints
Main Body
Para 2: points for & justifications
Para 3: points against & justifications
Conclusion
Para 4: sum up points & your opinion

VALUES
Knowledge
Technology is a useful servant but a dangerous master.
Christian Lous Lange

12 Culture

What Technology...

Secure

What technology museums are there in the San Francisco area?

Sign in 40

All Videos Images News More Settings Tools

About 2,572,000 results (0.72 seconds)

A • The Exploratorium

www.exploratorium.edu

Located in San Francisco itself with great views over the Bay, the Exploratorium is a favourite for both San Franciscans and visitors. **Explore** science in a fun interactive way. Some exhibits outside the museum are free. Open Tuesday-Sunday 10-5, or visit after dark on Thursdays (6-10pm, over 18s only).

B • Computer History Museum

www.computerhistory.org

Located in Silicon Valley at the south end of San Francisco Bay, the museum takes visitors through the history of computing, from the **earliest** computers to the latest silicon chip. Fly through a virtual world and try your hand at programming! Open Wednesday-Sunday 10-5 (plus Tuesdays in the summer – see website for details).

C • Chabot Space & Science Centre

www. chabotspace.org

Up in the hills to the east of the Bay, in the magnificent Redwood Regional Park, the Chabot Space & Science Centre **allows** visitors to find out about space. Admission includes two shows at the planetarium. Open Wednesday-Sunday 10-5. Friday and Saturday nights offer visitors the **chance** to see the stars through our telescopes (if the skies are clear).

D • Lawrence Hall of Science

www.lawrencehallofscience.org

The Lawrence Hall of Science is located on the campus of the University of California (Berkeley) on the north-east side of San Francisco Bay. Exhibits are always changing to show what Berkeley scientists are working on right now. With planetarium shows, 3-D films and the Ingenuity Lab (where kids can make stuff) this place is **perfect** for families and school groups. Open weekends and holidays 12-4.

Check these words

virtual world, hill, admission, ingenuity, stuff

Listening & Reading

1 **Look at the text. Where could you see it? What is it about?**

2 **Read the text. Which place (A, B, C or D) ...**

1 is visited by locals?
2 is in a park?
3 is open six days a week for part of the year?
4 has an attraction that depends on good weather?
5 has a special night for adults?
6 cannot usually be visited during the week?

Then, explain the highlighted words.

Speaking & Writing

3  **Listen to and read the webpage. Which of the places in Ex. 1 would you like to visit if you were in the San Francisco area? Why? Discuss with your partner.**

4 **ICT Collect information about a museum of technology in your country. Write a search engine entry for it, modelled on the ones in the text.**

Vocabulary

1 Choose the correct word.

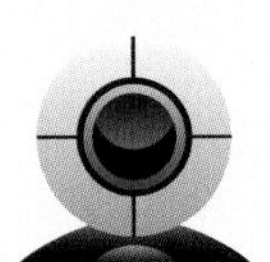

1 webcam/mouse
2 router/tower
3 hard drive/printer

4 headset/speaker
5 screen/keyboard

(5 x 3 = 15)

2 Fill in: *go, click, connect, detect, send, record, delete, download* **in the correct form.**

1 Could you please .... John a text and ask him to call me.
2 The game I .... yesterday is amazing.
3 How often do you .... online?
4 Where can I .... to a Wi-Fi hotspot nearby?
5 .... on the link to go to the webpage.
6 An anti-virus program can .... viruses on your computer.
7 You should .... any unknown emails.
8 How do I .... a voice message?

(8 x 2 = 16)

Grammar

3 Choose the correct item.

1 Programming is **so/such** easy these days.
2 **What/What a** lovely photo!
3 Thank you for fixing it! You're **so/such** an angel!
4 **How/What** quickly you type on this keyboard!
5 It's **so/such** a pity we don't have GPS!
6 You can't exchange my phone? **What/Such** nonsense!

(6 x 3 = 18)

4 Complete the second sentence in reported speech.

1 "First, log into your account," Marcus told me.
Marcus told me ....
2 "Don't use public Wi-Fi for company business, please," their manager said to them.
Their manager asked them ....
3 "Write a comment about my picture, please!" said Jasmine to her friend.
Jasmine asked her friend ....
4 "Don't tell anyone your password," our instructor told us.
Our instructor told us ....
5 "Give me the phone back!" Sue told George.
Sue told George ....

(5 x 3 = 15)

5 Write the correct question tag.

1 James bought a new tablet, ...?
2 They haven't left the computer room yet, ...?
3 You can write computer programs, ...?
4 We didn't find any good phones, ...?
5 You aren't taking ICT, ...?
6 We're both in our last year at college, ...?
7 The computer won't crash, ...?
8 Your laptop has a good graphics card, ...?

(8 x 2 = 16)

Everyday English

6 Match the sentences.

1 ☐ See, there you are.
2 ☐ That's the one, isn't it?
3 ☐ First click on the file.
4 ☐ What's the matter?
5 ☐ Let me show you.

A I can't work this out.
B Great. Thanks!
C OK. So what's next?
D Really? That's so easy!
E Yes, that's right.

(5 x 4 = 20)
Total 100

Competences

Lexical Competence
Understand words/phrases related to:
- computer parts & the Internet
- using a smartphone

Reading Competence
- understand texts related to technology (read for gist – matching headings to paragraphs); complete sentences

Listening Competence
- listen to and understand monologues related to technology (listen for specific information/gist – multiple matching)

Speaking Competence
- give instructions

Writing Competence
- write a leaflet
- write a for-and-against essay

Values: Cooperation

www.teamgames.com

Home | About Us | News | Games | Contact

Search...

TEAM GAMES

Once just for co-workers, team-building activities are now popular these days with sports teams, groups of friends and even families! They're a way to increase the feeling of closeness, unity and cooperation you share. And nowadays there are more choices than ever ...

A Competitions

The classic team-building activity, where your team **competes** together against one or more teams. It could be paintball, physical games like football or even a treasure hunt. These are great for sports teams or for co-workers.

Click for a list of team-building competitions

B Escape rooms

Probably the newest team-building activity, an escape room offers a short, high-energy game where you only win if you all work as one. The goal is to get out of a locked room within the time limit (usually around an hour). Perfect for people who can't leave town and don't have much spare time.

Click for a list of escape rooms

C Themed games

Some companies are now offering **experiences** straight from your favourite films and TV shows! For example, you might need to work together to escape from the Hunger Games or a forest full of mysterious creatures. These games **generally** last a day, but you'll all be talking about them for months after!

Click for a list of theme-based team-building activities

D Survival

Taking place over two or more days, **survival** team-building puts you into a physically and mentally difficult environment in the wild. Long-distance treks, **tough** climbs, shelter building and fire starting make this a great activity for group bonding.

Click for a list of survival team-building weekends

1 **What is the purpose of the text:** *to entertain*? *to inform*? *to persuade*? **Read through quickly to find out.**

2 **Listen to and read the text.**

Which team-building activity (A-D) ...

1 involves staying out overnight?
2 is suitable for busy people?
3 is recommended for athletes?
4 is based on well-known stories?
5 has not been around for very long?

Then, explain the words in bold.

3 THINK **In groups, create a team-building activity of your own. Think about:** *name – place – duration – what the team will do.*

4 **Present your team-building activity to the class. Once all groups have presented their activities, the class votes on the one they would prefer to do.**

Public Speaking Skills

1 a) **Read the task.**

You are at a technology fair. Give a presentation about a new piece of technology.

b) **Listen to and read the model. What techniques has the speaker used to start/end his presentation?**

Study Skills

Recapping key points

While you speak, repeat key points that you would like your audience to remember.

2 **Find the phrases the speaker has used in his presentation to recap key points. What are the key points that the speaker refers to?**

3 ICT **Collect information about a new piece of technology e.g. a computer, and complete the spidergram. Use your notes to prepare and give a presentation. Recap your main ideas.**

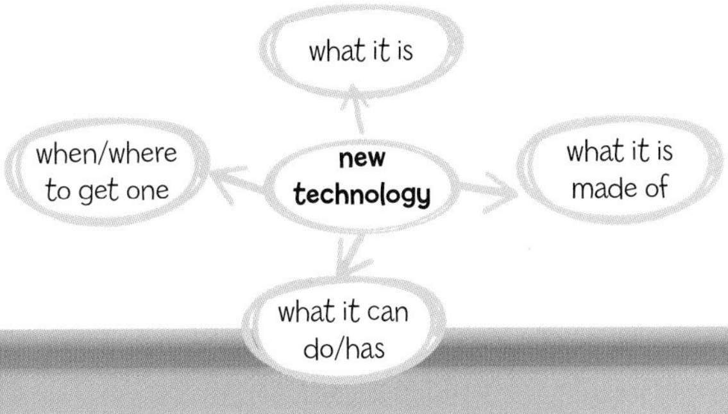

new technology
- what it is
- what it is made of
- what it can do/has
- when/where to get one

Good morning, everyone and thank you for joining me here at the 52nd Technology Fair. My name is Sam Hart. Let me ask you this. When I say 'mobile phone of the future', what comes to mind? ... perhaps a mobile that you wear as a bracelet? ... maybe a device that can fit into your wallet? Well, ladies and gentlemen, thanks to the work of my organisation, these ideas are now a reality. Let me present the XTVT mobile phone: the future of technology.

As you can see, it looks like your ordinary mobile phone. However, it is far from this. Some of the world's most amazing and unique materials which are flexible, strong, and above all, good for our environment make up this mobile phone.

It is because of these materials, this phone can change into different shapes, as I will demonstrate now. It can stretch into a large screen which is great for those days when your eyes are tired. Other than stretching, it can bend into a bracelet. This is particularly helpful when you are exercising. It can also become smaller to fit into your wallet, which means one less thing to carry around with you. But this is not all. Besides its flexibility, it also runs on solar power, so you never have to use a charger again. Sounds great, right? What's more, it also uses facial recognition, so in the event that someone steals your phone, they will not be able to use it. For those that are game lovers, the phone also has a built-in console.

So, when can you purchase this amazing new product? Well, from next week all electronic stores will sell the XTVT mobile phone. What's more, we are offering a 20 percent discount on all pre-orders today!

Without a doubt, this mobile phone with its flexibility, solar power feature, facial recognition and built-in console, will change the way we live. This mobile phone is the must-have device of the year!

Thank you all for being here today. If you have any questions on this amazing product, I'll be happy to answer them now ...

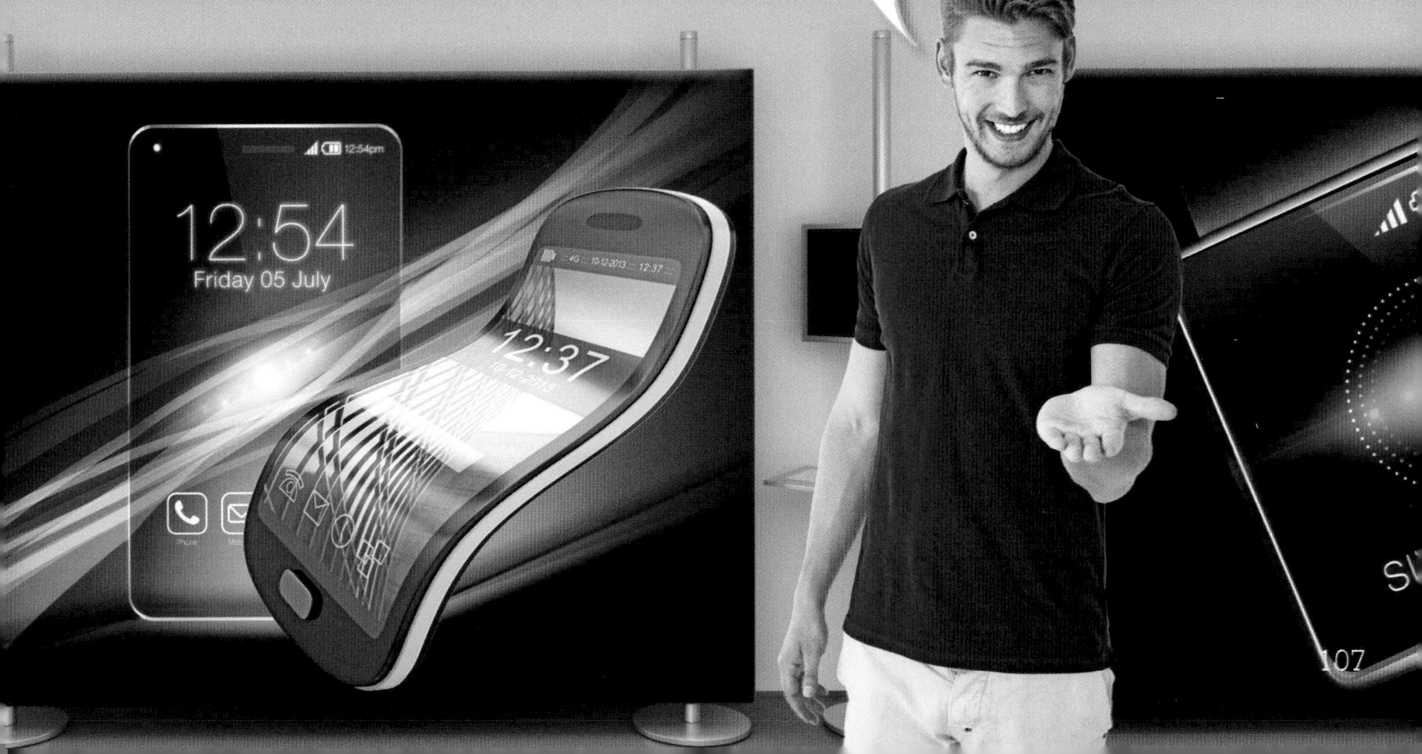

In England a century ago...

CLIL: History

An English High Street

Just after World War 1 (1914-1918), there were no big shopping centres or supermarkets. Instead, people visited a variety of small family-run shops on the high street to do their shopping. Today, a lot of the shops and jobs that existed back then don't **exist** anymore.

The Lamplighter

Each town had a lamplighter whose job was to light the town's streetlights when it got dark and put them out at 11 pm each night. Streetlights used gas and lamplighters carried around a ladder or a long pole to do their work.

The Butcher's

During and after the war, there wasn't enough meat, so as well as beef and chicken, butchers sold rabbits and pheasants. Usually, people came to order some meat, and then later in the day the butcher's boy delivered the meat to their homes on a bicycle.

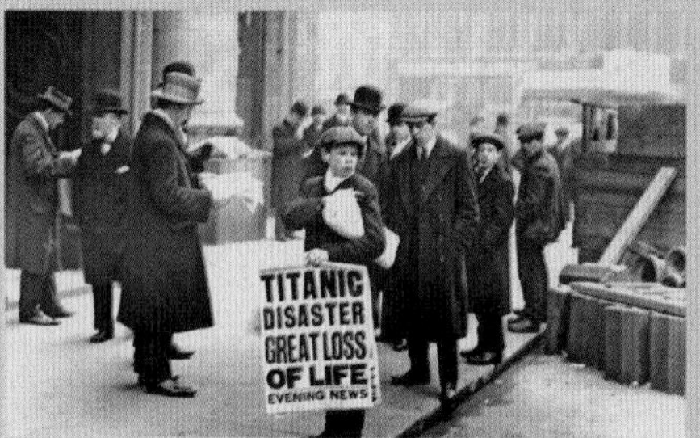

The Newsboy

On most high streets, it was common to hear young boys shouting 'Read all about it!' These boys got up at 4 am, bought newspapers, and sold them during the day. They often gave the money they **earned** to their parents.

The Tearoom

Tearooms were like modern-day cafés. They were especially popular with women from rich families. Groups of women drank tea (still England's favourite drink) and ate **freshly-baked** scones with jam.

The Tailor's

The tailor's sold clothes for men. Usually, customers didn't buy clothes on a hanger. Instead, the tailor **measured** a customer and made a suit to fit them perfectly. There were shops for women's clothes too, but a lot of women made their own clothes at home.

Listening & Reading

1 **Imagine you are in London 100 years ago. Look at the pictures and listen to the sounds. Where are you? What can you see, hear, smell?**

2 **Look at the text. Which of the shops and jobs in the text don't exist anymore?**

Listen and read to find out.

3 **Read the text again and decide if the sentences (1-5) are *T* for True or *F* for false. Then, explain the words in bold.**

1. Streetlights were left on throughout the night. ....
2. People usually returned to their butcher's to collect their order. ....
3. The money newsboys collected supported their families. ....
4. Only wealthy women visited tearooms. ....
5. Tailors made clothes for both men and women. ....

Check these words

pole, pheasant, scone, hanger

Speaking & Writing

4 ICT **What shops and jobs existed in your country 100 years ago? Collect information, then prepare a presentation.**

5 THINK **Compare shops and jobs in England and your country 100 years ago.**

B

CLIL: Food Preparation & Nutrition

Food Label

Apart from fresh fruit and vegetables, almost every food or drink product has two labels: the ingredients list and the nutritional information list.

The Nutritional Information List

The nutritional information list gives information about the nutrients in a food or drink. In the EU, this list must have the energy, fat, carbohydrates (including sugars), protein and sodium in a product. Sometimes, other information is given too, like vitamins. The list usually gives this information **per serving** (e.g. for a complete can of cola) or per 100 ml (for a drink) or 100 g (for a food).

Expert advice: This list is very useful when you want to decide which of two products is healthier. For example, you can read the amount of fat or sodium in two products and see which has less.

The Ingredients List

The ingredients list gives all of the ingredients in a food or drink product. Ingredients are listed by weight, so the heaviest ingredient comes first and the lightest comes last. Also, if a food is written in the name of the product (e.g. Strawberry Juice) then the ingredients list must show the **percentage** of this ingredient (e.g. strawberry extract [5%]). There must also be a list of allergens. These are ingredients which people can be allergic to.

Expert advice: Avoid products which have sugar or salt as one of their first ingredients and don't be **fooled** by a product's name. It might sound healthy, but check the ingredients list to see if it really is.

Nutrition Facts

Serving Size 5 oz. (144g)
Servings Per Container 4

Amount Per Serving	
Calories 310	**Calories** from Fat 100
	% Daily Value*
Total Fat 15g	**21%**
Saturated Fat 2.6g	**17%**
Trans Fat 1g	
Cholesterol 118mg	**39%**
Sodium 560mg	**28%**
Total Carbohydrate 12g	**4%**
Dietary Fiber 1g	**4%**
Sugars 10g	
Protein 24g	

Vitamin A 1% • **Vitamin C** 2%
Calcium 2% • **Iron** 5%

*Percent Daily Values are based on a 2,000 calorie diet. Your daily values may be higher or lower depending on your calorie needs:

	Calories	2,000	2,500
Total Fat	Less Than	65g	80g
Saturated Fat	Less Than	20g	25g
Cholesterol	Less Than	300mg	300mg
Sodium	Less Than	2,400mg	2,400mg
Total Carbohydrate		300g	375g
Dietary Fiber		25g	30g

Calories per gram:
Fat 9 • Carbohydrate 4 • Protein 4

INGREDIENTS: SUGAR, VEGETABLE OIL, HAZELNUTS (13%), SKIM MILK POWDER (8.7%), COCOA POWDER (7.4%), EMULSIFIER (SOY LECITHIN), FLAVOURING (VANILLIN).
CONTAINS: HAZELNUTS, MILK, SOY

Check these words

nutrient, weight, allergic

Listening & Reading

1 **Look at the label. Where can you see it? What does it show and why is it important to read it?**
Listen and read to find out.

2 **Read the text again. Decide if the sentences (1-5) are *T* (True) or *F* (False). Then, explain the words in bold.**

1 In the EU, the nutritional information list must have vitamins. ....
2 Nutritional information lists help people compare products. ....
3 The ingredients list only includes the heavier ingredients in a product. ....
4 All of the ingredients in the ingredients list have to have a percentage. ....
5 The ingredients list is important for people with allergies. ....

Speaking & Writing

3 THINK **Read the label again. What kind of product do you think it is attached to? Is it a healthy product? Give reasons for your answer.**

4 ICT THINK **Work in groups. Bring in clean food packaging from your home and compare the nutritional information list and the ingredients list on similar products. Which of the products are healthy/ unhealthy? Were you surprised by any of the results of your research?**

CLIL: Science

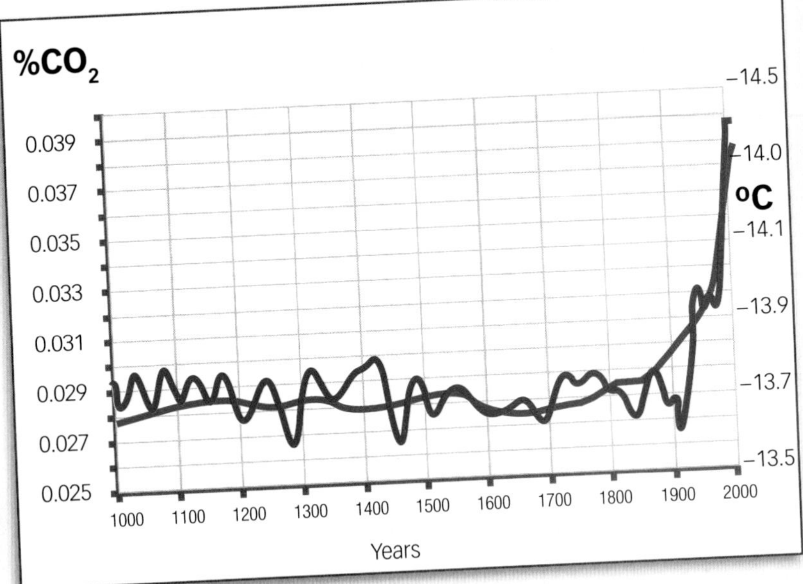

The Greenhouse Effect

Greenhouses are made out of glass, and people use them to grow crops in places where there is not a lot of sunlight. A greenhouse lets heat from the sun in, but it doesn't let it out again. So, it can hold heat and stay warm long after it has become cold outside.

Now, think of the Earth as a giant greenhouse. **Greenhouse gases** in the atmosphere act like the glass in a greenhouse. They allow heat from the sun to enter the atmosphere, but don't let all of it leave afterwards. This makes the planet warm and this is called the **greenhouse effect**.

More heat is trapped inside the planet when there are more greenhouse gases. Apart from water vapour, the most common greenhouse gas is carbon dioxide – and humans are responsible for a lot of it. In the graph, the blue line represents the percentage of carbon dioxide in the atmosphere. In 1000, it was 0.028% but from around 1700 we started to burn lots of **fossil fuels** such as oil, gas and coal. Burning fossil fuels causes carbon emissions, so the amount of CO_2 in our atmosphere began to rise. So, today, the number is over 0.04%.

The graph also shows the average global temperature – the red line – and we can see that it has risen a lot since 1700, too. In 1000, it was about 13.7°C but today it is around 14.5°C. There is a clear link between carbon dioxide emissions and the average global temperature, and this is called **global warming**.

Check these words

vapour, carbon dioxide, carbon emission, average

Listening & Reading

1 **Look at the graph. What does it show? What does it have to do with the greenhouse effect?**

Listen and read to find out.

2 **Read the text and complete the sentences (1-4) with words from the text.**

1 Greenhouses gases are similar to .... in a greenhouse.
2 .... and water vapour are greenhouse gases.
3 Oil, gas and coal are all ....
4 The greenhouse effect is linked to ....

Speaking & Writing

3 **Make sentences using the phrases in bold in the text.**

4 ICT **Research information about our carbon footprint, and how we can reduce the amount of carbon we produce in our lives. Tell the class.**

CLIL: Art & Design

ART
Movements of the 20th Century

The twentieth century was a time of great change. The world experienced two huge wars, but also some amazing technological developments which improved people's lives. And all of this was represented in the art movements of the century.

Abstract Expressionism

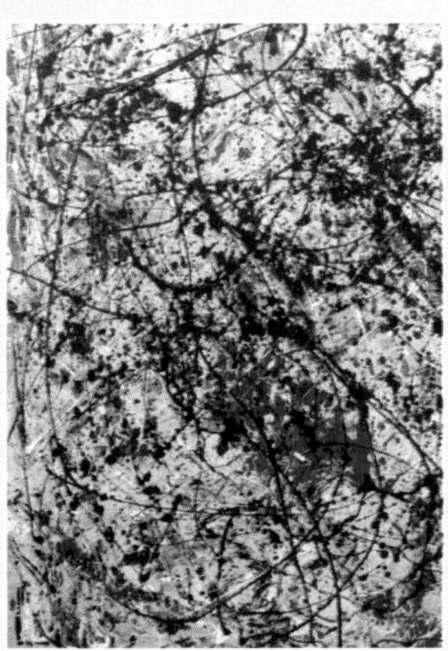

Abstract expressionism began in New York in the late 1940s. Artists created abstract paintings with images that didn't represent anything from the real world. These paintings often looked like simple splashes of colourful paint – and a lot of people **claimed** the movement was not 'real art'. The most famous abstract expressionist was Jackson Pollock. He created paintings like No. 5, 1948 by **dripping** paint onto huge canvasses on the floor.

Surrealism

Surrealism began in France in the late 1920s. It was an art movement which was interested in the human mind. A lot of surrealist artists **explored** dreams in their art, so surrealist paintings often look very strange with out-of-shape images and things which don't usually go together. For example, Salvador Dalí's Persistence of Memory shows **melted** clocks on a beach.

Pop Art

In the 1960s, a group of American artists started an art movement which represented people's everyday experiences. Pop artists used images of supermarket products, road signs or advertisements in their art. For example, Andy Warhol's Campbell's Soup Cans is **simply** 32 paintings of soup cans.

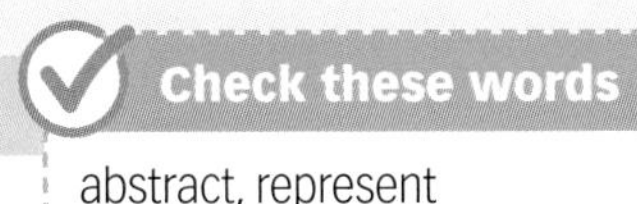

Check these words

abstract, represent

Listening & Reading

1 **Look at the title of the text and the subheadings. What characterises** *abstract expressionist*, *surrealist* **and** *pop art* **artworks?**

Listen and read to find out.

2 **Read the text and mark the sentences (1-5)** *S* **(surrealism),** *AE* **(abstract expressionism) or** *PA* **(pop art). Then, explain the words in bold.**

1 It caused a lot of disagreement. ....
2 It was inspired by the world of shopping. ....
3 It explored people's thoughts. ....
4 Its paintings did not show people or things. ....
5 It didn't start in the USA. ....

Speaking & Writing

3 THINK **Which style do you like the most/least? Why?**

4 ICT THINK **Collect information about another art movement of the 20th century and prepare a presentation. Use the headings:** *name – when started – where – features – famous painter/work of art*.

Word List

Unit 1 – Lifestyles

1a

aboard /ə'bɔːd/ (adv) = on a type of mass transportation
admire /əd'maɪə/ (v) = to really like and respect
break /breɪk/ (n) = a short rest
club /klʌb/ (n) = an organisation for people who have a common interest in a particular activity
crew /kruː/ (n) = a group of people who work together
equipment /ɪ'kwɪpmənt/ (n) = the tools needed to do a particular job or activity
fortunately /'fɔːtʃənətli/ (adv) = luckily
go back /ˌɡəʊ 'bæk/ (phr v) = to return
impossible /ɪm'pɒsəbəl/ (adj) = that cannot be done
involve /ɪn'vɒlv/ (v) = to take part or have a strong connection
member /'membə/ (n) = a part of a group
mission /'mɪʃən/ (n) = an important task
orbit /'ɔːbɪt/ (v) = to move around a planet
ordinary /'ɔːdənəri/ (adj) = usual, common
passenger /'pæsɪndʒə/ (n) = a person travelling on a bus, ship, etc
project /'prɒdʒekt/ (n) = a detailed study
properly /'prɒpəli/ (adv) = correctly
rise /raɪz/ (v) = (of the sun) to go up
running water (phr) = water supplied through pipes and taps
set /set/ (v) = (of the sun) to go below the horizon
shave /ʃeɪv/ (v) = to remove hair
space station /'speɪs ˌsteɪʃən/ (n) = a laboratory in space where people can live for long periods of time
spacesuit /'speɪssuːt/ (n) = an astronaut's outfit
spacewalk /'speɪswɔːk/ (n) = the act of an astronaut moving outside a spacecraft
spin /spɪn/ (v) = to turn round quickly
staff /stɑːf/ (n) = all the people who work in an office, company, etc
take over /ˌteɪk 'əʊvə/ (phr v) = to get control of sth
team /tiːm/ (n) = a group of people who work together
towel /'taʊəl/ (n) = a piece of material for drying your hands and body
typical /'tɪpɪkəl/ (adj) = ordinary

1b

advise /əd'vaɪz/ (v) = to tell sb what you think they should do
cruise /kruːz/ (n) = a holiday on a ship
delicious /dɪ'lɪʃəs/ (adj) = very tasty
divorced /dɪ'vɔːst/ (adj) = no longer married because the marriage has been legally ended
fix /fɪks/ (v) = to repair
flight /flaɪt/ (n) = a journey made by flying on an aeroplane
hang out /ˌhæŋ 'aʊt/ (phr v) = to spend time somewhere
harbour /'hɑːbə/ (n) = a small port
hiking /'haɪkɪŋ/ (n) = the act of going on a long walk in the countryside
lawyer /'lɔːjə/ (n) = sb who is trained in the law
mall /mɔːl/ (n) = a shopping centre
married /'mærid/ (adj) = having a husband or wife
mechanic /mɪ'kænɪk/ (n) = sb who repairs cars
salmon /'sæmən/ (n) = a large, silver-coloured fish with pink flesh
secretary /'sekrətəri/ (n) = sb who works in an office
serve /sɜːv/ (v) = to give food or drink to sb
shine /ʃaɪn/ (v) = to be bright
shrimp /ʃrɪmp/ (n) = a small shell fish with long tails and many legs
sight /saɪt/ (n) = an interesting place that tourists usually visit
single /'sɪŋɡəl/ (adj) = not married
souvenir /ˌsuːvə'nɪə/ (n) = sth you buy to remember an event or a holiday
treat /triːt/ (v) = to provide medical care

1c

appearance /ə'pɪərəns/ (n) = the way sb looks
bald /bɔːld/ (adj) = having little or no hair
branch /brɑːntʃ/ (n) = a local office of a big business
brave /breɪv/ (adj) = courageous
calm /kɑːm/ (adj) = relaxed, quiet
careful /'keəfəl/ (adj) = having the ability to avoid mistakes and problems
character /'kærəktə/ (n) = the particular qualities of a person that make them different from others
chubby /'tʃʌbi/ (adj) = a little fat in a pleasant way
clever /'klevə/ (adj) = having the ability to learn and understand things quickly
complexion /kəm'plekʃən/ (n) = the skin condition and colouring of one's face
fit /fɪt/ (adj) = in good physical condition
freckle /'frekəl/ (n) = a small brown spot on one's face or body
friendly /'frendli/ (adj) = kind and pleasant
full /fʊl/ (adj) = (of lips) large and rounded
jealous /'dʒeləs/ (adj) = envious of the achievements of others
kind /kaɪnd/ (adj) = generous and helpful
lazy /'leɪzi/ (adj) = sb who doesn't like working
look after /'lʊk ɑːftə/ (phr v) = to be responsible for sth/sb and keep them healthy and safe
make a difference (phr) = to play an important role
middle-aged /ˌmɪdəl 'eɪdʒd/ (adj) = sb between 40 and 60 years old
moustache /mə'stɑːʃ/ (n) = hair which grows on a man's upper lip
overweight /ˌəʊvə'weɪt/ (adj) = weighing more than one should
pale /peɪl/ (adj) = having a skin colour that is whiter than usual
plump /plʌmp/ (adj) = quite fat
relationship /rɪ'leɪʃənʃɪp/ (n) = the connection you have with sb
reliable /rɪ'laɪəbəl/ (adj) = trustworthy
roommate /'ruːmˌmeɪt/ (n) = sb living in the same room as sb else
sociable /'səʊʃəbl/ (adj) = enjoying spending time with other people
special /'speʃəl/ (adj) = unique
straight /streɪt/ (adj) = (of hair) not curly
support /sə'pɔːt/ (v) = to help
talkative /'tɔːkətɪv/ (adj) = talking a lot
vet /vet/ (n) = a doctor for animals
wavy /'weɪvi/ (adj) = (of hair) slightly curly
well-built /ˌwel 'bɪlt/ (adj) = having a large strong body

Culture 1

band /bænd/ (n) = a small group of musicians
chat /tʃæt/ (v) = to have a friendly conversation
contact /'kɒntækt/ (v) = to get in touch with, to communicate with
different /'dɪfrənt/ (adj) = not the same
festival /'festɪvəl/ (n) = a celebration
hang out /ˌhæŋ 'aʊt/ (phr v) = to spend time somewhere
hurling /'hɜːlɪŋ/ (n) = a game similar to hockey played by two teams of 15 players, popular in Ireland
interest /'ɪntrəst/ (n) = a hobby
international /ˌɪntə'næʃənəl/ (adj) = worldwide
outdoors /ˌaʊtdɔːz/ (adv) = taking place outside

preference /ˈprefərəns/ (n) = a choice, a thing one likes the best
single-parent /ˌsɪŋgəl ˈpeərənt/ (n) = a parent who looks after their children alone (without a partner)
teen /tiːn/ (n) = sb between 13 and 19 years old
tend to /ˈtend tə/ (v) = to be likely to have a particular quality
traditional /trəˈdɪʃənəl/ (adj) = existing for a long time without a change

Unit 2 – Shop till you drop

2a

alligator /ˈælɪˌgeɪtə/ (n) = a type of crocodile that lives in the USA
antique /ˌænˈtiːk/ (n) = valuable old furniture or other item
attraction /əˈtrækʃən/ (n) = a thing or place of interest
blanket /ˈblæŋkɪt/ (n) = a woollen bed cover
bouquet /bəʊˈkeɪ/ (n) = a bunch of flowers
caviar /ˈkæviɑː/ (n) = fish eggs eaten as food
comb /kəʊm/ (n) = a tool for untangling hair
customer /ˈkʌstəmə/ (n) = sb who buys goods from a shop
delivery service /dɪˈlɪvəri ˌsɜːvɪs/ (n) = the organisation that deals with taking things to a person or a place
doorman /ˈdɔːmən/ (n) = a person who offers help to people entering a building
employ /ɪmˈplɔɪ/ (v) = to give sb a job
entrance /ˈentrəns/ (n) = (of a building) the way in
fire brigade /ˈfaɪə brɪˌgeɪd/ (n) = the organisation in charge of putting out fires
grocer's /ˈgrəʊsəz/ (n) = a shop that sells food and other goods
hand out /ˌhænd ˈaʊt/ (phr v) = to give sth to people, to distribute
historic /hɪˈstɒrɪk/ (adj) = important in history
in addition to (phr) = as well as, extra to
lamp chop /ˌlæm ˈtʃɒp/ (n) = one of the cuts of lamb meat
landmark /ˈlændmɑːk/ (n) = a statue, building, etc that is easily seen and recognised
medicine /ˈmedsɪn/ (n) = a substance used to treat a disease or injury
miss the opportunity (phr) = to lose the chance to do sth
motto /ˈmɒtəʊ/ (n) = a phrase or short sentence used to show a particular belief
necklace /ˈnekləs/ (n) = a piece of jewellery that you wear around your neck
official /əˈfɪʃəl/ (adj) = agreed to or arranged by people in positions of authority
ordinary /ˈɔːdnri/ (adj) = common, usual
security guard /sɪˈkjʊərəti ˌgɑːd/ (n) = sb employed to protect a building and the people there
supplier /səˈplaɪə/ (n) = a company that provides sb with sth
take over /ˌteɪk ˈəʊvə/ (phr v) = to get control of sth
the sales /ðə ˈseɪlz/ (n) = a period of time during which a shop reduces the prices of goods
visitor /ˈvɪzɪtə/ (n) = a guest in a place

2b

ancient /ˈeɪnʃənt/ (adj) = belonging to times long ago
coach /kəʊtʃ/ (n) = a large comfortable bus
convenient /kənˈviːniənt/ (adj) = easy for particular purposes and needs
crowded /ˈkraʊdɪd/ (adj) = packed
distance /ˈdɪstəns/ (n) = the amount of space between two places
expensive /ɪkˈspensɪv/ (adj) = costing a lot of money
experience /ɪkˈspɪəriəns/ (n) = something happening to you
goods /gʊdz/ (pl n) = objects produced for sale
heavy /ˈhevi/ (adj) = of great weight
light /laɪt/ (adj) = not heavy
philosopher /fɪˈlɒsəfə/ (n) = a theorist
price /praɪs/ (n) = the money charged for things to buy
product /ˈprɒdʌkt/ (n) = an item which is made and sold on the market
side pocket /ˈsaɪd pɒkɪt/ (n) = a pocket in or at one side of a bag
spot /spɒt/ (n) = a small, round, coloured mark
sticker /ˈstɪkə/ (n) = a small piece of paper that sticks
strap /stræp/ (n) = a narrow piece of leather or cloth used to hold clothing in place
trader /ˈtreɪdə/ (n) = sb who owns and runs a shop or small business
upload /ʌpˈləʊd/ (v) = to transfer data onto a computer
variety /vəˈraɪəti/ (n) = many and different of sth
zip /zɪp/ (n) = a device for closing and opening parts of clothes and bags

2c

attachment /əˈtætʃmənt/ (n) = a file you send with an email
bookstall /ˈbʊkstɔːl/ (n) = a small shop with an open front that sells books
checked /tʃekt/ (adj) = having a pattern of coloured squares
discover /dɪˈskʌvə/ (v) = to find sth, to become aware of sth
driving licence /ˈdraɪvɪŋ ˌlaɪsəns/ (n) = a document showing sb is qualified to drive
exhausting /ɪgˈzɔːstɪŋ/ (adj) = extremely tiring
fitting room /ˈfɪtɪŋ ruːm/ (n) = a place in a shop where customers try on clothes
floral /ˈflɔːrəl/ (adj) = having a pattern or design with flowers on it
material /məˈtɪəriəl/ (n) = cloth used to make clothes
paradise /ˈpærədaɪs/ (n) = a place that seems perfect for a particular purpose
pattern /ˈpætən/ (n) = a design on clothes consisting of lines, shapes, etc
patterned /ˈpætənd/ (adj) = having shapes or colours
plain /pleɪn/ (adj) = (of material) having no pattern
rucksack /ˈrʌksæk/ (n) = a bag with straps that go over your shoulders so that you can carry things on your back
spotted /ˈspɒtɪd/ (adj) = decorated or covered with a pattern of spots
striped /straɪpt/ (adj) = having lines of different colours
tiny /ˈtaɪni/ (adj) = extremely small
trendy /ˈtrendi/ (adj) = fashionable, modern
wallet /ˈwɒlɪt/ (n) = a small flat container for paper money and credit cards, usually used by a man

Culture 2

anniversary /ˌænɪˈvɜːsəri/ (n) = a date which is celebrated because sth special happened on that date in the past
bank /bæŋk/ (n) = raised land on the sides of a river
beyond /bɪˈjɒnd/ (prep) = further in the distance than sth
borough /ˈbʌrə/ (n) = a district in a city responsible for its own schools, markets, etc
bridge /brɪdʒ/ (n) = a structure that is built over a river, etc so that people or vehicles can cross
brilliant /ˈbrɪljənt/ (adj) = excellent
celebrate /ˈselɪbreɪt/ (v) = to make a day or event special by doing sth enjoyable
chef /ʃef/ (n) = a professional cook

Word List

cross /krɒs/ (v) = to go from one side of sth to the other
history /ˈhɪstəri/ (n) = an account of events which happened in the past
location /ləʊˈkeɪʃən/ (n) = the place or position of sth
organised /ˈɔːɡənaɪzd/ (adj) = having things in order
philosophy /fɪˈlɒsəfi/ (n) = a belief
produce /ˈprɒdjuːs/ (n) = food or other things that are grown in large quantities
producer /prɒˈdjuːsə/ (n) = a person or company that grows food or makes goods to be sold
secret /ˈsiːkrɪt/ (n) = information that is not known by many people
storyteller /ˈstɔːriˌtelə/ (n) = sb who tells stories
success /səkˈses/ (n) = achieving your aims
waste /weɪst/ (n) = food that is thrown away

Unit 3 – Survival stories

3a

achievement /əˈtʃiːvmənt/ (n) = an accomplishment
blow /bləʊ/ (v) = (of the wind) to cause sth to move
brightly /ˈbraɪtli/ (adv) = vividly
coast /kəʊst/ (n) = land next to the sea
deck /dek/ (n) = the part of a ship which you can walk on
downstairs /ˌdaʊnˈsteəz/ (adv) = going down to a lower floor
drop /drɒp/ (v) = to become less
engine /ˈendʒɪn/ (n) = the machine that causes a car, boat, etc to move
flash /flæʃ/ (n) = a light that shines on and off very quickly
fog /fɒg/ (n) = a thick cloud of tiny drops of water that makes it difficult to see things
goal /gəʊl/ (n) = a target, sth you hope to achieve
head /ˈhed/ (v) = to go towards or in the direction of a place
heavily /ˈhevɪli/ (adv) = a lot
in trouble (phr) = in a difficult situation
land /lænd/ (n) = earth, soil
lie /laɪ/ (v) = to be in a flat position on a surface
luckily /ˈlʌkɪli/ (adv) = fortunately
mast /mɑːst/ (n) = (on a ship) a tall pole that the sails hang from
on board (phr) = on a ship
pick up /ˌpɪk ˈʌp/ (phr v) = to go and get sb/sth
pour /pɔː/ (v) = to rain heavily
proud /praʊd/ (adj) = pleased about sth good sb has done
reach /riːtʃ/ (v) = to arrive
realise /ˈriːəlaɪz/ (v) = to become aware of, to understand
relieved /rɪˈliːvd/ (adj) = happy because sth unpleasant hasn't happened
remote /rɪˈməʊt/ (adj) = isolated, far away from everything
rescue /ˈreskjuː/ (v) = to save sb from a dangerous situation
roll over /ˌrəʊl ˈəʊvə/ (phr v) = to turn to the other side
satellite phone /ˈsætəlaɪt ˌfəʊn/ (n) = a device that can send voice messages over extremely long distances
set sail (phr) = to begin a journey across the sea
signal /ˈsɪgnəl/ (n) = a sound or action which gives a message to the person who hears or sees it
snap /snæp/ (v) = to break with noise
storm /stɔːm/ (n) = bad weather with strong winds, rain and often lightning and thunder
suddenly /ˈsʌdənli/ (adv) = unexpectedly
violent /ˈvaɪələnt/ (adj) = happening with great force causing serious damage

3b

avalanche /ˈævəlɑːntʃ/ (n) = a large amount of snow, ice and rock that suddenly falls or slides down a mountain
bitterly /ˈbɪtəli/ (adv) = unpleasantly
carriage /ˈkærɪdʒ/ (n) = part of a train
crash /ˈkræʃ/ (v) = to fall and make a loud noise
dig /dɪg/ (v) = to make a hole by moving earth
elderly /ˈeldəli/ (adj) = the old people
emergency services /ɪˈmɜːdʒənsi ˌsɜːvɪsɪz/ (pl n) = public organisations such as the fire brigade, the ambulance service and the police
envelope /ˈenvələʊp/ (n) = a flat rectangular paper container for papers
grab /græb/ (v) = to take sth quickly
guest /gest/ (n) = a person who is staying at a hotel
manager /ˈmænɪdʒə/ (n) = a person responsible for a business
missing /ˈmɪsɪŋ/ (adj) = lost
resort /rɪˈzɔːt/ (n) = a place where a lot of people spend their holiday
set out /ˌset ˈaʊt/ (phr v) = to begin a journey
slope /sləʊp/ (n) = part of the side of a hill or mountain, especially as a place for skiing
strike /straɪk/ (v) = (of a disaster) to happen suddenly and without warning
vlog /vlɒg/ (n) = a video blog

3c

angry /ˈæŋgri/ (adj) = annoyed
anxious /ˈæŋkʃəs/ (adj) = nervous, worried
award /əˈwɔːd/ (n) = prize
bark /bɑːk/ (v) = (of a dog) to make a short loud noise
brake /breɪk/ (n) = what makes a vehicle stop or slow down
breeze /briːz/ (n) = a gentle wind
burglary /ˈbɜːgləri/ (n) = the act of entering a building and stealing things
canoe /kəˈnuː/ (n) = a small narrow boat
chase /tʃeɪs/ (v) = to run after sb or sth in order to catch them
cheerful /ˈtʃɪəfəl/ (adj) = happy
cover (with) /ˈkʌvə/ (v) = to put sth over sth else
crash /kræʃ/ (v) = to hit sth accidentally
disappear /ˌdɪsəˈpɪə/ (v) = to stop existing
footstep /ˈfʊtstep/ (n) = the sound or mark of a step when walking
forgive /fəˈgɪv/ (v) = to stop being angry with sb
frightened /ˈfraɪtənd/ (adj) = anxious or afraid of sth
gather /ˈgæðə/ (v) = to come together
gentle /ˈdʒentəl/ (adj) = calm, light
ground /graʊnd/ (n) = the soil or rocks which make up the floor of the Earth
helpful /ˈhelpfəl/ (adj) = willing to help
lie /laɪ/ (v) = to not tell the truth
parcel /ˈpɑːsəl/ (n) = sth wrapped in paper usually to be sent by post
pleased /ˈpliːzd/ (adj) = happy, satisfied
puzzled /ˈpʌzəld/ (adj) = confused
scream /ˈskriːm/ (v) = to shout because of fear
screech /skriːtʃ/ (v) = to make a loud and unpleasant noise
siren wailing (phr) = the long and loud sound of a siren (a warning device)
thrilled /θrɪld/ (adj) = very excited and happy
waterfall /ˈwɔːtəfɔːl/ (n) = a steep high cliff where water flows over the edge

Culture 3

alive /əˈlaɪv/ (adj) = not dead
Antarctica /ænˈtɑːrktɪkə/ (n) = the continent around South Pole
break up /ˌbreɪk ˈʌp/ (v) = to gradually divide into smaller pieces

camp /kæmp/ (v) = to stay somewhere for a short time in a tent
crazy /ˈkreɪzi/ (adj) = mad
crush /krʌʃ/ (v) = to push sth very hard
destroy /dɪˈstrɔɪ/ (v) = to damage sth badly
explorer /ɪkˈsplɔːre/ (n) = sb who travels to places that nobody has been to before
journey /ˈdʒɜːni/ (n) = trip
leave /liːv/ (v) = to go away from a place or a person
lifeboat /ˈlaɪfbəʊt/ (n) = a small boat on a ship for people to leave in if the ship is not safe or might sink
melt /melt/ (v) = to become liquid
reach /riːtʃ/ (v) = to arrive at
relieved /rɪˈliːvd/ (adj) = no longer worried
rescue /ˈreskjuː/ (v) = to save from danger or harm
save /seɪv/ (v) = to rescue sth/sb from danger
set out /ˌset ˈaʊt/ (phr v) = to begin a journey
sink /sɪŋk/ (v) = to go down below the surface of the sea
survive /səˈvaɪv/ (v) = to continue to live
tent /tent/ (n) = a shelter which can be folded up and carried
trap /træp/ (v) = to be kept in a place from which you cannot escape

Values A: Diversity

basically /ˈbeɪsɪkli/ (adv) = generally
belief /bɪˈliːf/ (n) = an opinion, sth a person believes in
culture /ˈkʌltʃə/ (n) = the lifestyle, beliefs and traditions of a group of people
depend on /dɪˈpend ɒn/ (phr v) = to rely on
diversity /daɪˈvɜːsəti/ (n) = variety
DNA /ˌdiː en ˈeɪ/ (n) = the chemical responsible for characteristics passed from parents to their children
enjoy /ɪnˈdʒɔɪ/ (v) = to get pleasure from sth
individual /ˌɪndɪˈvɪdʒuəl/ (adj) = personal, of one person
introduce /ˌɪntrəˈdjuːs/ (v) = to bring sth into a country for the first time
language /ˈlæŋgwɪdʒ/ (n) = the method of communication using spoken or written words
move away /ˌmuːv əˈweɪ/ (phr v) = to move house
physical /ˈfɪzɪkəl/ (adj) = relating to a person's body
population /ˌpɒpjʊˈleɪʃən/ (n) = all the people that live in a town, city, country, etc
religion /rɪˈlɪdʒən/ (n) = the belief in a god or gods
study /ˈstʌdi/ (n) = survey
tradition /trəˈdɪʃən/ (n) = a custom passed down from one generation to the next
unique /juːˈniːk/ (adj) = special, different from others

Public Speaking Skills A

clue /kluː/ (n) = a piece of evidence which helps to find the answer to sth
consist (of) /kənˈsɪst/ (v) = to be made up of
crop /krɒp/ (n) = plants or fruit grown in large quantities for food
curry /ˈkʌri/ (n) = a dish composed of meat or vegetables in a hot spicy sauce
delicate /ˈdelɪkət/ (adj) = small and beautifully shaped
exchange programme /ɪksˈtʃeɪndʒ ˌprəʊgræm/ (n) = an arrangement in which students from one country go to stay with students from another country
fascinating /ˈfæsɪneɪtɪŋ/ (adj) = very interesting
feature /ˈfiːtʃə/ (n) = a characteristic
field /fiːld/ (n) = an area of land used for growing crops
generous /ˈdʒenərəs/ (adj) = willing to give or share what one has with others
include /ɪnˈkluːd/ (v) = to contain
nickname /ˈnɪkneɪm/ (n) = an informal name for sb or sth
plant /plɑːnt/ (v) = to put a seed into the ground so that it will grow there
sandy /ˈsændi/ (adj) = covered in sand
spicy /ˈspaɪsi/ (adj) = with a strong flavour of spices
tanned /tænd/ (adj) = having brown skin by being in the sun
temple /ˈtempəl/ (n) = a building used to worship a god
tropical /ˈtrɒpɪkəl/ (adj) = (of a climate) very hot and wet
warm-hearted /ˌwɔːm ˈhɑːtɪd/ (adj) = kind and loving
welcoming /ˈwelkəmɪŋ/ (adj) = friendly

Unit 4 – Planning ahead

4a

agree /əˈgriː/ (v) = to have the same opinion with sb
ambition /æmˈbɪʃən/ (n) = a goal, a strong desire
arrange /əˈreɪndʒ/ (v) = to organise sth
arrangement /əˈreɪndʒmənt/ (n) = a plan
company /ˈkʌmpəni/ (n) = a business organisation
course /kɔːs/ (n) = a series of classes
decision /dɪˈsɪʒən/ (n) = the act of choosing what is the best to do
decoration /ˌdekəˈreɪʃən/ (n) = things put around a place to make it look more attractive
degree /dɪˈgriː/ (n) = the qualification you get when you finish a university or college
entrance test /ˈentrəns ˌtest/ (n) = a test that you take to join a school, university, etc
feedback /ˈfiːdbæk/ (n) = comments about how well or badly you are doing sth
fit /fɪt/ (adj) = healthy and in good physical condition
follow your dream (phr) = to pursue and try hard for what you want
full-time /ˌfʊl ˈtaɪm/ (adj) = working for the whole part of the working day or week
graduation /ˌgrædʒuˈeɪʃən/ (n) = successful completion of a course at college, university, etc
guest /gest/ (n) = sb who is invited somewhere
local /ˈləʊkəl/ (adj) = of the area sb lives in
long hours (phr) = for a long time
mistake /mɪˈsteɪk/ (n) = a wrong action
organisational skill (phr) = the ability to arrange things efficiently
otherwise /ˈʌðəwaɪz/ (adv) = or
pass /pɑːs/ (v) = to succeed in sth
quality /ˈkwɒləti/ (n) = a characteristic of sth
save /seɪv/ (n) = to rescue sth/sb from danger
set up /ˌset ˈʌp/ (phr v) = to establish
suit /suːt/ (v) = to be right/appropriate for a person
take care of (phr) = to look after
training /ˈtreɪnɪŋ/ (n) = the learning of skills you need for a particular job
university /ˌjuːnɪˈvɜːsəti/ (n) = an institution for higher education
venue /ˈvenjuː/ (n) = the place where an event takes place
work out /ˌwɜːk ˈaʊt/ (phr v) = to exercise

4b

appointment /əˈpɔɪntmənt/ (n) = an arrangement to see sb at a particular time
become /bɪˈkʌm/ (v) = to begin to have a particular job
board /bɔːd/ (n) = a group of people who have the responsibility for managing a business, etc
break down /ˌbreɪk ˈdaʊn/ (phr v) = to stop working

Word List

chairman /ˈtʃeəmən/ (n) = sb in charge of an organisation, etc
doorbell /ˈdɔːbel/ (n) = a button near the front door that you press to signal to the person in the house that you are there
episode /ˈepɪsəʊd/ (n) = each of the parts of a television story
flat /flæt/ (n) = apartment
join /dʒɔɪn/ (v) = to become a member of
lecture /ˈlektʃə/ (n) = a talk at university
part-time /ˌpɑːt ˈtaɪm/ (adj) = working less than the standard forty-hour week
plan /plæn/ (n) = an arrangement for the future
tour /tʊə/ (n) = an organised trip
volunteer /ˌvɒlənˈtɪə/ (v) = to offer to do sth without payment

4c

application /ˌæplɪˈkeɪʃən/ (n) = a document that you use to officially ask for a job, etc
available /əˈveɪləbəl/ (adj) = not busy
brave /breɪv/ (adj) = courageous
careful /ˈkeəfəl/ (adj) = cautious
caring /ˈkeərɪŋ/ (adj) = showing concern for other people
client /ˈklaɪənt/ (n) = a customer, a person using the services of a company, etc
communication skill (phr) = being good at exchanging information with sb orally or in writing
education /ˌedʒʊˈkeɪʃən/ (n) = the process of learning in a school, university, etc
enquire /ɪnˈkwaɪə/ (v) = to ask for information
exhibit /ɪgˈzɪbɪt/ (n) = an object shown to the public at a museum, etc
hard-working /ˌhɑːd ˈwɜːkɪŋ/ (adj) = putting a lot of energy into your work
have a seat (phr) = to sit down
imaginative /ɪˈmædʒɪnətɪv/ (adj) = able to come up with new original ideas
interested (in sth) /ˈɪntrəstɪd/ (adj) = caring about sth, wanting to know about sth
knowledge /ˈnɒlɪdʒ/ (n) = the information and understanding of a particular subject
look for /ˈlʊk fɔː/ (phr v) = to try to find, to search for
patient /ˈpeɪʃənt/ (adj) = not getting angry or easily annoyed
polite /pəˈlaɪt/ (adj) = kind
reply /rɪˈplaɪ/ (n) = a response
residence /ˈrezɪdəns/ (n) = home
salary /ˈsæləri/ (n) = the money that sb is paid each month by their employer
shop assistant /ˈʃɒp əˌsɪstənt/ (n) = sb who works in a shop and sells things to customers
sociable /ˈsəʊʃəbl/ (adj) = friendly, outgoing
work experience /ˈwɜːk ɪkˌspɪəriəns/ (n) = experience that sb already has of working

Culture 4

clash with /klæʃ wɪð/ (v) = to happen at the same time as sth else
customer /ˈkʌstəmə/ (n) = sb who buys goods from a shop
develop /dɪˈveləp/ (v) = to start to have sth
fit /fɪt/ (adj) = healthy and in good physical condition
have a head for figures (phr) = to be good at using numbers
industry /ˈɪndəstri/ (n) = the companies that produce goods for sale
outdoors /ˌaʊtˈdɔːz/ (adv) = taking place outside
promotion /prəˈməʊʃən/ (n) = getting a more important job
qualification /ˌkwɒlɪfɪˈkeɪʃən/ (n) = a particular skill in or knowledge of a subject
receipt /rɪˈsiːt/ (n) = a piece of paper that shows you have bought and paid for sth
scan /skæn/ (v) = (of a computer) to store information from a product
wage /weɪdʒ/ (n) = daily/weekly payment for work

Unit 5 – Food, glorious food!

5a

check out /ˌtʃek ˈaʊt/ (phr v) = to look at sth new
condition /kənˈdɪʃən/ (n) = the particular state that sth is in
cramped /kræmpt/ (adj) = small and uncomfortable
crate /kreɪt/ (n) = a box made of wood
crew /kruː/ (n) = the staff of a ship
cuisine /kwɪˈziːn/ (n) = the cooking style of a specific place
dish /dɪʃ/ (n) = a particular kind of food cooked as a meal
fatty /ˈfæti/ (adj) = (of food or drinks) that cause sb to gain weight
fresh /freʃ/ (adj) = (of food) made recently
frozen /ˈfrəʊzən/ (adj) = very cold, made into ice
healthy /ˈhelθi/ (adj) = good for your body
impressive /ɪmˈpresɪv/ (adj) = great, remarkable
ingredient /ɪnˈgriːdiənt/ (n) = a food item used to make a particular dish
junk food /ˈdʒʌŋk fuːd/ (n) = food such as crisps, hamburgers, etc which are bad for your health
keep one's spirits up (phr) = to keep oneself in a positive frame of mind
low-fat /ˌləʊ ˈfæt/ (adj) = without much fat
make sense (phr) = sth can be understood
midnight /ˈmɪdnaɪt/ (n) = 12 o'clock at night
mission /ˈmɪʃən/ (n) = an important task given to people, involving travelling to another country
navy /ˈneɪvi/ (n) = the part of a country's armed forces that can fight at sea
on board (phr) = on a ship
popular /ˈpɒpjʊlə/ (adj) = liked by many people
pot /pɒt/ (n) = a round container used for cooking food
prepare /prɪˈpeə/ (v) = to make sth ready
produce /ˈprɒdjuːs/ = (n) food or other things that are grown in large qualities
sailor /ˈseɪlə/ (n) = sb who works on a boat or ship
shift /ʃɪft/ (n) = a set period for a group or a person to work before another group or person replaces them
store cupboard /ˈstɔː ˌkʌbəd/ (n) = a piece of furniture used for keeping things for future use
submarine /ˈsʌbməriːn/ (n) = a ship that can travel both on the surface of the sea and under the sea
sunshine /ˈsʌnʃaɪn/ (n) = light and heat that come from the sun
tasty /ˈteɪsti/ (adj) = (of food) delicious
tinned /tɪnd/ (adj) = sealed in a can
typical /ˈtɪpɪkəl/ (adj) = usual, ordinary
vegetarian /ˌvedʒəˈteəriən/ (n) = sb who does not eat meat
voyage /ˈvɔɪɪdʒ/ (n) = a long journey by sea
wave /weɪv/ (n) = raised water
well stocked /ˌwel ˈstɒkt/ (adj) = (of a shop) having plenty of things to choose from

5b

add /æd/ (v) = to put in
boil /bɔɪl/ (v) = to cook in very hot water
bun /bʌn/ (n) = small sweet cake, usually in a round shape
dressing /ˈdresɪŋ/ (n) = a mixture of liquids such as oil and vinegar that you pour over a salad
drop /drɒp/ (n) = a small amount of a liquid
mix /mɪks/ (v) = to combine

order /ˈɔːdə/ (v) = to ask for food or drink in a restaurant, etc
pour /pɔː/ (v) = to make a liquid go out of a container you are holding
serving /ˈsɜːvɪŋ/ (n) = a portion of food for one person
shell /ʃel/ (n) = the hard covering of some animals
take off /ˌteɪk ˈɒf/ (phr v) = to remove

5c

affordable /əˈfɔːdəbəl/ (adj) = not too expensive
atmosphere /ˈætməsfɪə/ (n) = the mood or feeling that exists in a place and affects the people who are there
change /tʃeɪndʒ/ (n) = the money given back to you when you pay for sth with more money than it costs
countryside /ˈkʌntrisaɪd/ (n) = the land that is outside a city or town
delicious /dɪˈlɪʃəs/ (adj) = very tasty
dessert /dɪˈzɜːt/ (n) = sweet food eaten at the end of a meal
disappointing /ˌdɪsəˈpɔɪntɪŋ/ (adj) = not as good as you had hoped for
kick off /ˌkɪk ˈɒf/ (phr v) = to begin
located /ləʊˈkeɪtɪd/ (adj) = situated
mark /mɑːk/ (n) = score
menu /ˈmenjuː/ (n) = a list of food that is available in a restaurant, café, etc
portion /ˈpɔːʃən/ (n) = a serving
reasonable /ˈriːzənəbəl/ (adj) = (of a price) fair and not too high
recommend /ˌrekəˈmend/ (v) = to make a suggestion
retreat /rɪˈtriːt/ (n) = a quiet place where sb can relax
roast /rəʊst/ (n) = cooked meat
round off /ˌraʊnd ˈɒf/ (phr v) = to end sth in a satisfactory way
rude /ruːd/ (adj) = impolite
setting /ˈsetɪŋ/ (n) = a place or surroundings
takeaway /ˈteɪkəweɪ/ (n) = a shop or restaurant which sells hot food that you eat somewhere else
tempting /ˈtemptɪŋ/ (adj) = attractive
thumbs down /ˌθʌmz ˈdaʊn/ (n) = a reaction that shows you do not like sth
unpleasant /ʌnˈplezənt/ (adj) = that you do not like or enjoy
varied /ˈveərid/ (adj) = various, containing many different things
well worth doing (phr) = important to do

Culture 5

blow up /ˌbləʊ ˈʌp/ (phr v) = to destroy with explosives
celebrate /ˈselɪbreɪt/ (v) = to mark a day or event by doing sth special
cloth /klɒθ/ (n) = a material used for making clothes
clootie dumpling /ˈkluːtɪ dʌmplɪŋ/ (n) = a traditional dessert pudding made with dried fruit
complete /kəmˈpliːt/ (adj) = whole, with nothing missing
dried fruit /ˌdraɪd ˈfruːt/ (n) = fruit that has all the water removed from it so that it will last for a long time
fail /feɪl/ (v) = to not succeed
festive /ˈfestɪv/ (adj) = (of food) special, related to a celebration
fireworks /ˈfaɪəwɜːks/ (pl n) = small containers filled with explosive substances which produce a loud noise and brightly coloured patterns in the sky
groundnut /ˈgraʊndnʌt/ (n) = a peanut
invent /ɪnˈvent/ (v) = to create sth new
mixture /ˈmɪkstʃə/ (n) = several different things together
national /ˈnæʃənəl/ (adj) = relating to a whole country
oatmeal /ˈəʊtmiːl/ (n) = a type of flour made from oats
oven /ˈʌvən/ (n) = the enclosed part of a cooker where food is cooked
pan /pæn/ (n) = a round metal container with a large handle, used for cooking
parkin /ˈpɑːrkɪn/ (n) = a cake eaten in the north of England
shorten /ˈʃɔːtən/ (v) = to make shorter
simnel cake /ˈsɪmnəl keɪk/ (n) = a cake made with dried fruit
spice /spaɪs/ (n) = substance used in cooking to add flavour
spicy /ˈspaɪsi/ (adj) = having strong flavours from spices
suet /ˈsuːɪt/ (n) = beef or mutton fat
topping /ˈtɒpɪŋ/ (n) = food which is put on top of a dish to add flavour or make it look attractive
treat /triːt/ (n) = sth special
wrap /ræp/ (v) = to cover sth with paper

Unit 6 – Health

6a

ache /eɪk/ (n) = a feeling of pain that continues for a long time
advice /ədˈvaɪs/ (n) = an opinion about what you should do in a particular situation
antibiotic /ˌæntɪbaɪˈɒtɪk/ (n) = a medicine that cures illnesses and infections caused by bacteria
awful /ˈɔːfəl/ (adj) = terrible
come up /ˌkʌm ˈʌp/ (phr v) = to happen
complain /kəmˈpleɪn/ (v) = to express dissatisfaction about sth
cure /kjʊə/ (n) = a treatment that makes sb ill healthy again
disease /dɪˈziːz/ (n) = a serious illness
fever /ˈfiːvə/ (n) = a higher body temperature than usual
fluid /ˈfluːɪd/ (n) = a liquid
get rid of (phr) = to become free of sth that is unpleasant or annoying
illness /ˈɪlnəs/ (n) = a disease or health problem
in doubt (phr) = to not be certain
infection /ɪnˈfekʃən/ (n) = a disease that is caused by bacteria or a virus
liquid /ˈlɪkwɪd/ (n) = a substance, e.g. water, that is not solid
medical /ˈmedɪkəl/ (adj) = relating to the treatment of illnesses
nettle /ˈnetl/ (n) = a wild plant whose leaves hurt if you touch them
pain /peɪn/ (n) = an unpleasant feeling caused by an illness or injury
peppermint /ˈpepəˌmɪnt/ (n) = a type of mint plant with a strong smell and flavour used in medicine or drinks
plenty of (phr) = a large amount of sth
prescription /prɪˈskrɪpʃən/ (n) = a piece of paper written by your doctor that indicates the medicine you need to take
recipe /ˈresəpi/ (n) = a list of ingredients and a set of instructions that tell you how to cook sth
remedy /ˈremədi/ (n) = a medicine or treatment for a disease, illness or injury
smelly /ˈsmeli/ (adj) = having an unpleasant smell
soak /səʊk/ (v) = to leave in water for a long period
suffer (from sth) /ˈsʌfə/ (v) = to be affected and experience pain by a disease
temperature /ˈtemprətʃə/ (n) = how hot or cold sth is
treatment /ˈtriːtmənt/ (n) = medical attention given for a specific period of time
trick /trɪk/ (n) = a clever way of doing sth
vinegar /ˈvɪnɪgə/ (n) = a sour-tasting liquid made from malt or wine

6b

appointment /əˈpɔɪntmənt/ (n) = an arrangement to see sb at a particular time
bleeding /ˈbliːdɪŋ/ (n) = blood coming from a part of your body

Word List

career /kəˈrɪə/ (n) = sb's professional life
check-up /ˈtʃek ʌp/ (n) = a medical examination to see if you are healthy
for ages (phr) = for a long time
injured /ˈɪndʒəd/ (adj) = being hurt or having damaged a part of your body
patient /ˈpeɪʃənt/ (n) = a person who receives a treatment for illness
recently /ˈriːsəntlɪ/ (adv) = lately
regret /rɪˈgret/ (v) = to feel sad about sth you have done, or wish you had not done it
scholarship /ˈskɒləʃɪp/ (n) = an award of money given to a very good student for further study
training /ˈtreɪnɪŋ/ (n) = the process of learning the skills you need to do a particular job
wise /waɪz/ (adj) = smart and sensible

6c

bruise /bruːz/ (v) = to hit a part of your body causing a purple mark to appear
bump /bʌmp/ (v) = to accidentally hit by moving
burn /bɜːn/ (v) = to come in contact with fire or heat and make a mark on the skin
develop /dɪˈveləp/ (v) = to start having sth
injury /ˈɪndʒəri/ (n) = harm or damage to a person's body
side street /ˈsaɪd striːt/ (n) = a small street connected to a major street
sprain /spreɪn/ (v) = to damage the ankle or wrist by accidentally twisting or bending it

Culture 6

Aboriginal /ˌæbəˈrɪdʒnəl/ (adj) = relating to the original race of people who live in Australia
airfield /ˈeəfiːld/ (n) = a place where small aircraft can take off and land
bite /baɪt/ (v) = to close your teeth upon sth or sb
check-up /ˈtʃek ʌp/ (n) = a medical examination
clinic /ˈklɪnɪk/ (n) = a place where people go for medical treatment or advice
community /kəˈmjuːnəti/ (n) = a group of people living in a specific area
distance /ˈdɪstəns/ (n) = the amount of space between two points or places
donation /dəʊˈneɪʃən/ (n) = money given to a charity or other organisation
emergency services /ɪˈmɜːdʒənsi ˌsɜːvɪsɪz/ (pl n) = public organisations such as the fire brigade, the ambulance services and the police
equal (to) /ˈiːkwəl/ (adj) = the same as
location /ləʊˈkeɪʃən/ (n) = the place or position of sth
middle /ˈmɪdəl/ (n) = the central part of sth
the Outback /ði ˈaʊtbæk/ (n) = the central desert areas of Australia where few people live
profit /ˈprɒfɪt/ (n) = money that you get from selling services
provide /prəˈvaɪd/ (v) = to give, to supply sth to sb
remote /rɪˈməʊt/ (adj) = isolated, far away from everything
run /rʌn/ (v) = to operate sth
shot /ʃɒt/ (n) = an amount of medicine put into the body with a special needle
state /steɪt/ (n) = territory or area which is part of a country
transport /trænsˈpɔːt/ (v) = to take people from one place to another
trip /trɪp/ (n) = a journey that we make to a particular place

Values B: Volunteering

amnesia /æmˈniːziə/ (n) = memory loss
benefit /ˈbenɪfɪt/ (v) = to help sb to improve their life in some way
describe /dɪˈskraɪb/ (v) = to say or write what sth is like
faraway /ˈfɑːrəweɪ/ (adj) = being a long way away
independent /ˌɪndɪˈpendənt/ (adj) = self-sufficient, not controlled
life-changing /ˈlaɪf ˌtʃeɪndʒɪŋ/ (adj) = so important that it can affect your whole life
moment /ˈməʊmənt/ (n) = a point in time
purpose /ˈpɜːpəs/ (n) = a reason
quarter /ˈkwɔːtə/ (n) = each of the four equal parts that sth is divided into
reason /ˈriːzən/ (n) = an explanation
research /rɪˈsɜːtʃ/ (n) = work that involves studying sth and trying to discover facts about it
out of your shell (phr) = more interested in other people, more willing to talk and take part in social activities
stressed /strest/ (adj) = anxious
volunteer /ˌvɒlənˈtɪə/ (v) = to offer to do sth without payment
worry /ˈwʌri/ (v) = to feel anxious or troubled about sth

Public Speaking Skills B

ability /əˈbɪləti/ (n) = a skill
agree /əˈgriː/ (v) = to have the same opinion about sth as sb else
all-round /ˌɔːl ˈraʊnd/ (adj) = general
championship /ˈtʃæmpiənʃɪp/ (n) = a sporting event where competitors compete for top positions, involving a series of matches or races
charity /ˈtʃærəti/ (n) = an organisation which helps people in need
childhood /ˈtsaɪldhʊd/ (n) = the early years of sb's life
clear /klɪə/ (adj) = obvious
coach /kəʊtʃ/ (n) = the person who trains an athlete, team, etc
defender /dɪˈfendə/ (n) = sb in a sports team who tries to prevent the other team from scoring points, goals, etc
donate /dəʊˈneɪt/ (v) = to give money or things to charity
drop out (of) /ˌdrɒp ˈaʊt/ (phr v) = to leave school without finishing it
encourage /ɪnˈkʌrɪdʒ/ (v) = to try to persuade sb to do sth
event /ɪˈvent/ (n) = a happening
goal /gəʊl/ (n) = aim, purpose
hold /həʊld/ (v) = to organise (a meeting, etc)
introduce /ˌɪntrəˈdjuːs/ (v) = to make sth known to sb for the first time
offer /ˈɒfə/ (v) = to give, to provide
passer /ˈpɑːsə/ (n) = the player in a sports team responsible for passing the ball
position /pəˈzɪʃən/ (n) = a situation
rarely /ˈreəli/ (adv) = not often
scorer /ˈskɔːrə/ (n) = sb who scores a point or goal in a game
set up /ˌset ˈʌp/ (phr v) = to start an organisation to help people
similar /ˈsɪmələ/ (adj) = alike
talent /ˈtælənt/ (n) = a natural ability or skill to do sth

Unit 7 – Stick to the rules!

7a

allow /əˈlaʊ/ (v) = to permit, to let
annoy /əˈnɔɪ/ (v) = to make sb angry
campsite /ˈkæmpsaɪt/ (n) = an area where people stay in tents or caravans while on holiday
caravan /ˈkærəvæn/ (n) = a vehicle pulled by a car/van and which contains beds and cooking equipment so that people can spend their holidays in it

charge /tʃɑːdʒ/ (n) = an amount of money you have to pay for sth
daily /ˈdeɪli/ (adj) = happening every day
dangerous /ˈdeɪndʒərəs/ (adj) = unsafe
disturb /dɪˈstɜːb/ (v) = to bother sb
except /ɪkˈsept/ (prep) = apart from
extremely /ɪkˈstriːmli/ (adv) = very
fellow /ˈfeləʊ/ (adj) = of the same group
fire pit /ˈfaɪə pɪt/ (n) = a large hole in the ground in which a fire for cooking food is lit
free of charge (phr) = that does not cost anything
freely /ˈfriːli/ (adv) = without being limited
heating /ˈhiːtɪŋ/ (n) = the system for keeping a room, etc warm
lead /liːd/ (n) = a long narrow piece of leather, chain, etc that you fasten to the collar around a dog's neck in order to control the dog
light /laɪt/ (v) = (of a fire) to start
litter /ˈlɪtə/ (n) = rubbish
peaceful /ˈpiːsfəl/ (adj) = calm, quiet
pet /pet/ (n) = an animal which is kept at home
pick up /ˌpɪk ˈʌp/ (phr v) = to lift up
provide /prəˈvaɪd/ (v) = to make available
recycle /ˌriːˈsaɪkl/ (v) = to collect and process things such as paper and cans so that they can be used again
regulation /ˌregjʊˈleɪʃən/ (n) = an official rule or order
respect /rɪˈspekt/ (v) = to care about sb's wishes, beliefs and rights
rule /ruːl/ (n) = an official instruction about what you must or must not do
safety /ˈseɪfti/ (n) = the state of sth being safe to do or use
supply /səˈplaɪ/ (v) = to provide
tidy /ˈtaɪdi/ (adj) = orderly, neat

7b

adult /ˈædʌlt/ (n) = sb who is no longer a child, a mature person
allergic /əˈlɜːdʒɪk/ (adj) = becoming ill or getting a rash when you eat, drink or touch sth
avoid /əˈvɔɪd/ (v) = to try not to do sth
break the law (phr) = to commit a crime
custom /ˈkʌstəm/ (n) = an activity or way of behaving that is usual or traditional in a particular society
enter /ˈentə/ (v) = to go into a place
matches /ˈmætʃɪz/ (pl n) = small sticks of wood used to create fire
offend /əˈfend/ (v) = to do sth that upsets or annoys sb
passport /ˈpɑːspɔːt/ (n) = an official document allowing you to travel abroad
prison /ˈprɪzən/ (n) = the place where criminals are kept
rent /rent/ (n) = payment given to sb to live in their place temporarily
runway /ˈrʌnweɪ/ (n) = the long road where planes take off and land
settle in /ˌsetl ˈɪn/ (phr v) = to get used to living somewhere
sign /saɪn/ (v) = to write your name on a document to show that you agree with the content
support /səˈpɔːt/ (v) = to give help of some kind to sb or sth
up-to-date (phr) = the newest of its kind, the most recent
wildlife /ˈwaɪldlaɪf/ (n) = animals and other living creatures which live in the wild

7c

basement /ˈbeɪsmənt/ (n) = a floor built below ground level
cancellation /ˌkænsəˈleɪʃn/ (v) = the act of stopping sth arranged from happening
check out /ˌtʃek ˈaʊt/ (phr v) = to pay the bill and leave a hotel
damage /ˈdæmɪdʒ/ (n) = harm caused to sth
dust /dʌst/ (n) = very small bits of dirt on furniture, etc
equipped /ɪˈkwɪpt/ (adj) = including tools needed for a particular purpose
furniture /ˈfɜːnɪtʃə/ (n) = large moveable objects such as chairs and tables
latest /ˈleɪtɪst/ (adj) = the most recent
lock /lɒk/ (v) = to make sth safe by closing doors, windows, etc
overnight /ˌəʊvəˈnaɪt/ (adv) = during the night
property /ˈprɒpəti/ (n) = the things that belong to sb or sth
remove /rɪˈmuːv/ (v) = to take away
report /rɪˈpɔːt/ (v) = to state, to describe
sort /sɔːt/ (v) = to classify
view /vjuː/ (n) = sight, scenery
workspace /ˈwɜːkspeɪs/ (n) = a working area such as a desk, counter, room, etc

Culture 7

challenge /ˈtʃælɪndʒ/ (n) = sth that tests your abilities and strengths
competition /ˌkɒmpəˈtɪʃən/ (n) = a contest
competitor /kəmˈpetɪtə/ (n) = a person who takes part in a competition
crew member /ˈkruː ˌmembə/ (n) = a member of a group of people who work together
enormous /ɪˈnɔːməs/ (adj) = extremely large
excitement /ɪkˈsaɪtmənt/ (n) = a feeling of enthusiasm
face /feɪs/ (v) = to deal with
ferry boat /ˈferi bəʊt/ (n) = a boat or ship taking passengers across an area of water
finish line /ˈfɪnɪʃ laɪn/ (n) = the line at the end of a race
gather /ˈgæðə/ (v) = to come together
join /dʒɔɪn/ (v) = to participate
last /lɑːst/ (v) = to continue to happen
limit /ˈlɪmɪt/ (n) = the greatest amount allowed
miss /mɪs/ (v) = to lose the chance to do sth
race /reɪs/ (n) = a competition to see who is the fastest
sail /seɪl/ (v) = to move a boat across water
set sail (phr) = to begin a journey across water
shore /ʃɔː/ (n) = the land across the edge of the sea
spectator /spekˈteɪtə/ (n) = sb who watches a game, competition, etc
spot /spɒt/ (n) = a position
take part (phr) = to participate
wave /weɪv/ (n) = raised water
yacht /jɒt/ (n) = a medium-sized sailing boat

Unit 8 – Landmarks

8a

attraction /əˈtrækʃən/ (n) = an appealing feature which makes sb interested in visiting a place
canyon /ˈkænjən/ (n) = a deep narrow valley with steep sides usually with a river flowing through it
carve /kɑːv/ (v) = to make objects by cutting them out of wood or stone
chamber /ˈtʃeɪmbə/ (n) = an enclosed space; a large room
chance /tʃɑːns/ (n) = an opportunity
dig /dɪg/ (v) = to make a hole by moving earth
fall /fɔːl/ (n) = water dropping from a higher to a lower point
legend /ˈledʒənd/ (n) = a myth; a story
mine /maɪn/ (n) = a system of holes underground from where coal, salt, etc are removed
mine /maɪn/ (v) = to work underground digging for salt, coal, metal, etc

Word List

mineshaft /ˈmaɪnʃɑːft/ (n) = a narrow vertical hole or a tunnel that gives access to a mine
rainforest /ˈreɪnfɒrɪst/ (n) = a thick forest of tall trees in tropical areas with a lot of rain
servant /ˈsɜːvənt/ (n) = a person employed by another person to work at their house
shape /ʃeɪp/ (n) = a form
surface /ˈsɜːfɪs/ (n) = the outer top part or layer of sth
valley /ˈvæli/ (n) = a low flat area of land between hills
well /wel/ (n) = a deep hole in the ground to get water

8b

admission /ədˈmɪʃən/ (n) = the money that you pay to enter a place
charge /tʃɑːdʒ/ (n) = price
complete /kəmˈpliːt/ (v) = to finish
compose /kəmˈpəʊz/ (v) = to write music
confuse (with) /kənˈfjuːz/ (v) = to mistake for
exhibit /ɪgˈzɪbɪt/ (n) = a work of art in a gallery, museum, etc
invent /ɪnˈvent/ (v) = to create sth that did not exist before

8c

brick /brɪk/ (n) = a rectangular block of baked clay used for building walls
clay /kleɪ/ (n) = a kind of earth which is soft when wet and hard when dry
concrete /ˈkɒŋkriːt/ (n) = a building material made from stone, sand, cement and water
courtyard /ˈkɔːtjɑːd/ (n) = an open area surrounded by buildings or walls
glass /glɑːs/ (n) = a hard usually transparent substance used to make windows
marble /ˈmɑːbəl/ (n) = a type of very hard rock which shines when it is cut and polished
ruins /ˈruːɪnz/ (pl n) = ancient/old buildings that have survived over time
steel /stiːl/ (n) = a very strong metal whose major component is iron
stone /stəʊn/ (n) = a hard solid substance of which rocks consist
wood /wʊd/ (n) = the material that forms the trunks and branches of trees

Culture 8

beast /biːst/ (n) = an animal
ceramic tile (phr) = a piece of fired clay used for covering floors, walls, etc
chalk /tʃɔːk/ (n) = a soft white rock that we use to write or draw
emblem /ˈembləm/ (n) = sth that represents a particular person, a group of people or an idea
entrance /ˈentrəns/ (n) = a door, gate etc that allows access to a place
explorer /ɪkˈsplɔːrə/ (n) = a person who travels to places that very little is known about
figure /ˈfɪgə/ (n) = a drawing; an image
prehistoric times (phr) = the time period before recorded history
symbolise /ˈsɪmbəlaɪz/ (v) = to stand for
time capsule /taɪm ˌkæpsjuːl/ (n) = a container filled with objects that represent the present period of history
trade /treɪd/ (n) = the activity of selling and buying things
tribe /traɪb/ (n) = a group of people living together, sharing the same language, culture and history

Unit 9 – Live and let live

9a

bat /bæt/ (n) = a small flying animal that looks like a mouse with wings
beak /biːk/ (n) = the hard pointed part on a bird's face which is its mouth
claw /klɔː/ (n) = a sharp nail on an animal's toe
feathers /ˈfeðəz/ (pl n) = soft light coverings of a bird's body
fin /fɪn/ (n) = a wide thin part on each side and the back of a fish
hooked /hʊkt/ (adj) = bended
hoof (plural: hoofs/hooves) /huːf/ (n) = the hard lowest part of each foot of a horse, a cow, etc
horn /hɔːn/ (n) = the hard curved part on the top of some animals' head
hunt /hʌnt/ (v) = to chase an animal in order to kill it
ivory /ˈaɪvəri/ (n) = a hard cream-coloured substance which forms elephant tusks
kitten /ˈkɪtn/ (n) = a young cat
logger /ˈlɒgə/ (n) = a person who cuts down trees
oil spill /ˈɔɪl spɪl/ (n) = leakage of oil into the sea
paw /pɔː/ (n) = an animal's foot
peacock /ˈpiːkɒk/ (n) = a large bird the male of which has got long blue and green tail feathers
response /rɪˈspɒns/ (n) = a reply
seal /siːl/ (n) = a large fish-eating mammal with thick fur that lives in cold areas in the sea
stripe /straɪp/ (n) = a line
treetop /ˈtriː tɒp/ (n) = the upper part of a tree
trunk /trʌŋk/ (n) = the body of a tree
tusk /tʌsk/ (n) = a long pointed tooth of an elephant, a walrus, etc
webbed /webd/ (adj) = having the toes connected with a membrane
whiskers /ˈwɪskəz/ (pl n) = long hairs on the face of a cat, a seal, etc

9b

bin /bɪn/ (n) = a container for rubbish
safely /ˈseɪfli/ (adv) = securely
turn round /ˌtɜːn əˈraʊnd/ (phr v) = to cause to change direction
waste /weɪst/ (n) = rubbish

9c

bagful /ˈbægfʊl/ (n) = the amount that a bag contains
cycle path /ˈsaɪkəl pɑːθ/ (n) = a narrow road for bicycles
encourage /ɪnˈkʌrɪdʒ/ (v) = to make sb more likely to do sth
greenery /ˈgriːnəri/ (n) = trees
litter /ˈlɪtə/ (n) = rubbish
public transport /ˌpʌblɪk ˈtrænspɔːt/ (n) = buses, trains, etc for people to use
recycle /riːˈsaɪkəl/ (v) = to collect and process things such as cans, glass or paper, so that they can be used again

Culture 9

celebrate /ˈseləbreɪt/ (v) = to mark a day or event by doing sth special, usually with other people
free of charge (phr) = without paying any money
gather /ˈgæðə/ (v) = to come together
in the heart of (phr) = in the centre of
outfit /ˈaʊtfɪt/ (n) = a set of clothes worn together
pedal /ˈpedl/ (v) = to move the bicycle with your feet
service /ˈsɜːvɪs/ (v) = to examine a machine and repair it if needed
swap /swɒp/ (v) = to exchange

Values C: Good Citizenship

avoid /əˈvɔɪd/ (v) = to keep away from
can't stand (phr) = to dislike
coach /kəʊtʃ/ (v) = to teach or train sb
impact /ˈɪmpækt/ (n) = an effect
law /lɔː/ (n) = a system of rules by a government or society
look after /ˈlʊk ɑːftə/ (phr v) = to take care of
obey /əʊˈbeɪ/ (v) = to follow rules/instructions

nder arrest (phr) = in legal custody

ublic Speaking kills C

rain /dreɪn/ (n) = a pipe that carries water or sewage
aking /li:kɪŋ/ (adj) = letting water escape
our /pɔ:/ (v) = (of a liquid) to come out of sth
inse /rɪns/ (v) = to wash sth in clean water to remove dirt or soap from it
ap /tæp/ (n) = the part at the end of a pipe which controls the flow of water

Unit 10 – Holiday time

0a

right /braɪt/ (adj) = full of light
udget /bʌdʒɪt/ (n) = an amount of money that you have available to spend
eal /di:l/ (n) = an arrangement
ine /daɪn/ (v) = to eat dinner, usually at a restaurant
xpedition /ˌekspəˈdɪʃən/ (n) = an organised journey for a specific purpose
et sb down /ˌget ˈdaʊn/ (phr v) = to cause sb to be exhausted
ook after /lʊk ɑ:ftə/ (phr v) = to take care of
nemorable /memərəbəl/ (adj) = notable
n board (phr) = on a ship
ight /saɪt/ (n) = a place of interest
taff /stɑ:f/ (n) = all the people who work for a company
troll /strəʊl/ (v) = to walk in a leisurely way
hunderstorm /θʌndəstɔ:m/ (n) = a storm with lightning and thunder and usually heavy rain
wet /wet/ (adj) = not dry

10b

admire /ədˈmaɪə/ (v) = to show respect
guest /gest/ (n) = a person staying at a hotel
guidebook /gaɪdbʊk/ (n) = a book for tourists giving information about a place
look forward to /ˌlʊk ˈfɔ:wəd tə/ (phr v) = I can't wait
melt /melt/ (v) = to become liquid
provide /prəˈvaɪd/ (v) = to give
thermal /θɜ:məl/ (adj) = relating to or caused by heat

10c

airport shuttle (phr) = a hotel bus that takes passengers to and from the airport
laundry service (phr) = the service in a hotel that washes and irons clothes for guests
polite /pəˈlaɪt/ (adj) = kind
recommend /ˌrekəˈmend/ (v) = to suggest
reservation /ˌrezəˈveɪʃən/ (n) = an arrangement to have a hotel room, a ticket, etc kept for you
seafront /si:frʌnt/ (n) = the part of a town on the coast that is next to the beach

Culture 10

break /breɪk/ (n) = a short period of rest
capital /kæpɪtl/ (n) = the most important city of a country or region
eagle /i:gəl/ (n) = a large bird with a hooked bill and long broad wings
otter /ɒtə/ (n) = a small mammal with four short legs, short brown fur and a long tail that swims well and eats fish
peaceful /pi:sfəl/ (adj) = quiet
puffin /pʌfɪn/ (n) = a black and white seabird with a large brightly-coloured beak
wander /wɒndə/ (v) = to walk around a place without any specific purpose

Unit 11 – Join in the Fun

11a

be caught in the moment (phr) = to be completely focused on a specific event
come alive (phr) = (of a place) to become full of activity
come true (phr) = to happen
float /fləʊt/ (v) = to lie on or just below the surface of a liquid
full moon /ˌfʊl ˈmu:n/ (n) = the moon when it is in the shape of a complete disc
give thanks to (phr) = to show appreciation that sth has happened
harvest /hɑ:vɪst/ (n) = the amount of crops gathered when they are mature
in full swing (phr) = at the highest level of an activity
out of sight (phr) = where sb/sth can't be seen
release /rɪˈli:s/ (v) = to set free
tree trunk /tri: trʌŋk/ (n) = the body of the tree
truly /tru:li/ (adv) = really
wish /wɪʃ/ (n) = a hope; a desire

11b

march /mɑ:tʃ/ (v) = to walk with very regular steps
parade /pəˈreɪd/ (n) = a procession in order to celebrate a special day, an event, etc
wonder /wʌndə/ (v) = to ask yourself

11c

circus /sɜ:kəs/ (n) = a group of clowns and acrobats that travel to various places and perform a show
concert /kɒnsət/ (n) = a music performance
escape room /ɪˈskeɪp ru:m/ (n) = a game where people are locked into a room and have to find a way to escape solving puzzles
fashion show /fæʃən ʃəʊ/ (n) = an event where models wear new styles of clothes
highlight /haɪlaɪt/ (n) = the most interesting part of an event
ice show /aɪs ʃəʊ/ (n) = an event in which ice-skaters perform, usually with musical accompaniment
opera /ɒpərə/ (n) = a musical play in which all words are sung
waist-deep /weɪst di:p/ (adv) = at a depth to reach the middle part of your body

Culture 11

annual /ænjuəl/ (adj) = happening every year
bushfood /bʊʃfu:d/ (n) = any food native to Australia and eaten by the original inhabitants
experience /ɪkˈspɪəriəns/ (v) = to be in a situation
fancy /fænsi/ (v) = to like
gathering /gæðərɪŋ/ (n) = the act of getting together
inhabitant /ɪnˈhæbɪtənt/ (n) = a dweller
sample /sɑ:mpəl/ (v) = to taste
sandstone rock /sændstəʊn ˌrɒk/ (n) = a rock that contains mainly sand

Unit 12 – Going online!

12a

access /ækses/ (v) = to open a computer file
anti-virus program /ænti ˈvaɪərəs ˌprəʊgræm/ (n) = a type of utility for scanning and removing programs introduced secretly into a computer system in order to alter or destroy data
attachment /əˈtætʃmənt/ (n) = a file sent with an email message
click /klɪk/ (v) = to select using the left button of a mouse
complex /kɒmpleks/ (adj) = complicated
delete /dɪˈli:t/ (v) = to remove
detect /dɪˈtekt/ (v) = to find
download /ˌdaʊnˈləʊd/ (v) = to receive data over the Internet
exchange /ɪksˈtʃeɪndʒ/ (v) = to give and receive
exposed /ɪkˈspəʊzd/ (adj) = not covered
familiar /fəˈmɪliə/ (adj) = known
flash drive /flæʃ draɪv/ (n) = a portable data storage device
hacker /hækə/ (n) = a person who accesses other people's computers illegally

Word List

hard drive /hɑːd draɪv/ (n) = the part of a computer which contains all the programs
headset /ˈhedset/ (n) = a set of headphones
interconnected /ˌɪntəkəˈnektɪd/ (adj) = joined
keyboard /ˈkiːbɔːd/ (n) = the part of a computer where you type in order to operate it
link /lɪŋk/ (n) = an HTML object that allows you to visit a new location when you click or tap it
mouse /maʊs/ (n) = a device attached to the computer, which moves the cursor around the screen
network /netwɜːk/ (n) = a group of computers which are connected to each other
pop-up advert /ˌpɒp ʌp ˈædvɜːt/ (n) = an announcement that appears unexpectedly on the screen and tries to persuade people to buy a product or service
printer /ˈprɪntə/ (n) = a device attached to the computer which produces a written copy of a file
purchase /ˈpɜːtʃəs/ (n) = what one buys; a product
record /rɪˈkɔːd/ (v) = to copy
router /ˈruːtə/ (n) = a device which connects computer networks to each other, and sends information between networks
scanner /ˈskænə/ (n) = a device that captures images from physical items and converts them into digital formats
screen /skriːn/ (n) = a flat surface as part of a computer, on which pictures and words are shown
speakers /spiːkəz/ (pl n) = the part of a computer through which the sound comes out
tower /ˈtaʊə/ (n) = a metal case that holds all of the computer's components
trick /trɪk/ (n) = an action that intends to cheat sb
upload /ʌpˈləʊd/ (v) = to send a file from your computer to another computer
USB /juː es ˈbiː/ (n) = a part that connects other devices to a computer
virus /ˈvaɪərəs/ (n) = a small program or script that can cause your computer not to function correctly
webcam /ˈwebkæm/ (n) = a video camera that takes pictures which can be viewed on a website

12b

crash /kræʃ/ (v) = to stop functioning properly
password /ˈpɑːswɜːd/ (n) = a secret word or phrase used to gain access to sth
pity /ˈpɪti/ (n) = a feeling of sadness
unreasonable /ʌnˈriːzənəbəl/ (adj) = illogical
up-to-date /ˌʌp tə ˈdeɪt/ (adj) = recent

12c

addictive /əˈdɪktɪv/ (adj) = of sth which a person cannot stop using, doing or taking
background /ˈbækgraʊnd/ (adj) = behind the main subject
calculator /ˈkælkjuleɪtə/ (n) = an electronic device used to do mathematical calculations
GPS /ˌdʒiː piː ˈes/ (n) = (global positioning system) a system that shows the exact position of sth using signals from satellites
note /nəʊt/ (n) = a short piece of writing
obviously /ˈɒbviəsli/ (adv) = surely; without doubt
online shopping /ˌɒnlaɪn ˈʃɒpɪŋ/ (n) = buying things on the Internet
pretend /prɪˈtend/ (v) = to act as if sth were real or true when it is not
setting /ˈsetɪŋ/ (n)= a place on a mobile phone or other electronic device where you can set a function
social media /ˌsəʊʃəl ˈmiːdiə/ (pl n) = websites that allow people to communicate on the Internet using a computer or mobile phone
steal /stiːl/ (v) = to take sth which belongs to sb else without their permission

Culture 12

admission /ədˈmɪʃən/ (n) = entrance
explore /ɪkˈsplɔː/ (v) = to search and discover
hill /hɪl/ (n) = an area of land not as high as a mountain
ingenuity /ɪnˌdʒəˈnjuːəti/ (n) = the ability to think of clever ways to solve a problem
stuff /stʌf/ (n) = things
virtual world /ˌvɜːtʃuəl ˈwɜːld/ (n) = a computer-based online community environment designed and shared by individuals

Values D: Unity

compete /kəmˈpiːt/ (v) = to take part in a race or a competition
experience /ɪkˈspɪəriəns/ (n) = an event that happens to sb
generally /ˈdʒenərəli/ (adv) = usually
survival /səˈvaɪvəl/ (adj) = remaining alive
time limit /ˈtaɪm lɪmɪt/ (n) = an amount of time within which sth has to be done
tough /tʌf/ (adj) = difficult

Public Speaking Skills D

close /kləʊs/ (adv) = near
craftwork /ˈkrɑːftwɜːk/ (n) = the act of making decorative or practical objects by hand
gather /ˈgæðə/ (v) = to come together
mankind /ˌmænˈkaɪnd/ (n) = the human race
tribe /traɪb/ (n) = a group of people of the same race, language and customs

CLIL A: History

earn /ɜːn/ (v) = to receive money in return for work that you do
hanger /ˈhæŋgə/ (n) = a piece of wood, plastic or metal with a hook at the top that we use to hang clothes
measure /ˈmeʒə/ (v) = to be a specific size, length, etc
pheasant /ˈfezənt/ (n) = a bird with a long tail
pole /pəʊl/ (n) = a long piece of wood or metal used to support things
scone /ˈskɒn/ (n) = a small cake

CLIL B: Food Preparation & Nutrition

allergic /əˈlɜːdʒɪk/ (adj) = covered in a rash when you eat, smell or touch sth
fool /fuːl/ (v) = to trick sb
nutrient /ˈnjuːtriənt/ (n) = a substance that helps animals and plants to grow
weight /weɪt/ (n) = the amount of heaviness of sth

CLIL C: Science

average /ˈævərɪdʒ/ (adj) = typical or normal of sth
carbon dioxide /ˌkɑːbən daɪˈɒksaɪd/ (n) = the gas that comes from animals and people breathing out and from chemical reactions
emission /ɪˈmɪʃən/ (n) = the sending out of fumes
reduce /rɪˈdjuːs/ (v) = to make smaller in size or amount
vapour /ˈveɪpə/ (n) = tiny drops of liquid in the air which appear as mist

CLIL D: Art & Design

abstract /ˈæbstrækt/ (adj) = based on a general idea or thought
claim /kleɪm/ (v) = to say that sth is true without proving it
drip /drɪp/ (v) = to fall in drops
explore /ɪkˈsplɔː/ (v) = to examine; to look into
melt /melt/ (v) = to become liquid because of heat
represent /ˌreprɪˈzent/ (v) = to show; to act as an example of

Pronunciation

Vowels

a	/eə/	care, rare, scare, dare, fare, share
	/eɪ/	name, face, table, lake, take, day, age, ache, late, snake, make
	/æ/	apple, bag, hat, man, flat, lamp, fat, hand, black, cap, fan, cat, actor, factor, manner
	/ɔ:/	ball, wall, call, tall, small, hall, warn, walk, also, chalk
	/ɒ/	want, wash, watch, what, wasp
	/ə/	alarm, away, America
	/ɑ:/	arms, dark, bar, star, car, ask, last, fast, glass, far, mask
e	/e/	egg, end, hen, men, ten, bed, leg, tell, penny, pet, bell, pen, tent
i	/ɪ/	in, ill, ink, it, is, hill, city, sixty, fifty, lip, lift, silly, chilly
	/ɜ:/	girl, sir, skirt, shirt, bird
	/aɪ/	ice, kite, white, shine, bite, high, kind
o	/əʊ/	home, hope, bone, joke, note, rope, nose, tone, blow, know, no, cold
	/ɒ/	on, ox, hot, top, chop, clock, soft, often, box, sock, wrong, fox
	/aʊ/	owl, town, clown, how, brown, now, cow
oo	/ʊ/	book, look, foot
	/u:/	room, spoon, too, tooth, food, moon, boot
	/ʌ/	blood, flood
	/ɔ:/	floor, door
u	/ɜ:/	turn, fur, urge, hurl, burn, burst
	/ʌ/	up, uncle, ugly, much, such, run, jump, duck, jungle, hut, mud, luck
	/ʊ/	pull, push, full, cushion
	/j/	unique, union
y	/aɪ/	sky, fly, fry, try, shy, cry, by

Consonants

b	/b/	box, butter, baby, bell, bank, black
c	/k/	cat, coal, call, calm, cold
	/s/	cell, city, pencil, circle
d	/d/	down, duck, dim, double, dream, drive, drink
f	/f/	fat, fan, first, food, lift, fifth
g	/g/	grass, goat, go, gold, big, dog, glue, get, give
	/dʒ/	gem, gin, giant
h	/h/	heat, hit, hen, hand, perhaps BUT hour, honest, dishonest, heir
j	/dʒ/	jam, just, job, joke, jump
k	/k/	keep, king, kick
l	/l/	lift, let, look, lid, clever, please, plot, black, blue, slim, silly
m	/m/	map, man, meat, move, mouse, market, some, small, smell, smile
n	/n/	next, not, tenth, month, kind, snake, snip, noon, run
p	/p/	pay, pea, pen, poor, pink, pencil, plane, please
q	/kw/	quack, quarter, queen, question, quiet
r	/r/	rat, rich, roof, road, ready, cry, grass, bring, fry, carry, red, read
s	/s/	sit, set, seat, soup, snow, smell, glass, dress, goose
	/z/	houses, cousin, husband
t	/t/	two, ten, tooth, team, turn, tent, tool, trip, train, tree
v	/v/	veal, vet, vacuum, vote, arrive, live, leave, view
w	/w/	water, war, wish, word, world
y	/j/	youth, young, yes, yacht, year
z	/z/	zoo, zebra, buzz, crazy

Diphthongs

ea	/eə/	pear, wear, bear
	/ɪə/	ear, near, fear, hear, clear, year, dear
	/i:/	eat, each, heat, leave, clean, seat, neat, tea
	/ɜ:/	earth, pearl, learn, search
ee	/i:/	keep, feed, free, tree, three, bee
	/ɪə/	cheer, deer
ei	/eɪ/	eight, freight, weight, vein
	/aɪ/	height
ai	/eɪ/	pain, sail, tail, main, bait, fail, mail
ie	/aɪ/	die, tie, lie
ou	/ʌ/	tough, touch, enough, couple, cousin, trouble
	/aʊ/	mouse, house, round, trout, shout, doubt
oi	/ɔɪ/	oil, boil, toil, soil, coin, choice, voice, join
oy	/ɔɪ/	boy, joy, toy, annoy, employ
ou	/ɔ:/	court, bought, brought
au	/ɔ:/	naughty, caught, taught

Double letters

sh	/ʃ/	shell, ship, shark, sheep, shrimp, shower
ch	/tʃ/	cheese, chicken, cherry, chips, chocolate
ph	/f/	photo, dolphin, phone, elephant
th	/θ/	thief, throne, three, bath, cloth, earth, tooth
	/ð/	the, this, father, mother, brother, feather
ng	/ŋ/	thing, king, song, sing
nk	/ŋk/	think, tank, bank

Rules of punctuation

Capital letters

A capital letter is used:

- to begin a sentence. *It is cold today.*
- for days of the week, months and public holidays.
  Sunday, August, May Day Bank Holiday
- for names of people and places.
  This is Paul and he's from New York.
- for people's titles.
  Mr and Mrs Jones, Dr Miller, Prince William, etc.
- for nationalities and languages.
  She is Mexican.
  Can you speak Spanish?
  Note: The personal pronoun ***I*** is always a capital letter.
  Jenny and I are friends.

Full stop (.)

A full stop is used to end a sentence that is not a question or an exclamation.

Sue is away on holiday. She's in Brazil.

Comma (,)

A comma is used:

- to separate words in a list.
  There's lettuce, tomatoes, cucumber and olives in the salad.
- to separate a non-essential relative clause (i.e. a clause giving extra information which is not essential to the meaning of the main clause) from the main clause.
  Mary, who has moved here, is a teacher.
- after certain joining words/transitional phrases (e.g. ***in addition to this***, ***moreover***, ***for example***, ***however***, ***in conclusion***, etc).
  For example, I like playing tennis and swimming.
- when a complex sentence begins with an ***if*-clause** or other dependent clauses.
  If Bob isn't there, ask for Ann.
  Note: No comma is used, however, when they follow the main clause.
- to separate questions tags from the rest of the sentence.
  It's hot, isn't it?
- before the words ***asked***, ***said***, etc when followed by direct speech.
  Max said, "It was late to call them."

Question mark (?)

A question mark is used to end a direct question.

What time does Sheila arrive?

Exclamation mark (!)

An exclamation mark is used to end an exclamatory sentence (i.e. a sentence showing admiration, surprise, joy, anger, etc).

He's so tall!

What a nice dress!

Quotation marks (' ' " ")

- Single quotes are used when you are quoting someone in direct speech (nested quotes).
  'She got up, shouted 'I'm late' and ran out of the room,' Bob said.
- Double quotes are used in direct speech to report the exact words someone said.
  "Nora called for you," Mark said to me.

Colon (:)

A colon is used to introduce a list.

To make an omelette we need the following: eggs, milk, butter, cheese, salt and pepper.

Semicolon (;)

A semicolon is used to join two independent clauses without using a conjunction.

We can go to the aquarium; Tuesdays are quiet there.

Brackets ( )

Brackets are used to separate extra information from the rest of the sentence.

The Taj Mahal (built between 1622 and 1653) is in India.

Apostrophe (')

An apostrophe is used:

- in short forms to show that one or more letters or numbers have been left out.
  She's (= she is) *sleeping now.*
  This restaurant opened in '99. (= 1999)
- before or after the possessive ***-s*** to show ownership or the relationship between people.
  Charlee's dog, my dad's sister (singular noun + ***'s***)
  the twins' sister (plural noun + ***'***)
  the children's balls (irregular plural + ***'s***)

American English – British English Guide

merican English	British English
ccount	bill/account
irplane	aeroplane
nyplace/anywhere	anywhere
partment	flat
athrobe	dressing gown
athtub	bath
ill	banknote
illion=thousand million	billion=million million
usy (phone)	engaged (phone)
ab	taxi
all/phone	ring up/phone
an	tin
andy	sweets
heck	bill (restaurant)
loset	wardrobe
onnect (telephone)	put through
ookie	biscuit
orn	sweetcorn, maize
razy	mad
esk clerk	receptionist
essert	pudding/dessert/sweet
owntown	(city) centre
rapes	curtains
rugstore/pharmacy	chemist's (shop)
uplex	semi-detached
ggplant	aubergine
levator	lift
all	autumn
aucet	tap
irst floor, second floor, etc	ground floor, first floor, etc
lashlight	torch
rench fries	chips
ront desk (hotel)	reception
arbage/trash	rubbish
arbage can	dustbin/bin
as	petrol
as station	petrol station/garage
rade	class/year
ntermission	interval
ntersection	crossroads
anitor	caretaker/porter
erosene	paraffin
awyer/attorney	solicitor
ine	queue
ost and found	lost property
nail	post
nake a reservation	book
notorcycle	motorbike/motorcycle
novie	film
novie house/theater	cinema
ews-stand	newsagent
ffice (doctor's/dentist's)	surgery
ne-way (ticket)	single (ticket)
veralls	dungarees

American English	British English
P	
pants/trousers	trousers
pantyhose/nylons	tights
parking lot	car park
pavement	road surface
pedestrian crossing	zebra crossing
(potato) chips	crisps
public school	state school
purse	handbag
R	
railroad	railway
rest room	toilet/cloakroom
S	
sales clerk/sales girl	shop assistant
schedule	timetable
shorts (underwear)	pants
sidewalk	pavement
stand in line	queue
store, shop	shop
subway	underground
T	
truck	lorry, van
two weeks	fortnight/two weeks
V	
vacation	holiday(s)
vacuum (v.)	hoover
vacuum cleaner	hoover
vest	waistcoat
W	
with or without (milk/cream in coffee)	black or white
Y	
yard	garden
Z	
(pronounced, "zee")	(pronounced, "zed")
zero	nought
zip code	postcode

Grammar

American English	British English
He just went out./ He has just gone out.	He has just gone out.
Hello, is this Steve?	Hello, is that Steve?
Do you have a car?/ Have you got a car?	Have you got a car?

Spelling

American English	British English
aluminum	aluminium
analyze	analyse
center	centre
check	cheque
color	colour
honor	honour
jewelry	jewellery
practice(n,v)	practice(n) practise(v)
program	programme
realize	realise
tire	tyre
trave(l)ler	traveller

Expressions with prepositions and particles

American English	British English
different from/than	different from/to
live on X street	live in X street
on a team	in a team
on the weekend	at the weekend
Monday through Friday	Monday to Friday

Irregular Verbs

Infinitive	Past	Past Participle
be /bi:/	was /wɒz/	been /bi:n/
bear /beə/	bore /bɔ:/	born(e) /bɔ:n/
beat /bi:t/	beat /bi:t/	beaten /ˈbi:tən/
become /bɪˈkʌm/	became /bɪˈkeɪm/	become /bɪˈkʌm/
begin /bɪˈgɪn/	began /bɪˈgæn/	begun /bɪˈgʌn/
bite /baɪt/	bit /bɪt/	bitten /ˈbɪtən/
blow /bləʊ/	blew /blu:/	blown /bləʊn/
break /breɪk/	broke /brəʊk/	broken /ˈbrəʊkən/
bring /brɪŋ/	brought /brɔ:t/	brought /brɔ:t/
build /bɪld/	built /bɪlt/	built /bɪlt/
burn /bɜ:n/	burnt (burned) /bɜ:nt (bɜ:nd)/	burnt (burned) /bɜ:nt (bɜ:nd)/
burst /bɜ:st/	burst /bɜ:st/	burst /bɜ:st/
buy /baɪ/	bought /bɔ:t/	bought /bɔ:t/
can /kæn/	could /kʊd/	(been able to /bɪn ˈeɪbəl tə/)
catch /kætʃ/	caught /kɔ:t/	caught /kɔ:t/
choose /tʃu:z/	chose /tʃəʊz/	chosen /ˈtʃəʊzən/
come /kʌm/	came /keɪm/	come /kʌm/
cost /kɒst/	cost /kɒst/	cost /kɒst/
cut /kʌt/	cut /kʌt/	cut /kʌt/
deal /di:l/	dealt /delt/	dealt /delt/
dig /dɪg/	dug /dʌg/	dug /dʌg/
do /du:/	did /dɪd/	done /dʌn/
draw /drɔ:/	drew /dru:/	drawn /drɔ:n/
dream /dri:m/	dreamt (dreamed) /dremt (dri:md)/	dreamt (dreamed) /dremt (dri:md)/
drink /drɪŋk/	drank /dræŋk/	drunk /drʌŋk/
drive /draɪv/	drove /drəʊv/	driven /ˈdrɪvən/
eat /i:t/	ate /eɪt/	eaten /ˈi:tən/
fall /fɔ:l/	fell /fel/	fallen /ˈfɔ:lən/
feed /fi:d/	fed /fed/	fed /fed/
feel /fi:l/	felt /felt/	felt /felt/
fight /faɪt/	fought /fɔ:t/	fought /fɔ:t/
find /faɪnd/	found /faʊnd/	found /faʊnd/
fly /flaɪ/	flew /flu:/	flown /fləʊn/
forbid /fəˈbɪd/	forbade /fəˈbeɪd/	forbidden /fəˈbɪdən/
forget /fəˈget/	forgot /fəˈgɒt/	forgotten /fəˈgɒtən/
forgive /fəˈgɪv/	forgave /fəˈgeɪv/	forgiven /fəˈgɪvən/
freeze /fri:z/	froze /frəʊz/	frozen /ˈfrəʊzən/
get /get/	got /gɒt/	got /gɒt/
give /gɪv/	gave /geɪv/	given /ˈgɪvən/
go /gəʊ/	went /went/	gone /gɒn/
grow /grəʊ/	grew /gru:/	grown /grəʊn/
hang /hæŋ/	hung (hanged) /hʌŋ (hæŋd)/	hung (hanged) /hʌŋ (hæŋd)/
have /hæv/	had /hæd/	had /hæd/
hear /hɪə/	heard /hɜ:d/	heard /hɜ:d/
hide /haɪd/	hid /hɪd/	hidden /ˈhɪdən/
hit /hɪt/	hit /hɪt/	hit /hɪt/
hold /həʊld/	held /held/	held /held/
hurt /hɜ:t/	hurt /hɜ:t/	hurt /hɜ:t/
keep /ki:p/	kept /kept/	kept /kept/
know /nəʊ/	knew /nju:/	known /nəʊn/
lay /leɪ/	laid /leɪd/	laid /leɪd/
lead /li:d/	led /led/	led /led/

Infinitive	Past	Past Participle
learn /lɜ:n/	learnt (learned) /lɜ:nt (lɜ:nd)/	learnt (learned) /lɜ:nt (lɜ:nd)/
leave /li:v/	left /left/	left /left/
lend /lend/	lent /lent/	lent /lent/
let /let/	let /let/	let /let/
lie /laɪ/	lay /leɪ/	lain /leɪn/
light /laɪt/	lit /lɪt/	lit /lɪt/
lose /lu:z/	lost /lɒst/	lost /lɒst/
make /meɪk/	made /meɪd/	made /meɪd/
mean /mi:n/	meant /ment/	meant /ment/
meet /mi:t/	met /met/	met /met/
pay /peɪ/	paid /peɪd/	paid /peɪd/
put /pʊt/	put /pʊt/	put /pʊt/
read /ri:d/	read /red/	read /red/
ride /raɪd/	rode /rəʊd/	ridden /ˈrɪdən/
ring /rɪŋ/	rang /ræŋ/	rung /rʌŋ/
rise /raɪz/	rose /rəʊz/	risen /ˈrɪzən/
run /rʌn/	ran /ræn/	run /rʌn/
say /seɪ/	said /sed/	said /sed/
see /si:/	saw /sɔ:/	seen /si:n/
sell /sel/	sold /səʊld/	sold /səʊld/
send /send/	sent /sent/	sent /sent/
set /set/	set /set/	set /set/
sew /səʊ/	sewed /səʊd/	sewn /səʊn/
shake /ʃeɪk/	shook /ʃʊk/	shaken /ˈʃeɪkən/
shine /ʃaɪn/	shone /ʃɒn/	shone /ʃɒn/
shoot /ʃu:t/	shot /ʃɒt/	shot /ʃɒt/
show /ʃəʊ/	showed /ʃəʊd/	shown /ʃəʊn/
shut /ʃʌt/	shut /ʃʌt/	shut /ʃʌt/
sing /sɪŋ/	sang /sæŋ/	sung /sʌŋ/
sit /sɪt/	sat /sæt/	sat /sæt/
sleep /sli:p/	slept /slept/	slept /slept/
smell /smel/	smelt (smelled) /smelt (smeld)/	smelt (smelled) /smelt (smeld)/
speak /spi:k/	spoke /spəʊk/	spoken /ˈspəʊkən/
spell /spel/	spelt (spelled) /spelt (speld)/	spelt (spelled) /spelt (speld)/
spend /spend/	spent /spent/	spent /spent/
stand /stænd/	stood /stʊd/	stood /stʊd/
steal /sti:l/	stole /stəʊl/	stolen /ˈstəʊlən/
stick /stɪk/	stuck /stʌk/	stuck /stʌk/
sting /stɪŋ/	stung /stʌŋ/	stung /stʌŋ/
swear /sweə/	swore /swɔ:/	sworn /swɔ:n/
sweep /swi:p/	swept /swept/	swept /swept/
swim /swɪm/	swam /swæm/	swum /swʌm/
take /teɪk/	took /tʊk/	taken /ˈteɪkən/
teach /ti:tʃ/	taught /tɔ:t/	taught /tɔ:t/
tear /teə/	tore /tɔ:/	torn /tɔ:n/
tell /tel/	told /təʊld/	told /təʊld/
think /θɪŋk/	thought /θɔ:t/	thought /θɔ:t/
throw /θrəʊ/	threw /θru:/	thrown /θrəʊn/
understand /ˌʌndəˈstænd/	understood /ˌʌndəˈstʊd/	understood /ˌʌndəˈstʊd/
wake /weɪk/	woke /wəʊk/	woken /ˈwəʊkən/
wear /weə/	wore /wɔ:/	worn /wɔ:n/
win /wɪn/	won /wʌn/	won /wʌn/
write /raɪt/	wrote /rəʊt/	written /ˈrɪtən/